THE BOOK OF WANDERINGS

THE BOOK

of

WANDERINGS

A Mother-Daughter Pilgrimage

KIMBERLY MEYER

LB

Little, Brown and Company

New York   Boston   London

Little, Brown and Company
Hachette Book Group
1290 Avenue of the Americas
New York, New York 10104
littlebrown.com

First Edition: March 2015

Little, Brown and Company is a division of Hachette Book Group, Inc. The Little, Brown name and logo are trademarks of Hachette Book Group, Inc.

The publisher is not responsible for websites (or their content) that are not owned by the publisher.

The Hachette Speakers Bureau provides a wide range of authors for speaking events. To find out more, go to hachettespeakersbureau.com or call (866) 376-6591.

Map by John Barnett

ISBN 978-0-316-25121-1
LCCN 2014955746

10 9 8 7 6 5 4 3 2 1

RRD-C

Printed in the United States of America

For Ellie, who went with me
And for Terry and Mary Martha and Sabine,
who let us go

Mon enfant! I give you my hand!
I give you my love, more precious than money,
I give you myself, before preaching or law;
Will you give me yourself? Will you come travel with me?
Shall we stick by each other as long as we live?

—Walt Whitman, "Song of the Open Road"

CONTENTS

Contents

V. INTO THE VOID
Sinai Desert

VI. PARADISE, WHEREVER THAT MAY BE
Cairo, Alexandria

EPILOGUE
Home

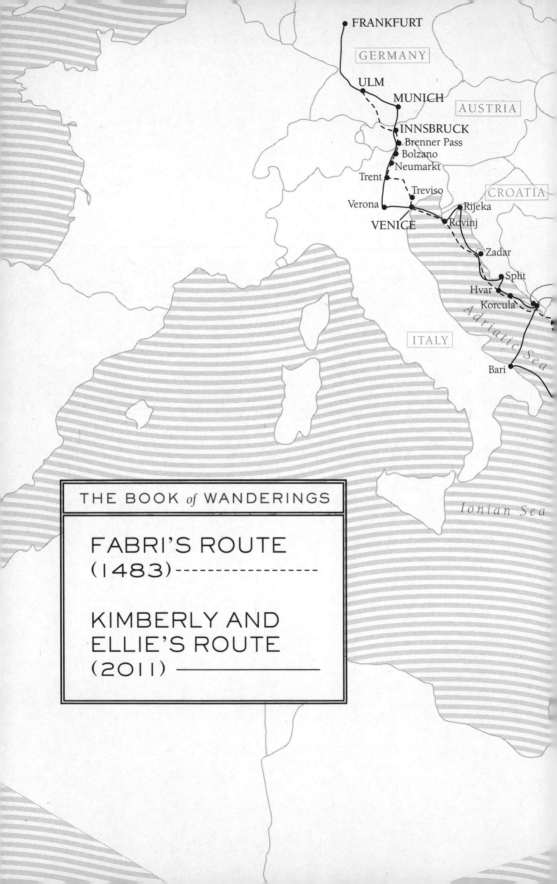

FRANKFURT

GERMANY

ULM

MUNICH

AUSTRIA

INNSBRUCK

Brenner Pass

Bolzano

Neumarkt

Trent

Treviso

CROATIA

Verona

Rijeka

VENICE

Rovinj

Zadar

Split

Hvar

Korcula

Adriatic Sea

ITALY

Bari

Ionian Sea

THE BOOK *of* WANDERINGS

FABRI'S ROUTE
(1483) - - - - - - - - - - - - -

KIMBERLY AND
ELLIE'S ROUTE
(2011) ——————————

ISRAEL

Tel Aviv
(Jaffa)

Jericho
Bethany
Bethlehem
JERUSALEM
Gaza
Judean Desert
Dead Sea
Hebron

Mediterranean Sea

BOSNIA
HERZEGOVINA

SINAI

Be'er
Sheba

JORDAN

*Negev
Desert*

Medjugorje
DUBROVNIK
Shkodër

Durrës

Vlorë

GREECE

Corfu/Kérkyra

Darb al-hajj

Eilat
Taba

*Gulf of
Aqaba*

area of detail

*Aegean
Sea*

TURKEY

Patras
Peloponnese
Kalamata

Methoni

Rhodes

Iraklio
Crete

CYPRUS

Lefkosia/Nicosia

Stavrovouni   Larnaca

Mediterranean Sea

Tel Aviv
(Jaffa)

ISRAEL

JERUSALEM

Gaza   Jericho

*Dead
Sea*

ALEXANDRIA   Rosetta

SINAI

Darb al-hajj

CAIRO   Suez

Gulf of Suez

Tor

Eilat
Taba

Gulf of Aqaba

Nuweiba

EGYPT

Saint Catherine's Monastery
Mount Sinai/Jebel Musa

Sharm el-Sheikh

Red Sea

I. GENESIS

New Mexico, Texas, Kansas, Oklahoma,
Missouri, Frankfurt, Ulm

And he placed at the east of the garden of Eden
    Cherubim,
and a flaming sword which turned every way,
    to keep the way of the tree of life.

—Genesis 3:24

IN THE CHAPEL OF MIRACULOUS
HEALING

IT HAD NEVER occurred to me before to bless a car. Babies and old people and strangers when they sneezed, perhaps, but never a car. We rarely even washed ours. With three little girls, all still in one form of car seat or another, if our station wagon were ever freed of the broken crayons and melted chocolate kisses ground into the floor mats, this would be miracle enough. But outside El Santuario de Chimayó, in the foothills of the Sangre de Cristo ("the Blood of Christ Mountains of New Mexico"), we watched a priest in his black suit and white surplice sprinkling a navy blue Ford Fairlane with holy water and intoning a prayer in Spanish as the family to whom the car belonged—grandparents, parents, children—stood around in a semicircle, heads bowed. Was it new, at least to the owners? Was this a kind of baptism? Or had the car broken down? Had there been an accident? Was it being healed? Or exorcised of some grief that had happened in it?

Strange are the instruments of revelation.

This was our first official family road trip, not one in which we were traveling to see relatives or attend a wedding, but a journey just our own. A few days before, my husband, Terry, and our daughters and I had driven away from Houston, away from the shroud of humid air, away from the concrete and the billboards and the suburbs that sprawled incessantly for miles, always bordered by the same stores and restaurants and gas stations that bordered all the suburbs of all the cities of the country. In West Texas, the flat earth opened up onto the Palo Duro Canyon, a jagged tear, and we camped there and listened in the dark to the thrum of crickets and the strumming of a guitar from another campsite nearby. My bones pressed against the hard ground until they forgot they were something separate and I fell asleep.

Days later, outside Santa Fe, dry hills spotted with scrub juniper and piñon pine and wooden crosses, we passed a sign for Chimayó, and I vaguely remembered having heard something about a chapel there where miracles happened. "Should we go back?" Terry asked. And perhaps to prove to ourselves that, despite the three little girls in the backseat, we could still be spontaneous, we turned around and onto the two-lane road lined with cottonwood trees and small frame houses and gardens with rows of corn and peppers and zinnias.

The legend of El Santuario de Chimayó begins in the year 1810, on the night of Good Friday. In the hills near the village of El Potrero, a landscape that had been sacred to the Tewa and Pueblo Indians before Europeans arrived, Don Bernardo Abeyta, a member of Los Hermanos Penitentes, the Penitent Brothers, is performing his lonely atonements, most likely flagellating himself with a whip made from leaves of the yucca plant. Sometime during that night, Don Bernardo Abeyta sees a light flare from the hillside, and when he reaches the spot, he begins to dig with his bare hands and unearths a crucifix. Three times he carries the crucifix in procession to the church, and three times, by morning, it is gone, buried again in the sandy earth. Finally, the congregation understands what God is trying to tell them: The crucifix must remain where He placed it, and a chapel should be erected around that sacred spot. Then the miraculous healings can begin.

When we arrived, not quite two centuries later, an air of festivity suffused the parking lot of the adobe chapel. Several stands draped with strands of red chili peppers offered burritos and cold drinks for sale, and people wandered in and out of the little souvenir stores. We went into one and looked at the rosaries and matchbox shrines, the bundles of piñon incense and Famous Holy Chilies. I picked through trays spread with *milagros,* small silvery devotional charms, each about the size of a dime and stamped out in various shapes—eyes, arms, legs, angels, the Virgin Mary at prayer, even (oh my, was that what I thought it was?) a penis and scrotum. *Milagros, the sign read, is the Spanish word for "miracles." Milagros are offered to a favorite saint as a reminder of the petitioner's particular need, or they are offered to the saint in thanks for a prayer answered.*

Back outside, we wandered through an arched gateway and into the small adobe chapel with its hand-hewn pews and ceiling beams and its altar screen, primitively painted in blues and greens and reds, at the center of which hung a crudely carved crucifix. But while our fellow tourists and pilgrims genuflected and crossed themselves and even sat in the wooden pews of the chapel for a few moments in silent prayer, the mood itself felt provisional. This wasn't the destination, and everyone seemed to know it but us. So after a polite interval, we too followed the stream of people stooping as they passed through a doorway off the altar into the sacristy.

We found ourselves in a low-ceilinged, cave-like room whose walls were plastered with the offerings of the grateful and the yearning: crutches and braces, poems and photographs, votive candles, baby shoes, dolls, and all the varied tin *milagros* signifying broken bodies and inflamed hearts. An elderly man sat on a bench, his head in his hands. Middle-aged white women with fanny packs, Hispanic women, children, and teens all knelt around a pit in the center of the earthen floor—it must have been the spot where Don

Bernardo Abeyta found the crucifix two centuries ago. Before the pilgrims stood to leave, they scooped some of the sand from the pit into a Ziploc plastic bag or a snack container. Later, back at home, they would sprinkle it over an ailing loved one or perhaps even swallow it themselves. I understood then—it's the dirt here that's miraculous, the earth itself that is holy.

When I think of myself and my husband on that trip, standing there in the doorway to the sacristy watching from the other side of belief with our daughters in our arms, it makes me wonder if what we thought was our own spontaneous act of resistance to our staid life in Houston with three little girls was actually an attempt by the universe to reveal something to us. *Wake up!* was it saying? *Pay attention!* It makes me wonder if meaning exists embedded in the world, and we need only the eyes to see it. The Spanish word *mirar,* "to look," comes from the same Latin root as *miracle,* after all. To look carefully is to see the marvel of our existence. Was that the lesson of Chimayó? Or was it instead that we imagine we see in material things signs from a world beyond—a world beyond that doesn't actually exist?

Afterward, we wandered back out into the heat of the August afternoon. Ellie, only six then, was crying for a drink. Mary Martha, thumb in her mouth and blankie slung across her shoulder, kept reaching up her arms to be held. Sabine, the baby on my hip, was in dire need of a new diaper and a nap. Our accidental pilgrimage was over. We had to get back on the road. But all the rest of that day, driving through the barren hills away from Santa Fe, our daughters asleep in the backseat of the air-conditioned car, we thought about Chimayó and what we'd witnessed there.

For both of us, the chapel became a sign of what we were seeking in traveling with our daughters: remnants of something genuine that suburban sprawl had not yet swallowed up in its ravenous maw. But for me, there was more. Months and years afterward, it would come back to me, our journey to this odd sanctuary of kitsch and piety. What was it that haunted me? The irrational belief that God lurked in this sacred soil? That healing miracles could be wrung from it? The inadequacy of my own skepticism in the face of such devotion? What if there really was an unseen world beneath this world that I'd been too blind to see?

I am always late to the miracle, always doubtful, unconvinced. But something in me had wanted to gather the earth anyway, a fistful of soil. To swallow it. Rub it into my wounds.

PILGRIMS AND STRANGERS

MAYBE THE JOURNEY begins here: I am sitting on the carpeted floor of my bedroom in the tract home on Echo Street in the Woodlands, Texas. I must be seven or eight. I am alone. It is afternoon. I am running my hand over the carpeting, maybe tracing out the pattern of sunlight and shadow that the shimmering leaves outside my window have cast on the floor. I don't remember. I remember only how, for a moment, the pattern of leaves disappears and everything becomes shadow, the sun having passed behind a cloud. I am suddenly aware that I am tired. I have never been aware that I am tired before. I have never noticed before the way the light can disappear and return. It is both beautiful and very sad, very sad because it's beautiful and because it does not stay.

Much later I will read in Homer's *Iliad* that

Human generations are like leaves in their seasons.
The wind blows them to the ground, but the tree
Sprouts new ones when spring comes again.
Men too. Their generations come and go.

And I will recall the pattern of shadow and light on the floor of my bedroom in the house on Echo Street, and me running my hand back and forth across what can't be held.

*   *   *

Maybe it is with me from the beginning, like the eggs in my ovaries that became my daughters. On Tanzania's Laetoli plain, not far from Olduvai Gorge, where paleontologists believe human life took shape, the footprints of two early humans—*Australopithecus afarensis*—are embedded in what was once wet volcanic ash, now turned to stone. Three point six million years ago, two hominids walked side by side. A third, a child perhaps, walked in their footsteps. What are they walking away from? Where are they going? We, their descendants, still have a restlessness embedded in us. We try to heal the restlessness by wandering.

Maybe, though, more precisely, it begins here: With me riding my bike to the little jadeite green rental house of my former boyfriend, the one I've just broken up with because, as I had written in my notebook, "My thoughts have been hovering uncertainly around the idea of solitude. I feel somehow that I am closing in on myself, closing inward, turning in." The irony of this entry will perhaps become apparent when I tell you that the reason I am riding my bike to the house of my former boyfriend in Lawrence, Kansas, on this fall day in 1991, when the leaves are just beginning to turn and the geese are flying south through the blue sky in a V like the wake behind some unseen force pulling itself through the air, is that I am pregnant. I am pregnant and I think that I don't know what to do. I think that at this moment I have two choices before me: to abort the mass of cells dividing frantically inside me, even as the branches of the turning maples lose their leaves and swell with wind, or to have the baby the dividing cells will become by spring, after a bitter winter.

The summer before, Steve and I would drive out through farmland, fields of corn and wheat and milo, to the beach at Clinton Lake, windows rolled down, Van Morrison singing "Cypress Avenue" on a cassette tape. We would make stir-fries and watch *Twin Peaks* and sit eating ice cream on the porch of the old brick house that had been subdivided into apartments where I lived. That was the summer I learned to drink coffee and love Miles Davis and fall asleep to someone else's breathing next to mine in a twin bed.

But this fall day, Steve is in law school at the university where I am a senior majoring in English, and we have plans for our lives that don't necessarily include each other—clerkships and internships and Teach for America, maybe the Peace Corps, maybe backpacking across Europe. Nothing has been decided. The future still exists as pure possibility, or so I think. I will do something interesting, something exceptional, something unconventional. "I feel the need to travel and experience the beauty and mystery of other worlds, other cultures," I had written in my notebook the same day I confessed my need for solitude. "I feel this pull for a bohemian-explorer-intellectual kind of life." And I signify my gypsy spirit to the conventional world by the Birkenstocks that I wear and by the lyrics to the Indigo Girls song that I copy into my notebook. "There's more than one answer to these questions / pointing me in a crooked line," they sing over and over to me, speaking to both the questing restlessness I feel inside and the many possible paths, none exclusive, that this restlessness could take.

But now I am pregnant and I think I don't know what to do, and so I have come to Steve, who tries to comfort me as we lean against his desk, saying, "It's your body..." and "I'll support whatever you want to do." These platitudes, though, are spoken in a dazed kind of way, and, really, how can I blame him? We've just broken up and now there's this between us and it might be my body, but it's his life too. As I leave, there is vague talk of making "an appointment" and about how everything will be okay. But when I get back to the apartment in the old house and lie down on the couch beneath the window, I cry and cry, because I know that there will be no appointment, just as I know there will be no Peace Corps, no Teach for America, no backpacking across Europe, no *bohemian-explorer-intellectual kind of life*. There was never going to be any of that, there had never been a time when I was going to do any of that. Becoming pregnant my senior year in college was always what was going to happen to me, and part of what I'm crying over this fall day is my own gullibility.

What I am trying to say here is that this was not a moral decision. I had been raised Catholic, it's true. My parents and their siblings had all gone to Catholic school, and my brother and sister and I loved to hear our father tell stories about how he and the other boys would torment Sister Mary Ivan, who reminded them hourly that only "good Catholics" would ever find salvation. One aunt of mine, a Poor Handmaid of Jesus Christ, had served in the refugee camps in the killing fields of Cambodia and had later met Mother Teresa. Another aunt left the Sisters of Mercy after Vatican II to marry a former priest who'd studied in Rome. I found both of their stories terribly romantic. My father's parents donated regularly to the Pink Sisters in St. Louis, cloistered nuns in rose-colored habits who were dedicated to the contemplative life and the perpetual adoration of the Blessed Sacrament. My mother's parents attended Mass every Saturday evening after an early dinner at Pope's Cafeteria. When I visited, they would encourage me to pray for the canonization of a nun up for sainthood whose prayer card my grandmother kept on a bedside table along with her rosary. But when I prayed, it did not seem to me that anyone was listening— God or the Virgin Mary or Jesus or the saints. There was no presence, only absence, a silence, a void where they should have been.

Anyway, by the time I discovered I was pregnant, I had already read Nietzsche's *The Antichrist* in a Great Books class, the experience of which was a little like falling in love—this recognition of the doubt already inchoate within me that I had been waiting for someone to come along and articulate. In *The Antichrist,* Nietzsche argues that Christian morality has its roots in the rejection of reality. Our earthly existence is suffering, he claims, and "sufferers have to be sustained by a hope which cannot be refuted by any actuality—which is not *done away with* by any fulfillment: a hope in the Beyond." Christians cling to this hope, this expectation that in the kingdom of God their suffering will finally find relief. So, says Nietzsche, the Beyond drains value away from this world. It makes us lazy. We grow fat on grace.

I did not want to be fat and lazy. I wanted to be intellectually agile and lithe. And when one of the smartest guys from class invited me for a beer at Free State Brewery, and there he parroted Nietzsche, saying casually, matter-of-factly, "We're just afraid to die. So we make up this idea called heaven to keep from having to face the truth," I thought, *Oh my God! He's right! He has such beautiful blue eyes. And he's right!*—proving just how intellectually rigorous I was.

But on a practical level, the implications of reading Nietzsche for me were this: If we invented God and heaven and Jesus and the angels and saints in order to cope with our inevitable suffering and our fear of death, then the moral codes by which we live, the inhibitions that fetter us, are not necessary. If we think this through rationally, what we'll find is that we don't have to be good Catholics. We don't have to be good at all, because there's no divinity judging our actions, weighing our immortal souls. But instead, Nietzsche says, "The great lie of personal immortality destroys all rationality, all naturalness of instinct, all that is salutary, all that is life-furthering, all that holds a guarantee of the future in the instincts henceforth excites mistrust. *So* to live that there is no longer any *meaning* in living: *that* now becomes the 'meaning' of life." This was, perhaps, an all too convenient reading, but what I began to see through Nietzsche was that Christianity had been keeping me from acting on my instinctual urges—natural erotic impulses that generate, that propel us all forward. In fact, in some strange way, Nietzsche's insistence on the *naturalness of instinct* may have been partly responsible for my pregnancy.

Maybe it was instinct too, some evolutionary drive toward self-preservation, that made me keep the cells inside my womb that, even as I lay on the couch weeping for the lives I wouldn't live, were splitting apart and coalescing to form the beating heart of the baby that would become my daughter Ellie. At any rate, I kept the cells. Not because of some injunction from the priests or anything they claimed the scriptures said. I did not know if there was a God beyond me, if He was speaking to me, if He was witnessing my suffering. There was no annunciation from the angels to make my path clear. Instead, I heard a voice from deep inside call out to me as if through water. It was not my voice, or the voice of the replicating cells. But it said that something vulnerable existed now because of me, needing my protection. And I listened.

Perhaps I was destined to be a pilgrim. Perhaps my mother knew something I didn't when she sewed me a somber black Pilgrim dress with a white bonnet and snap-on collar and cuffs from a Butterick pattern, a costume I wore for a couple of Halloweens. My sister was Robin Hood; my brother Superman. My cousins, two sisters, were both Raggedy Ann. Why did I want to be a Pilgrim? Neither my mother nor I can remember. Maybe, though, she was calling into being my true identity through this initiation. Or maybe I became a pilgrim the way we are given a name at birth, which we must then grow into.

Some say that we are all pilgrims. *Pilgrims,* from the Latin *peregrini*—*per*, "through"; *ager*, "field, land, country." We're wanderers and strangers, foreigners, aliens, exiles. We're on a journey, trying to return to some spiritual home.

The book of Genesis is the story of the origin of our exile from a home with God and of the pilgrimage that then becomes our life. *In the beginning,* in Eden, the Lord God commands His human creations not to eat of the Tree of Knowledge at the center of the Garden, for if they do, He says, they will surely die. But the serpent, most cunning of all the beasts, suggests to Eve that by eating the fruit of the Tree of Knowledge, instead of dying, she will find that her eyes are opened and she will be as a god, knowing good and evil. When she eats of it and gives it to her husband and he eats of it, their eyes are fully opened, just as the serpent had said. What was once hidden is finally revealed. *O taste,* sings the Psalmist, *O taste and see* . . .

But God knows that now human curiosity cannot be restrained, that having eaten of the fruit of the Tree of Knowledge and become like gods knowing good and evil, Adam and Eve will next reach out to pluck the fruit from the Tree of Life, and then they, like Him, will live forever. But this God is a jealous God. And so these creatures, though He has shaped them in His own image, must be banished. He drives them out of the Garden of Eden to roam the land of thorn and thistle, to till the soil from which they were made, to feel the pangs of hunger and, for Eve, of bearing children, to suffer; that is, to suffer and die. To the east of Eden, He places cherubim with a whirling sword of flame to bar the way to the Tree of Life.

From Eve we inherited a legacy of restless curiosity and exile. We are all pilgrims, wandering through the mortal world, longing to return to our original homeland where we once dwelled without the necessity of death and in the presence of God. But the time of timelessness is over. And the homeland unattainable here.

After Ellie's birth in May—on Mother's Day, as it happened—and after my graduation a week later, I returned to my parents' home in the Woodlands for the summer. Not the tract home on Echo Street anymore but another house that my father had built later, when I was in junior high, the one with the sunken living room and the walk-in closets and the detached garage, the one whose front yard was shaded by trees grown from saplings he'd dug up in the woods and transplanted. In August I would begin a graduate program in English literature back at the University of Kansas, which seemed, oddly, the most practical solution: the tuition was cheap, I could survive on student loans, and I'd have to be away from Ellie only during the hours I spent in class. My sister had transferred to the university when I found out I was pregnant, and she'd be nearby to help. In this way, I could buy myself two years before I'd need to find a real job and full-time day care, and I wouldn't be too much of a burden on my parents.

In the meantime, that summer, I lived with them, staying with Ellie in my sister's old room, which looked out over the backyard and the drainage ditch lined with concrete and the sweet gum and yaupon and pine trees separating the ditch from the golf course beyond. Though I had been bored and desperate to leave this place years before, now I was simply grateful not to be alone. My mother did our laundry and cooked for me. I nursed the baby and dressed her like I'd once dressed my dolls. High school friends and aunts and uncles and cousins dropped by with gifts. I went to the swimming pool, where I used to lifeguard, and swam laps while Ellie slept in her stroller. I painted a rocking chair white. I started reading to my tiny daughter—*Goodnight Moon*, *The Runaway Bunny*. She was the most beautiful creature I'd ever beheld. In the evening, my mother and I, sometimes my sister or brother, would take her for walks through the thick, still air on the golf course paths. Or we'd rent a movie and watch it on the VCR in the TV room upstairs while my father slipped Ellie illicit Blue Bell ice cream— spoonful after illicit spoonful. When she fell asleep, I'd lay her in her carrier and we'd all stare. My parents' reassurances, when I'd first told them I was pregnant, were proving true: "This is good news," they'd said. If they felt I was a burden, it went unspoken; if I had brought some shame upon them, it was never acknowledged; and what I had to offer them in recompense for that and for all the teenage years I'd been so difficult, for all the years I'd wanted desperately to leave behind this master-planned community in the suburbs of Houston where there was nothing to do, was this small child.

But though I was back at home, I was not at rest. As the air conditioner clicked off and on at night, Ellie in the white iron crib beside my bed, I would lie awake consumed with terror, my heart banging around in the cage of my chest like a desperate prisoner. It was as if giving birth had cleaved open something in me that had not closed back up. In hauling Ellie into this world of light and shadow I had once seen mapped out on the floor of my bedroom as a child, I seemed to have pulled the abyss along with her. I kept imagining my own death obsessively as a disintegration into that same merciless dark from which she'd come. Staring at Ellie's sleeping face, I think I knew already that I was the cloud gazing at its own dissolving image on the surface of some still body of water down below. I knew, in looking at this creature I'd shaped out of my own substance, *flesh of my flesh,* that I was witnessing my erasure.

When I was pregnant, her existence cut off certain possibilities I'd envisioned for my life. But her birth initiated me into the dark mystery of mortality; an equivocal gift, as wisdom always is, but a gift nevertheless. The love I felt for her was plied irrevocably with an understanding of the possibility of her loss that felt palpable, concrete. I loved her so intensely that the thought of parting from her, of leaving her alone and unprotected, became unbearable. In loving her, in seeing myself reflected in her face, I became fully aware of the fragility of that love, fully aware that she could at any moment be reclaimed by that vast darkness from which she'd been delivered.

And yet, upon her arrival, I was also filled with a hope that in shaping my daughter with my own hands the way God shaped Adam from the soil, I had the chance to start over, to fix things, to make one small part of creation flawless this time. For as long as I could remember, I'd had a hunger that my parents, and later my boyfriends, could never feed. It had made me restless and impatient. It had made me push them away. What was this restless hunger for? Knowledge? Experience? The whole wide world? Profound love and connection? To keep my daughter from that same hunger, I would read to her, and take her to museums. I'd sign her up for art classes and teach her a foreign language. We'd sew. We'd knit. We'd bake together. We'd make a garden, be in tune with the natural world. She'd eat her vegetables. She'd play piano. She'd be well-rounded. She'd never watch too much TV. God had shaped humans in His image; I'd make Ellie the me I had wanted to be. Like God, I craved a clean slate. Over and over again in Genesis, He sends flood and fire and brimstone to wipe out the wicked but preserves a holy remnant and, as with a sourdough starter, begins the world anew. "Not that my life is such a mess," I'd written in my notebook a few months before Ellie was born, "but this new life will give me a chance to try to do things better, more purely— to create a more perfect life than my own." Of course I, like God, would fail.

But that would come later. For the moment, let's face it: I was lucky. I was in grad school on student loans so I could be with Ellie most of every day. My parents drove up to Kansas as often as they could, or flew us down to see them. They bought me groceries. They bought Ellie clothes. Steve and I had briefly reconciled and shared his house together, but when we broke up for good, he took Ellie every other weekend and once during each week, which gave me a break. Now she and I were living in student-family housing in a second-floor apartment with a window air conditioner and a galley kitchen and linoleum-tile floors. I sewed curtains, a periwinkle slipcover for the hand-me-down couch, throw pillows in a knockoff Pierre Deux print, a quilt for Ellie in white. She and I ate our meals together at a narrow kitchen table beneath a poster of Matisse's *Blue Nude*. In Ellie's bedroom were the iron crib and the rocking chair I'd painted, and a shelf of books and puzzles. My room was just big enough for my desk and my bed. Outside on the porch, I tried to grow basil in terra-cotta pots, but the sun burned it all up. I planted red geraniums instead.

Who needed to travel? Student-family housing turned out to be a low-income mini-UN. On one side of us lived a young Bangladeshi couple who showed me photos of their wedding filled with red saris and orange marigolds, a marriage arranged by their parents. On the other side, a couple from Ghana who had left their young son in Africa in the care of grandparents so they could continue their studies in the United States. At the far end, an extended family from India who squeezed into a one-bedroom unit and were always cooking something fragrant—a dal, basmati rice—while the ancient grandmother sat on her pallet in a nook of the living room and smiled at me and Ellie through the open front door. Downstairs was a Chinese couple, usually in flip-flops, and their little girl, about Ellie's age. The girls played together once or twice.

Maybe it was stressful standing at the card catalog in the library with Ellie in a back carrier chewing on her plastic key chain as I tried to do research. Maybe I would have liked to linger after seminars to talk to other students, grab a beer and sit in the sun with them, cook dinner with them and play penny poker, eat a No-Student-Loan Special of vegetarian chili at Yello Sub. Maybe I did confess in my notebook, in a moment of desolation, "I love being with Ellie and watching her grow and learn. I think about her when I'm not with her and I enjoy every minute when I am with her. But I'm also so interested in grad school and I want to throw myself into my studies." Maybe I was so sleepy after reading to Ellie and singing to her and putting her to bed at night that afterward I'd struggle blearily through the Romantic poets or the Moderns— Eliot, Pound, Stevens, Yeats. Maybe papers got written between changing diapers and trips to Wal-Mart for socks and tights, and to Checkers Foods, and to Duds 'n Suds, where we did our laundry each week. At least the owner always came over and held Ellie for me while I folded clothes. And overall, I felt proud of the life I was struggling to make for myself and my daughter, and capable, precisely because it was hard.

Ellie was the wound, but she was also the salve, the balm. She kept me from some vast aloneness I'd often felt, some disconnection from other people. It was probably out of that sense of disconnection that I'd written in my notebook just before I broke up with Steve, *My thoughts have been hovering uncertainly around the idea of solitude. I feel somehow that I am closing in on myself, closing inward, turning in.* But in the afternoons, I'd lay down a quilt in the wagon and put Ellie in it with a plastic baggie filled with Goldfish crackers, and we'd walk up to campus to the Natural History Museum to see the taxidermied buffalo and the prairie dogs in the diorama and the dinosaur fossils in the glass cases. Fridays after my last class, I would strap Ellie into her bike seat and we would ride to Massachusetts Street and I would treat myself to a coffee and Ellie to a cookie at La Prima Tazza, then we would visit one of the used-books stores and sit and read. Sometimes we'd end up at Papa Keno's for pizza. Sometimes we'd stop at the farmers' market in the parking lot off Vermont Street and buy something to cook for dinner and get pastries for the morning from the Mennonite women in long calico dresses and white caps. And on the weekends when the weather was nice, we'd drive out to the beach at Clinton Lake where Steve and I used to go, and I'd let her splash around in the shallow muddy waters. Afterward I'd wash her feet in the outdoor shower and buy her a slushy drink from the Clinton Store, with its aged gas pump out front and its screen door and sandy floors. Once, when I was sick, unable to get out of bed, she listened to my heart with the stethoscope from her doctor's kit and brought me "tea" in a pink plastic cup. Once, when I was lonely and crying on the edge of the tub, she put her chubby arms around my neck and told me, "It's going to be okay. I'm going to make you better." She was my constant companion.

But the loneliness was always there, a low hum. And sometimes it would erupt into waves of oppressive despair and yearning no one could make better. A cold Sunday in spring at the metal playground in student-family housing, with no classes to break up the monotony and Ellie's nap hours off, the bright blue day like a heavy burden I would have to carry across the endless prairie that stretched toward the horizon. A summer afternoon outside a fraternity house on Tennessee Street, the brothers playing Frisbee on the wide front lawn, a scene provoking a sentimental ache in me that I couldn't explain, the only Greeks with whom I'd ever connected being the ancients. At the crux of my longing and my sadness at those moments was this paradox: I had Ellie with me all the time, and I still felt alone.

Into this paradox, enter Terry. It is Christmas. He's on leave from his post at Fort Sill near Lawton, Oklahoma, where he has been stationed since graduating from West Point a few years before. He's visiting his parents in their split-level house in the Woodlands, where he grew up too. They're hosting their annual holiday party to which my family has been invited. I am in the kitchen. Ellie is crawling on the floor. Terry, whom I've known since the days of sunlight and shadow in the house on Echo Street, comes in to get a drink, and we end up leaning against the counter talking about history and politics the rest of the evening until my parents, with whom I've come, are ready to leave. We think about each other off and on for a year. We meet again the following Christmas. We write each other. We talk by phone. We become an item. We visit a few times—Lawrence, Lawton, Topeka. But I am filled with some indefinable doubt that is perhaps a fear of the inevitable, perhaps a fear of some life of stasis that I'm still trying to avoid. We break up. For months we don't speak. But then one night, near Thanksgiving, I feel so lonely I don't know what to do. And this voice like the one that spoke to me through water speaks his name and I call him in Oklahoma and two months later we're engaged.

We were apart the entire engagement. Terry had been deployed to Guantánamo Bay, Cuba, to help run a refugee camp there for Cubans and Haitians attempting to enter the United States. This was in 1995, long before Gitmo became what it is now. Back then, the INS was interviewing refugees, trying to process them in an orderly fashion to avoid overwhelming the system the way the Mariel boatlift had in 1980. Terry served as an aide to the ranking colonel who oversaw the running of migrant operations. As such, he was also the public affairs officer in charge of leading visiting journalists from all over the world through the camps. The upshot of all this was that he had access to a phone he could use to call me, which he did a couple of times a week, always around five a.m., before anyone else had arrived in the hangar where he worked. But in those days before the Internet became widely available, we also wrote letters, both of us, every single day of the nearly six months he was gone.

In the letters, Terry sometimes told of his encounters in the camps—the afternoon some Cuban migrants gave an impromptu concert to smiling crowds, first a quartet in flip-flops and T-shirts and pompadours singing classical Spanish music and playing guitars and tambourines, later a lone man chanting folk songs about Guantánamo Bay, Bill Clinton, and the United States. Another day, somber, he told of when his battalion forcibly repatriated about

115 Haitians. That morning, two platoons of soldiers were dressing in riot gear. Watching them, Terry said, was like observing preparations for combat. It gave him chills. "I hope I never have to see men prepare for battle. It must be terrifying for the migrants. The very people taking care of them are now waking them up early in the morning, packing their belongings, and with a strong show of force present, escorting them to a large truck for the trip to the Coast Guard cutter. By this afternoon they will be back in Haiti."

Terry enjoyed interacting with the visiting journalists and the NGO personnel posted at the base. He liked trying to translate the strangeness of the army for those outside of it. Because—and this is one of the qualities that drew me to him—Terry could stand back with those not a part of it and see the idiosyncrasies, but at the same time he could interpret them so that they made sense. Most of his colleagues did not have this wide-angle perspective. One guy, a captain with whom he spent some of his free time early on, a fervent Southern Baptist, reacted incomprehensibly to an art gallery set up to display the migrants' work. "He said it was 'sick,' 'perverse.' He 'didn't know why we let them display it,' 'it was below the U.S.,'" Terry wrote. "I thought I was with Jesse Helms." When Terry went to see the art, he couldn't fathom the reason for the captain's reaction. "Naturally it was not all pro-U.S., and there were a couple of naked women, but nothing that far out there. I just kept quiet. Not worth talking about with him. When religion is involved, there is no gray area; it is all black and white, right or wrong."

But mostly our letters were filled with an ache for each other that we tried to bridge by writing about the quotidian—trips to the Naval Exchange for yogurt and pastries, running routes and workout routines, *Sesame Street* episodes, details of the wedding, the plan for the garden I planted in the backyard of Terry's house in Lawton that spring before he returned, the itinerary for our Ireland honeymoon. Now that I'd finished grad school, I complained about my job at a nonprofit in Topeka, half an hour away, where I was supposed to be editing newsletters and monographs but where I ended up taking care of the mail and answering phones instead. When cable TV was hooked up in the tent where Terry slept on a cot he padded with his sleeping bag, he felt distraught over the noisy distraction and even tried to get the guys to watch PBS instead of stock-car races or *America's Funniest Home Videos*. Usually he'd have to put on headphones and listen to music to drown out the sound: Shawn Colvin, Robert Johnson, Johnny Cash, Beethoven, Bach, Mozart, Chopin.

"Writing, sharing my mind, brings me somehow closer to you," I wrote. "I feel connected to you in some way while writing and I don't want that feeling to end," Terry admitted. In his loneliness and isolation, he would often walk down to the water and sit on the black rocks, the surf and the breeze, the stars and the moon and the distant lights, calming him. He'd read, too, from the list of books I'd sent: Willa Cather's *My Ántonia;* Toni Morrison's *Beloved; Love in the Time of Cholera* by Gabriel García Márquez. Back in my bed in Lawrence, Kansas, late at night while Ellie slept in the next room, I read Tobias Wolff's *In Pharaoh's Army,* which he'd sent me, and I wrote him letters in which I quoted E. E. Cummings ("it is so long since my heart has been with yours / shut by our mingling arms through / a darkness where new lights begin and / increase") and "The River-Merchant's Wife: A Letter," by Ezra Pound ("I desired my dust to be mingled with yours / Forever and forever and forever").

The life we would live, Ellie and Terry and me, we mapped out in intricate detail: the drives through the low red hills of Oklahoma, the hikes in the wildlife refuge near Fort Sill, the afternoons in the vegetable garden bordered by sunflowers and nasturtiums and zinnias. Terry would build a shed for his tools. I'd teach at

Cameron University. We'd buy a used Volvo. We'd have another baby, maybe two. We'd read to them and put them to bed. We'd sit on the couch and drink tea. That life seemed to exist even then, in some other world; we just needed to arrive there and take our places. "We already are a family," I wrote to him in May as his return neared, "we just need to be together."

This vision of the life we wanted to live might seem the opposite of that *bohemian-explorer-intellectual kind of life* I had once craved. It might seem to embody the stasis I feared early on with him, and from which I initially wanted to back away. And yet, in the end, we both saw that a life together offered not stasis at all but possibility; not stillness, but relentness movement forward of another kind. Homer says,

> *Human generations are like leaves in their seasons.*
> *The wind blows them to the ground, but the tree*
> *Sprouts new ones when spring comes again.*

I wanted to be part of that cycle of regeneration and then join my dust to my husband's *forever and forever and forever*.

We were married in an old stone chapel, in sunlight, at Fort Sill, an outpost established to protect pioneer settlements in Kansas and Texas from "hostile" native tribes. It was here that the Comanche formally surrendered, ending the Indian Wars on the southern plains. Geronimo, the Apache chief, was buried here. Before Terry left for Guantánamo, he'd taken me to see his grave. "'Now there is no loneliness for you / Now there is no more loneliness,'" I had written to him, the words of the Apache blessing, while he was gone. Ellie had just turned three.

During the two years we lived in Oklahoma, I taught English composition at the university to former soldiers and machinists at the Goodyear plant, and I volunteered at the Fort Sill museum, cataloging photographs, mostly of young privates wearing brown wool uniforms and standing on the cobblestoned streets of tattered European villages during the Second World War. Once I came across a photograph of the chapel where we'd been married, which early on had also served as a school. The children, lined up in front, wore calico dresses or short pants and had bare feet; their teachers, in dark skirts cinched tight at the waist and white cotton-lawn blouses, bracketed them like parentheses. Terry and I found that we loved places layered with history, like that chapel, and it meant something to us both that we'd been married there.

The vision Terry and I described to each other in our letters was materializing. The summer after we married, during a break in my teaching, I tried to capture the rhythm of our days in my notebook:

Waking up to Ellie crawling sleepy-eyed and tangle-haired into bed with me in the mornings while Terry showers. And then the three of us eating breakfast together at the kitchen counter. Waving goodbye to Terry from the front porch. Then Ellie playing in her room or painting in the kitchen while I straighten the house and get ready for the day. And then the day: maybe story time at the library, swimming at the YMCA, tea and cookies at the bookstore, working in the garden, playing in the sandbox. Then dinnertime approaches and I begin chopping and grating and mixing and stirring. And maybe Ellie helps me and maybe she writes letters and words on sheets of paper or plays in her room with her dolls. And Terry comes home and we eat and talk. And Ellie dances for us (jigs, ballet, jazz) or we all play "Memory Game." Then Ellie takes a bath and we all read books and I lay with Ellie and sing her to sleep.

On the weekends, we'd take Ellie hiking in the Wichita Mountains, in the wildlife refuge that shelters American bison and Rocky

Mountain elk as well as a remnant of native prairie that escaped the plows of pioneers because the ground beneath was too full of stones. Like our love for the chapel, we found, too, that we loved the places that had been discarded, places that were hard to love. On our hikes, we would often head to an area called Charon Gardens, which the guidebook described as "an untamed garden of Eden, a pristine, primeval wilderness." There, massive oval boulders of red granite balanced precariously on ridges, and a sheer cliff dropped down to a pool of deep water. We would stand at the edge of the precipice, blue sky above us, cold, dark water below, and look out upon everything and behold that it was very good. How could we know how happy we were?

The other daughters we'd imagined in our letters arrived quickly, just over a year apart. Mary Martha, then Sabine. Ellie was four, then five. Those were the years of restless movement. Terry left the army and we left Fort Sill. We returned to the Woodlands for a while. My father built us a small house on an overlooked lot surrounded by sweet gum and pines. Terry built us a bed from a set of plans I found in a magazine. His grandmother lived next door with Baby, the little dog for whom she cooked hot dogs. Our parents, some siblings, lived nearby. Terry took the bus into the city every morning in the dark, and returned in the dark as well. I took Ellie to school and fed the babies and walked them in the double stroller and read to them and lay with them in the afternoon until they fell asleep. Then I folded some laundry and wrote in my notebook, "It's a little like observing a death, watching infancy pass on." It was all going too fast, and though I kept the floor swept and the beds made, I felt largely out of control. We tried to put in a garden in the backyard, but there was too much shade, so Terry laid a brick patio instead. Sometimes as soon as he drove home from the bus station in the evening, I would hand him a baby and he'd hand me the car keys and I'd drive into the city for a poetry reading—Adam Zagajewski, I recall, and Marie Howe. Afterward, I'd buy their books and go to a café and sit and read. I loved being anonymous. Loved knowing that no one there knew that back home I had a husband and babies waiting for me. I loved not thinking about them, loved remembering, for a few hours, who I had once been. But then I'd picture my hand on Sabine's soft tummy; Mary Martha's hair, frowsy after her nap . . .

When I decided to go back to graduate school, we bought a bungalow in Houston near the elementary school and spent a summer ripping out old cabinets, sanding floors, painting. Then we drove away from the city and the heat and humidity toward the Sangre de Cristo Mountains of New Mexico. There we stood in the doorway of El Santuario de Chimayó watching pilgrims gathering holy dirt, and I saw how I had always stood on the outside of faith, my face peering in through the bars of the gates of the garden, while the cherubim with their whirling swords of flame kept me at bay. But I saw, too, how in my exile, I had been haunted. By God, maybe. Or maybe by a longing for evidence to refute my fear that this material world and those people I love— so beautiful and so quickly passing—are all there is. Perhaps God and this longing are one.

I think that my doctoral dissertation was an attempt to understand what I'd witnessed in El Santuario de Chimayó, the obscure revelation I received there. I was writing about America's sacred places— Plymouth and Jamestown, the Fountain of Youth in St. Augustine, the Grand Canyon, Chaco Canyon, Mesa Verde, the redwood forest, Monticello, Graceland, the Little Houses of Laura Ingalls Wilder throughout the Great Plains. The religious impulse to gather holy dirt and be healed did not seem so different to me from the yearning to experience the sublime in the Grand Canyon or among the redwoods. Laura Ingalls Wilder (like Thomas Jefferson, perhaps; Elvis, of course) seemed to have become a kind of iconic saint to her devotees, among whom I counted myself and, by this point, my three little girls.

The dissertation was a way out into the world beyond that I still craved, despite the external premises of my life: afternoon naps and snacks in plastic baggies and baths at night, hair smelling of chlorine in the summer, and teacher's gifts for the holidays and Halloween costumes in the fall. So every summer after that first accidental pilgrimage and for most of the rest of my daughters' childhoods (which is about how long it took me to get my PhD), Terry and I would pack up the Volvo station wagon with camping gear and coolers and Barbie dolls and baby dolls and backpacks and set out from Houston so that Mommy could do "research." We loved the back roads that we traveled, the discarded places. We loved the sense of self-containment, of having our daughters all to ourselves. But binding Terry and me together was this unacknowledged understanding: we were also traveling in part to assuage some vague loss we both felt for the freedom we would never have because of that fall day years before when I had kept the cells that were becoming Ellie, and in part to assuage the restlessness in me that couldn't be completely stilled by the quaint old bungalow, and the fruit trees we had planted out front, and the adored children, and even by him, the man who had rescued me from being alone.

Once I began to see these sacred places across the country as shrines and the travelers to them as pilgrims, I wanted to understand the phenomenon of pilgrimage in the Middle Ages, that great age of faith when the pious and the battered set out for holy places seeking comfort and healing and absolution, seeking to reconnect with the divine who had banished them. And so I read—in the pool while the girls, bodies growing lean, splashed around in the water; at the playground after school; at all the doctors' offices as we waited to be called; on the couch in the sunroom in the evening when I really should have been getting dinner started; in bed at night. Most pilgrims, I learned, limited by mundane practicalities of time and money, settled for traveling to the nearby shrines of local saints, while the more discerning or the more desperate journeyed farther—to Santiago de Compostela in northern Spain, to Walsingham or Canterbury in England, to Aachen in Germany, to Lourdes in France, to Rome. The pilgrimage to Jerusalem, the most distant, the most arduous, and the most costly, was also by far the most spiritual. Jerusalem was, after all, the omphalos, meaning, literally, "the navel of the world," where Christ was crucified and where Christianity was born. Medieval cartographers frequently signified its import by placing the Holy Land at the very center of their *mappae mundi*, their maps of the world, with all the continents and rivers and seas emerging from its source.

In my research, I read accounts written by Jerusalem pilgrims themselves—Egeria and the Holy Paula, women of the Roman Empire who traveled in the late fourth century, the latter with her daughter; Arculf, a native of France, and Saint Willibald, the first English pilgrim, and the Russian Abbot Daniel; the twelfth-century Germans John of Würzburg and Theoderich; Margery Kempe, who arrived in Jerusalem in 1436 and who was reviled by her fellow pilgrims for her constant hysterical weeping at all the holy places. But one voice, the intimacy and specificity of it, really caught my ear, and that was the voice of Friar Felix Fabri, a Dominican of the Order of Preachers, a member of a convent in Ulm. I discovered an English translation of his 1,300-page *Fratris Felicis Fabri Evagatorium in Terrae Sanctae, Arabiae et Egypti Peregrinatoniem (The Book of the Wanderings of Brother Felix Fabri in the Holy Land, Arabia, and Egypt)* in the university library one winter break and read it by the fire while the girls played dress-up and read Harry Potter books and watched *Aquamarine* on the VCR.

Fabri begins his *Book of Wanderings* by briefly charting the first pilgrimage he'd made, from southern Germany to Jerusalem back in 1480, but he says he returned from this grueling journey dissatisfied. It was short. It was hurried. It was incomplete. Though gone from Ulm for seven months, he was in the Holy Land itself for only nine days. His guides managed to arrange a quick visit to Bethlehem and Bethany, but it took place in the dark. When he returns home and tries to remember the landscape and the sites he visited, he is maddened to find that "the Holy Land and Jerusalem with its holy places appeared to me shrouded in a dark mist, as though I had beheld them in a dream." So he begins to read everything he can find on Jerusalem. He collects accounts of the crusaders and tracts of pilgrims and treatises by natural historians. And the more he reads, the more he realizes how superficial and confused his own pilgrimage had been without that knowledge to guide him and help him see.

Fabri is driven by a consuming desire to return to Jerusalem. "I call God to witness that for many years I was in such a fever of longing to perform that pilgrimage that whether I was asleep or awake I hardly ever had any other subject before my mind," he writes in the epistle dedicatory to the *Book of Wanderings*. "And I may say with truth that while engaged in these thoughts I lay awake for more than a thousand hours of the night and time of rest." Fabri surreptitiously obtains letters of permission to return to the Holy Land from both the master general of the Dominican Order and the pope, so when, in the early spring of 1483, a group of noblemen from Ulm ask Fabri to join them on their pilgrimage to the Holy Land as their chaplain, he is able to produce his letters and beg leave to go. After all of this effort and torment, how can the prior say no? So Fabri adorns his scapular with red crosses sewn on by virgins dedicated to God, and, as the custom for pilgrims then dictated, lets his beard begin to grow.

Determined not to forget anything this time, determined to have some tangible evidence of his travels for both himself and his Dominican brethren who must remain behind, Fabri reveals his plan of action. He'll begin with his departure and end with his return and will set down what he does day by day. "For I never passed one single day while I was on my travels without writing some notes, not even when I was at sea, in storms, or in the Holy Land; and in the desert I have frequently written as I sat on an ass or a camel; or at night, while the others were asleep, I would sit and put into writing what I had seen." Fabri's account goes on for nearly ten months and is driven by his restless curiosity and a desire to preserve the particulars of everything he sees. These particulars are portholes onto an enchanted world, alive with miracles and meaning, as the Oklahoma landscape was for Terry and me, inhabited in our imagination by Comanche warriors and pioneer schoolchildren in calico and, later, by our own memories.

Once, when Ellie was little and learning to write, after I had explained something to her about which she'd been curious, she announced in all seriousness, "I'm going to write that down." When I asked her why, she said, "So I can remember it and explain it to my children like you explained it to me." I remember that Ellie told me this because I wrote it down in my own notebook, which I filled with things I saw and learned and did not want to forget, things I might want to explain to my children someday. Ellie understood what Fabri understood and what I understood: that the created world is full of strange fascination we should try to observe and remember.

But to document is also to acknowledge that this world is fleeting. And in trying to preserve the fleeting world, we write as if with water on sand. This is something else I wrote down in my notebook, back when we lived in Oklahoma and had a garden and Ellie would help me weed and water, wearing her swimsuit and blue galoshes: "Two sunflowers opened yesterday. Ellie and I were looking at the flowers last night and she was explaining to me that 'First they grow and bloom then die, bloom and die, bloom and die.'" *Human generations are like leaves in their seasons,* wrote Homer. *Their generations come and go.* I am a mother of children I carried across this vast country in search of sacred shrines, children who once were babies in car seats, who once lay between my husband and me in our tent as the stars blinked in the dark sky above. But all that is now a long time ago. I understand Fabri's obsessive need to record what he witnessed, all those details. I understand the craving, almost physical, to preserve memory from being *shrouded in a dark mist as though beheld in a dream.* By preserving those fleeting moments—say, of a child's upturned face as she tells you she's going to write down what you said—you try to remove them from time and make them eternal, even if you know this is a futile task.

We were lucky. The bungalow in the city. Daughters who bound us together. Jobs that sustained us. But things had not been perfect. For though I said that Ellie was both my wound and my balm, she herself suffered because of the way that she came into existence, and that suffering I have no desire to preserve or remember. I don't want to remember, for example, how, after Terry and I got married, and Ellie and I moved to Oklahoma and away from Steve, and Steve got married to Tracy, who had two children of her own, and I had Mary Martha and Sabine, and we moved to Texas, and Steve and Tracy had another child, Ellie—three, four, five years old— became increasingly lost in a confusion and rage whose source she felt but could not articulate, at least not with words. I don't want to remember the tantrums at every family gathering, how she never had any friends at school. I don't want to remember how my mother told me, "Ellie seems to be drifting away from us. Sometimes she doesn't seem to be there at all." I don't want to remember the dream Ellie had of driving through the mountains with those she loved and everyone being blown away by the wind so that, on the mountaintop overlooking an endless abyss, "I was left all alone." Or the one in which she got lost and tried to find her way home because she knew we would be looking for her there. But where was home? With me or with her dad? When I told her I'd never let her get lost, she pointed to the window and said she wanted to jump out. I don't want to remember that. Nor how, when she was seven or eight, she grabbed a paring knife from the kitchen drawer and told me she didn't want to live. I don't want to remember how she would ride off, barefoot, on her pink bike with streamers flying from the handlebars, behind neighbors' houses and onto busy streets, me chasing her with the little ones in tow, one on my hip, one holding my hand. And how, when I would finally catch her, I'd see in her eyes both fury and a flicker of relief. I don't want to remember how she would begin every diary she kept with "My name is Ellie Rose Meyer. My parents are divorced"—which technically wasn't true, since Steve and I had never married, but which I found to be a shattering way for a little girl to conceive of herself. Shattering, too, was her hope that Steve and I would one day reunite, that Terry and Tracy would marry. In my mind, the window and the paring knife and the pink bike with streamers, the diary entries and the hopelessness, were all related, and all traceable back to me.

I don't want to remember the stealing, little trinkets from schoolmates' cubbies—a plastic pig, an invisible-ink pen, a rock painted gold. I don't want to remember the yelling and the fighting. I don't want to remember the lying. Or, in middle school, the black clothes, the black eyeliner, the black nail polish, the black boots, the black belt with the skull-and-crossbones buckle. Or the cutting, the cutting, the cutting, so deep across her wrist one night that she needed stitches from the clinic by the highway. Terry dressed and drove her while I lay in our bed with Mary Martha and Sabine, who cried inconsolably until they fell asleep. The triage nurse asked them why the mother hadn't come, Terry told me later. Why hadn't I? And was I absent in some deep way I hadn't even realized? Is that why this had happened? And why, one summer day, she rode her bike to the house of a boy, longing for some connection? Is that how he was able to force her to do things she was ashamed to do, the boy unaware, untroubled by how this destroyed her? Is that why she didn't tell me until years later?

I had failed her. My immense love couldn't keep her from suffering. I remember thinking that. And how I felt responsible, in some distant but unswerving way, for that suffering. My leaving Lawrence, my marriage to Terry, my having Mary Martha and Sabine, had been the cause of this effect, even if Terry and I kept telling ourselves that our lives were better this way. At any rate, all this now existed. And I would never unwish it. Did that hurt Ellie? Did she feel rejected? Was that why she was smashing up the perfect life that I, like God, had been trying to shape for us all? And when she smashed things, did she feel ashamed? Did she know that my intentions were rooted in love, so she turned her anger and fear of abandonment inward against herself?

I remember, too, that even in my hopelessness, I was determined to carry Ellie, violently, if necessary, across this wasteland of our own creation until she was safe. And I would like to recall how, in the end, Ellie did return to us. How she went to therapy. How she chose, despite my own religious doubt, to attend an all-girls Catholic high school. How she was loud and funny and driven by passionate emotion. How she started a Save Darfur club her junior year. How she realized, about the same time, that she wanted to become a public defender for the poor and the forgotten, like her father. "You have a big heart," I would tell her, "and you know how to use it." I would like to note, for the record, how the nuns, in their compassion and mercy, consoled her when she worried about the stealing, the cutting, the boys. "God knows what the heart intends," they said. How they told her, when she worried about the way she'd entered this world, that it was obvious she was "made with love."

When Ellie left for college, the heartbeat at the center of our house grew still. I missed her, of course. But there was more to my grief than her absence. She was approaching the age I had been when I set out into the world that lay, full of possibility, before me and found myself instead on a road that led inexorably to her. I began to understand that this was the end of an era that had defined me. Ellie and the other daughters who came later were the center out of which the self I became was born. We'd been tied together, umbilically, in the dark abyss where they connected me to some tenuous sense of the infinite, of a presence beyond myself. But now these little gods were abandoning me. One by one, they'd have to be cut away. Who was I without them? And anyway, who had I been before? Was there a *milagro* I could pin to a wall in the chapel of miraculous healing? Was there holy dirt I could gather for what had been lost?

Could I go on a pilgrimage? Set out like Fabri? Set out *with* him? Use his journey as a guide? I was teaching a Great Books course at the university and had all summer off. Why not? When I asked this of Terry, did he have any idea what he was getting into when he said he thought I should go? Or did he, in fact, understand that longing I felt for the life that had been interrupted? Did he wish for me the chance to reconnect with the person I never got to be?

At first, I imagined walking through cities, climbing up mountains, crossing desert sands, sailing the sea alone. Aside from the nights here and there in cafés reading poetry, I had not really been by myself for nearly twenty years and hardly remembered what that was like. Maybe this trip would help show me the way. In the end, though, I took Ellie. I didn't really want to be so completely on my own. But Terry couldn't leave work. And Mary Martha and Sabine weren't old enough to go. So I took Ellie because she was free. I took her because one of her New Year's resolutions when she was twelve read: "Be alive." And because back on August 30, 1991, when I wrote in my notebook about the pull toward solitude and the pull toward the mystery of other worlds, I also wrote about traveling, about living a *bohemian-explorer-intellectual kind of life:* "I wish I was brave enough to do this alone. Yet I know I am not, nor will I ever be." And then, as if in answer to an inarticulate prayer, Ellie was conceived.

Something had been forged between my daughter and me all those years ago. We were marked by her genesis and by all the suffering afterward that her conception had wrought. And as she left me and began making her own life, separate from the one we'd made for her, I wanted to give her a gift, an inheritance. Maybe, like Eve, I wanted to pass on to my daughter a legacy of hunger, a curiosity, a chance to taste and see. So I gave her the journey for which I'd longed and that her arrival had forestalled.

I know that there is a logic that explains *how* cells divide and differentiate to become embryos that become babies that become children who then grow up and leave. But I still haven't found an explanation for *why*. I try to trace it back—past braces, past gangly arms and legs, past round bellies, past the days of crawling, past the days of nursing, past the twinges in the womb, to the moment of conception—and the *why* remains. It's the same *why* we can ask of our expanding universe, traced back through heat and density and time to the Big Bang. In those moments of potential and possibility, before there is anything, when there is nothing, maybe that's where God resides. I don't know. But doubting is a form of hoping.

It's not that I thought that I would find answers for my doubts or solace for my fears by retracing a medieval Dominican friar's pilgrimage path across the Mediterranean and around the Holy Land and through the desert. It's not that I thought that by taking this trip I could resurrect the person I had been before I had children. It's not that I thought that by taking Ellie with me I'd fill the void I'd felt at her departure or prove to her that she herself was not alone. It's not that I thought that I would, in some sacred shrine or some deserted place beneath the stars, finally find a lasting home in God.

Still, I went.

DEPARTURE FROM HOME,
WHEREVER THAT MAY BE

WHEN I CALLED Ellie to ask her if she wanted to come with me, she was in the library at school in Austin and had tried to answer sotto voce as she hurried toward the door to talk outside. But before she could make it out, she was shrieking "Yes!" while the other students glared. I felt so close to her at that moment, so aligned. She *got* it. My daughter *got* it. We'd be a great pair. We'd take notes in our notebooks together. She'd be staff photographer, and once we got to Israel and Egypt, she'd help translate, using the beginning Arabic she was learning that year. I'd coordinate with hostels and hotels and tour guides, and get us from point to point. It's true, as I recall, that I left the length of the journey a little vague, mainly because I was still in the middle of planning and didn't quite have it all plotted out. Weeks later, when it became clear that we'd have to be gone two months, Ellie's enthusiasm seemed tempered. That was a long time to be away from a boyfriend. But by then she had committed and it was too late to back out without hurting me.

Not that I didn't have my own doubts. In the months leading up to our departure, I grew increasingly agitated. All day long as I was driving Mary Martha and Sabine to school, as I was grading student papers, as I was chopping onions for dinner, as I was folding laundry or sweeping the kitchen floor, my mind would wander toward unsettling visions. Of our plane going down in a valley of green hills. Of our train plunging from a bridge strung across a gorge in the Alps. Of our ferry hitting a reef and sinking to the bottom of the sea. Maybe in Jerusalem there would be a suicide bombing on the exact bus we were taking to Jericho. Maybe the Bedouin in the Sinai would hold us hostage, or maybe they would abandon us and we would die of thirst. Maybe in Tahrir Square we'd be trampled by demonstrators or get shot by military police in riot gear.

Whatever fears Terry had for us I think he tried to calm by making intricately detailed schedules of summer camps and sleepovers for Mary Martha and Sabine and visits with family near and far away, of the feeding of dogs and cats and the watering of plants, of the ordering of prescriptions and the purchasing of face wash and shampoo and feminine-hygiene items. Only once did he say to me, "You just can't take any chances." He was worried, he told me later, after I'd returned safely, about the American journalist, the blonde, who'd been raped during the demonstrations in Cairo. And about the old cities full of dark corners. About the impatience Ellie and I shared for inefficiency and narrow-mindedness—bureaucratic and human traits we were fairly likely to encounter as travelers in foreign lands.

While Terry made spreadsheets, I charted our route by sifting through Fabri's *Book of Wanderings* for all the place-names I could find and marking them on an atlas of the Mediterranean I'd come across in an old *National Geographic* magazine. Sometimes the names Fabri used were obsolete Latin designations. Sometimes the names referred to places that no longer existed. But slowly, thanks to the sleuthing abilities that returned to me from a childhood spent reading Nancy Drew along with my relentless searches on the Internet, our itinerary began to take shape.

I got in the habit, after the girls and Terry had gone to bed, of sending e-mails across all those time zones to hostels and convents in the many towns and cities to which we would travel, to tour guides and drivers, to a friend in Frankfurt, to a Franciscan friar and to a guide in Jerusalem, to a wilderness outfitter in the Sinai, to friends of friends in Cairo and friends of friends in Cyprus, to the Italian and Croatian and Greek shipping lines. While they slept, I made my inquiries: *Are you available…? Do you have vacancies…? Is it possible…? Can we follow* this *route through the desert? Can we use camels? Will you provide sleeping bags? A translator? A balm for my fears?* And while I slept fitfully and dreamed of the varieties of our destruction, they replied. I would wake to their notes in broken English, and another piece of the intricate jigsaw puzzle of this wandering route would click into place.

But how much I missed everything, even before we departed — the faces of my younger daughters, the body of my husband beside me in our bed at night, my books and my thrift-store oil portraits and my clawfoot tub, the one Terry had re-enameled just for me. I missed everything as if it were already slipping over the edge of the horizon, far from my sight. It all became imbued with nostalgia because of its impending loss.

Sometimes, too, I would try to picture myself without the others, in some foreign city or on a boat or beneath the desert stars that were even now illuminating the sand. Or I would try to picture my husband and daughters and our house and the shady backyard without me. It was as if, in imagining my imminent disappearance, I was imagining my afterlife, the days here, in this particular place, continuing to dawn without me in them.

What was I doing, chasing after a celibate Dominican friar who surely would not have approved of the travels of a religious skeptic and married woman who had daughters still at home? And those daughters — Mary Martha and Sabine — would they feel abandoned? Or, being teenagers, would they even notice that I was gone? And Terry? What would he do without me for two months?

He had no cooking skills to speak of. Would he remember to feed the girls fruit? What if one of them had an emotional crisis? What if *he* did? Still, as soon as classes ended that May, Ellie came home and we packed and repacked the matching backpacks that I'd bought from the wilderness outfitter with our clothes and toiletries, trying to discard everything inessential. Ellie kept taking out shoes to make room for her books—one for every week of our journey. Back when she was fifteen, as she was beginning to put aside her Harry Potter novels, she had told me, "I'm working on building my library." She slowly filled the shelves in her room with an indiscriminate mix of the classics and contemporary fiction, keeping a running count of the number of books she possessed at any given time. Now, as she packed, she made a list in her notebook of those she was bringing:

1. Flannery O'Connor's *Complete Stories*
2. Jhumpa Lahiri's *The Namesake*
3. Jhumpa Lahiri's *Interpreter of Maladies*
4. Umberto Eco's *The Mysterious Flame of Queen Loana*
5. John Irving's *The World According to Garp*
6. Ian McEwan's *Atonement*
7. José Saramago's *Death with Interruptions*
8. Isabel Allende's *Eva Luna*

I brought only my knitting, Steinbeck's *East of Eden,* whose descriptions of the land Ellie thought I might like, and Fabri.

The departure, when it finally came, was all wrong. Terry had to go out of town on business and would not return until after we'd left, so he and I had ended up saying good-bye days before, when my leaving did not yet feel real. It was my parents, then, who would pick Ellie and me up and take us to the airport for our flight to Frankfurt. That afternoon, as Ellie and I waited for them, our luggage piled in the entryway, I gave Mary Martha and Sabine each a locket with my picture in it, just like the locket I would wear with their photos all through the trip. And then my parents pulled up, and I had to just leave the girls standing on the curb outside, their arms draped around each other for comfort, as we drove off. Terry would return in a few hours, but I cried the whole way to the airport, recalling the Elizabeth Bishop poem "Questions of Travel" that I'd looked up and scribbled into my notebook at the last minute:

> *Think of the long trip home.*
> *Should we have stayed at home and thought of here?*
> *Where should we be today?*
> *Is it right to be watching strangers in a play*
> *in this strangest of theatres?*
> *What childishness is it that while there's a breath of life*
> *in our bodies, we are determined to rush*
> *to see the sun the other way around?*

And as we checked our bags and as we went through security and as we sat on the runway in the plane, that line—*Should we have stayed at home and thought of here?*—kept running through my mind, an accusing refrain.

I have implied that the birth of Ellie at the end of my senior year in college cut off certain possibilities for me, including foreign travel. But that is not entirely true. The *bohemian-explorer-intellectual kind of life* was no longer an option, that's for certain. And yet there had been the Ireland honeymoon with Terry, in the days before the rise of the Celtic Tiger—and then its collapse—when we'd rented a car and driven along the west coast photographing derelict castles and unkempt sheep and piles of drying peat, stopping for tea and scones in every little village. And before that, the summer of the year I finished graduate school, just after Ellie turned two, my mother had driven up to Lawrence and stayed with her for a couple of weeks so that I could backpack around Europe with my friend Sabine Mahr, a German exchange student I'd met at the university the year before. My parents bought my plane ticket as a graduation gift, and I paid for the rest with the five-hundred-dollar inheritance I'd received from my grandmother Elvina, who'd died when I was pregnant with Ellie, and whom I'd named my daughter for.

Sabine and I wandered the cobbled streets of Prague and went across the Charles Bridge in the brand-new Czech Republic and then returned at night to our oddly configured apartment carved from a much larger space in the Communist era but with the grace of its porcelain plates, hand-painted in blue and pink and gold, and its tall, narrow windows covered in lace and overlooking a grassy courtyard still intact. In Vienna, we visited Schönbrunn Palace and a Klimt exhibit and drank coffee and ate pastries in rococo cafés. In Venice we roamed the maze of canals lined with decadent and decaying palazzi and cathedrals and took the ferry to Saint Mark's Square every morning from the island of Giudecca, where we stayed in a convent run by tiny nuns who spoke no English. In Naples, we spent our last lira on gelato and pizza and stayed in an overcrowded hostel room with girls from Australia who came in late and loud and drunk. The next day we took the train to Pompeii and walked the excavated streets of that ancient, doomed city and saw, in the stone storerooms, piles of amphorae and plaster casts of the huddled bodies whose flesh had been buried in volcanic ash.

In the years since that trip we'd taken together, Sabine and I had kept in touch. She visited Terry and me in Houston after we had married. I named, as you will have noticed, my youngest daughter after her. Later, Terry and I traveled to Frankfurt to attend her wedding to Martin and bowed our heads as the choir sang a Bach cantata in the muted light of a September afternoon. Now Sabine and Martin and their children lived in a graceful old apartment in Frankfurt with high ceilings and parquet floors, furnished with Sabine's grandmother's antiques and sleek modern couches and lamps, children's artwork, and floor-to-ceiling bookshelves filled with books. Ellie and I stayed there for a couple of days to allow our bodies time to adjust before heading to Fabri's hometown of Ulm.

The morning after we arrived, Sabine drove us out to Kloster Eberbach, a former Cistercian monastery nestled in the Kisselbach Valley near the Rhine. She thought this might be a good way for us to ease into our travels—with a tangible vision of the sort of home Fabri would have left. The monastery was enclosed by walls and hedges, and we wandered the grounds within, shaded by enormous fir trees and small conical spruces and birches pruned like umbrellas, listening to the audio guide.

Built up in the twelfth and thirteenth centuries, this monastery was more than a place of devotion and education and care for the poor and the sick; in its seclusion, it was its own complete and self-sustaining world. We toured the dormitory, a light-filled space of vaulted Gothic ceilings and deep recessed windows and cold stone floors where, after compline, the last divine office of the day, the monks would lay themselves down to sleep on rough pallets until called again to the chancel shortly after midnight to sing the Psalms and recite the prayers for matins. We passed through the refectory, where the brothers would eat their spare meals in the fullness of silence. We sat in the Romanesque basilica with its sturdy walls and clerestory windows, the light from the stained glass refracting, breaking, broken, no ornamentation to distract from contemplation and connection with the divine. The gardens in the center of the cloister complex were, the audio guide told us, a stand-in for paradise.

We passed through the garden and then had lunch in the sun in a café with a cobblestoned patio overlooking the grounds of the monastery while elegant elderly Germans drank Riesling and talked in the early-afternoon light, and I thought of the opening stanza of T. S. Eliot's *The Waste Land,* that poem of displacement and spiritual wandering through a world that has been shattered into fragments:

Summer surprised us, coming over the Starnbergersee
With a shower of rain; we stopped in the colonnade,
And went on in sunlight, into the Hofgarten,
And drank coffee, and talked for an hour.

That night after dinner and after the children were tucked into their beds, Ellie and I talked with Sabine and Martin about traveling. Perhaps with the Elizabeth Bishop line still in my head, I asked them why we feel compelled to leave home on these journeys. "I have this map of the world in my mind," Sabine offered, "and I am slowly filling it in with all the places I've been. When I travel somewhere, I suddenly have a connection with that particular place. And then later, I remember things that happened in certain cities or I remember the view from the train. And the map fills in and becomes very personal. It is my *own* map of the world."

The next day, Sabine made tomato and brie sandwiches on brown bread for Ellie and me and she drove us to the train station, where we would board the 14:18 for Ulm. The blue sky of the day before had turned gray and it was starting to rain, delicately, poignantly. We were all quiet and sad at this departure, which would separate us again after such a short time. "There is a word for what I am feeling now," Sabine turned to me and said. "We say *Wehmut.* This is like..."—she paused and pressed her hand to her chest, to her heart—"a feeling in the body. It's an ache. Like a longing to be with someone. Like a sadness of parting."

The familiarity of home is like sanded wood. We pass smoothly through our days hardly noticing the particulars. Traveling, we get snagged on splinters. We are in a constant state of awakening and revelation, and we notice details that those whose home we are traveling through cannot see, so accustomed are they to it all. In Germany, the long, narrow sugar packets and tiny spoons served with coffee. The flowers spilling from window boxes. The cut of all the men's jackets. The women in office attire pedaling bikes and still looking fabulous. And yet, when we depart from our homes and from those we love, when we travel to places unfamiliar to us, home remains like a film covering our eyes that we can't quite wipe away. We see through its lens.

For Felix Fabri, the lens through which he measures all that he sees, from the palazzi of Venice to the slave markets in Alexandria, is Ulm. Ulm is a city in the Swabian region of what is now southern Germany but was then, during the friar's lifetime, a free imperial city of the Holy Roman Empire, beholden to no petty feudal princes or dukes, only to Emperor Frederick III himself. Fabri was sent to Ulm in 1474 from the Dominican convent in Basel, where he had first professed his vows at fifteen or sixteen years of age and taken the habit of the Preaching Friars after a year's novitiate. The ceremony occurred on the feast day of Saint Catherine of Alexandria, when Fabri "out of love for her . . . bound myself for ever to the service of God and of this virgin" as his spiritual spouse. A detail that I love, one of the few biographical scraps that have survived: before taking his vows and rejecting the temporal world, Fabri had been Felix Schmidt, a member of the ruling class of Zurich. The family's coat of arms was "a globe argent on a field sable"—that is, a silver world framed by black, the earth spinning through the dark universe. Like the Pilgrim costume my mother sewed me, perhaps his family's arms had called this wanderer of the globe into being.

The Ulm Fabri enters and quickly embraces as his adoptive city—with its cobblestoned streets, and *fachwerk* houses, half timbered and plastered in between, with its roof tiles like fish scales, with its stone wall rising above the left bank of the Danube punctuated by entry gates and towers, with its footbridges over the rivers Blau and Iller, which wind through the city and spill into the Danube, with its spired minster church, its public fountains and market squares and *Rathaus*—this Ulm is in the midst of a cultural and religious flowering with which much of Germany stirs, having crawled out of the dark years of waste and devastation wrought by the Black Death the century before.

Because the Dominicans are a mendicant order, devoted to a life of active engagement with the world through preaching the Gospel and serving the poor, the Dominican priory, unlike the serene and remote Kloster Eberbach of the Cistercians, has been built right in the midst of the tumult of Ulm, where priests and monks and nobles move among book printers and mapmakers and glove makers, dyers and spinners and weavers, tailors, glaziers, tanners, cobblers, blacksmiths and goldsmiths and locksmiths and farriers, millers and barbers, innkeepers, butchers and bakers and candlestick makers. In this frenetic, thriving city, the lowly find justice equally with the nobility. Here, Fabri says, "One hears the news of the day from the East and the West more than in any city in Swabia. Here there is joy and sorrow, life and death, here, virtue and vice."

Beyond this cultural vitality, which surrounds and invigorates him, Fabri participates in the Observant Movement, a drive toward religious revitalization and reform dominating the region at the time. To turn away from the world's vanities and return to the principles of apostolic life by keeping more exactly the rules of

the orders, to kindle an inner desire for union with the divine—
these were, broadly speaking, its goals. But the Observant Movement, though it sought reform, was not a harbinger of things to
come, said Kathryne Beebe, a Fabri scholar, when we met one day
in Fort Worth at the café at the Kimbell Art Museum. For though
it was Germany, and though the Reformation would arrive within
decades, and the monasteries and priories and friaries and convents of Ulm would be forced to dissolve in the new dispensation,
the Observant Movement seemed neither to anticipate this revolution nor to nourish it. Instead it looked back to a more perfect past
and tried to resurrect it. It could not imagine the new world on the
horizon just beginning to come into view.

In some ways, this disappoints me. I want the pilgrim in whose
footsteps I'm walking to be heading forward, not back. "Fabri
would have been blindsided by the Reformation," Kathryne Beebe
said over coffee. "He was quite orthodox. He was an amalgamation
of the Late Middle Ages and the Renaissance. He was interested in
natural history, for example. He'd read Pliny. But at the same time,
he *loved* his indulgences." Yet as Beebe told me more about Fabri's
involvement with the Observant Movement and about his sermons
to the nuns in the numerous convents ringing Ulm, cloistered nuns
for whom he served as spiritual pastor, I was moved. "He urged
them not to be so intent on following the rules but instead to focus
on the spirit of them," Beebe explained.

And I am moved, as well, by the great affection Fabri feels for
his adopted city, the place by which he measures all that he encounters on his travels, the lens through which he sees the world.
Fabri even envisions the final section of his *Book of Wanderings* to be
a treatise devoted to the history of Swabia and the city of Ulm, so
that the written narrative, like the journey itself, will end at home.
In Ulm, Hans Eugen Specker, a historian of the city, would tell me
that when Fabri returned from his pilgrimage and approached the

Danube, the silhouette of the city rising up just beyond, he called Ulm his *Mutterland,* his "mother country." Meaning the place that gave birth to who he was. The place of comfort and familiarity for which he had longed when he was a stranger in a strange land.

In Fabri's Ulm, Ellie and I got off the 14:18 and lumbered toward the town center under the weight of our backpacks, the cathedral's spire our north star. Evening bells were ringing and American pop music was playing somewhere and the sounds of a soccer game filtered out from the bars and kebab restaurants. We dropped off our bags at our hotel and then set out to find something to eat in the remnants of the medieval quarter—cobblestoned streets, half-timbered houses, entry towers—that Fabri would still have recognized. Where the Herdbrücke, the Herd Bridge, crossed the Danube near the old city walls, we shared a pizza at an outdoor café while a Bier Bike, one of those bars on wheels pedaled by drunk young men, passed back and forth across the bridge.

Afterward, as we walked the cobblestoned streets eating gelato, Ellie and I wondered what Terry and Mary Martha and Sabine were doing in Houston. It was early afternoon there. The sun would have burned off the morning humidity. The bungalows and cottages of our neighborhood would be quiet in the lull after lunch. Terry would be working. Without me there to wake them up, the girls might still be sleeping. "So what is home for you now, Ellie?" I asked. She thought for a minute and then answered, "I don't really feel like I have a *home* home right now." It wasn't Houston, she confessed, where we were giving her old room to Sabine so that she and Mary Martha no longer had to share. It wasn't Austin, where she'd lived in a dorm her freshman year and where all of her belongings were in storage until her apartment lease began in the fall. "I used to think home was with the people you love—like wherever those people are, that's your home," she continued. "But

I think there's actually a *physicalness* to home. Home has to be a physical space with objects in it. Because objects have memories attached to them. And we're human beings and our physical things remind us of who we are."

We talked about how, growing up, Ellie had always been split between two homes—ours in Houston and Steve and Tracy's in Kansas City. "I remember going between the two houses was like going between two planets," she told me. "In Kansas, we had seven TVs for six people—and we had cable." In Houston, we had one television with rabbit ears. "And open up the pantry in Kansas: Cinnamon Toast Crunch, Frosted Flakes, Lucky Charms," Ellie remembered. "In Houston, the most exciting thing you might find would be Panda Puffs. Mostly it was Life or Cheerios."

This movement back and forth between homes seemed to create in Ellie a persistent sense of dislocation and confusion. Maybe that dislocation is what Ellie was referring to when, at age seven, she'd cried out in a rage to me, "You don't know what's inside my mind! You don't know how hard my life is!" Later, when she calmed down, she sobbed about all the coming and going between Houston and Kansas City, about not being with her dad.

Ellie told me about a dream she had had years later, when she was sixteen and building her library. In it, I decide that I want to radically simplify our life. This requires moving to the country, where we no longer live in a house but in the trees, in a structure made of rope. We sleep on hammocks of strings. I have decided that this move must take place immediately, so the girls have time to pack only two outfits and no chance to phone anyone to say good-bye. After we leave town, I bring them to a bookstore and tell them they can each buy two books. Ellie chooses Italo Calvino and Gabriel García Márquez.

What does this dream signify? At the time, we'd been reading the book of Genesis in my class at the university. Were the girls and

I like Noah and his three sons, compelled by God to gather the animals, two by two, and escape the floods that He will send to wipe away the corrupt creation He's made, another radical simplification? Was I the Lord Himself, forcing this uprooting, my daughters at the mercy of my inexplicable jealousy to have them all to myself in a kind of garden? Was this dream a reflection of Ellie's own sense of deep instability, her fear that at any moment she would have to abandon those she loves, her fear that she could be abandoned by them to live in a dwelling made of rope that is never fixed in one place? Or was it instead an expression of some deep restlessness in her to grab only what was necessary and escape?

Books, maps, notebooks. These were the essentials. On our trips across America when the girls were younger, that's what I always packed for them in the bags that sat by their feet in the station wagon. You're bored? Read. Where are we? How long till we get there? Look at the map I've copied from the atlas and laminated just for you. You see something strange or beautiful or unsettling, something you want to remember? Write it down before it escapes you. Though in the dream we seem to be at cross-purposes, I love that in it Ellie and I both recognize the necessity to carry two books into the apocalypse.

What could I claim as my home, my mother country? What was home for me now?

The summer before my kindergarten year, my parents, who had both been raised in St. Louis by parents who had themselves grown up in St. Louis, packed up a U-Haul and left behind their brothers and sisters and nieces and nephews and the small Missouri town where my father had been coaching football and wrestling and teaching driver's ed on the side to make ends meet, and headed south to Texas to try to make a better life for their children than they were likely to find in the dying Midwest. "Dear Mother and

Pop," my dad wrote to his parents in the midst of preparations for the move as they grappled with the loss of their only son and his growing family, "Received your letter yesterday and it helped relieve my apprehensions of how you felt about it all. I know how you feel. Our children mean all there is to us and someday we'll have to make the same sacrifice. But because they mean so much to us now I feel I must give them more than what this present situation can afford."

Along with other transplanted families, like Terry's from Detroit, we settled in the Woodlands, then a new development north of the city of Houston being built on land in the Piney Woods that had once been part of a large logging operation. Before that, native Atakapan tribes had ranged through the area, hunting and gathering and smearing their bodies with alligator grease to protect them from mosquitoes, though they don't appear to have formed any permanent settlements. And anyway they were all gone by the time settlers began arriving in the early 1800s. We drove up in our U-Haul in 1974 at the beginning of a regional boom. In the Woodlands, whose marketing campaign declared it "A Real Hometown," my father, in a great American act of reinvention, eventually made a life for himself and our family neither coaching nor teaching, but building houses.

So I became a child of the suburbs—a child of sawdust and cul-de-sacs and concrete slabs, of the new utopia. And though I was not overtly conscious that something was missing in the flat and humid Gulf Coast where we had gone to live, nevertheless I missed the hills, I missed the seasons, I missed the cousins and aunts and uncles of the Missouri that I barely remembered. When my grandfather sent me some leaves from his backyard that he'd pressed one fall, glued to mat board and labeled in his slanting, architectural *ALL CAPS* hand, I treasured it for some reason I couldn't name then but now suspect was that it represented the lost world that had been fractured. "Should we have stayed at home," Elizabeth Bishop asks again at the end of "Questions of Travel," "wherever that may be?" I felt a similar wandering dislocation.

In the Woodlands, where everything was new and blank, I craved history and complexity and texture. Instead of Barbies, I played with the Sunshine Family, all three generations of whom—grandparents, parents, and children—wore Birkenstocks and lived on the Sunshine Family Farm, traveled the country in their Sunshine Family Van with Piggyback Shack, and made a living spinning yarn and throwing pottery in their Sunshine Family Craft Store. I read the Laura Ingalls Wilder Little House books obsessively, over and over again, and wore my hair in two long braids. My mother sewed me a calico pioneer outfit—sunbonnet, pinafore, apron—as she would sew me a Pilgrim costume a year or two later. Despite living in Houston, I fantasized about eating the tail of a freshly butchered pig roasted over a fire and about making candy by drizzling hot molasses over milk pans filled with snow. I took quilting classes. I taught myself needlepoint and embroidery. I sat on the floor of my bedroom one afternoon and watched the shadowy pattern of leaves disappear and ran my hand across what was not there. In another letter to his parents, sent after the move, my father wrote, "Kim still baffles our understanding at times. Growing up 'is painful' as she says."

Despite my family, who loved me though I baffled them, I felt alone. Books helped. They were a way to live life elsewhere, to feel the conflict and the mystery lacking in the banal place where my body resided, where there was almost nothing to do except go to the mall or the Cineplex, both miles down the highway. But it wasn't until the spring day in my freshman year in high school when my English teacher, Mignon Walker, her long auburn hair wound up into a loose nest on the top of her head, perched herself on a stool at the front of the room and read us Ezra Pound's

"The River-Merchant's Wife: A Letter" that I began to see how the world of words might bring me solace by leading me into a community of other minds like mine. I wasn't conscious of this yet. I didn't really know what it was that drew me, later that summer on humid nights, air oppressive as wet wool, to pull out my photocopy of "The River-Merchant's Wife" and sit in my window, reading it over and over again. I knew I loved the sounds the words made. But I see now that there is a sort of ache in the words that matched the ache I felt—those blue plums, that river of swirling eddies, all those sorrowful monkeys, the paired butterflies in the West garden in autumn that the river-merchant's wife writes to her husband about when he is far away. The poem did not bring solace by helping me escape from the ache I felt but by embodying it so precisely in words. Those were the same words that, years later, I would send to Terry, when I ached for him, *forever and forever and forever.*

But if words had become for me a comfort in my exile, still, where was my home? Was it really the Woodlands? Was it St. Louis, where almost none of my family still lived? Was it the cluster of German villages near the Rhine that my father's family had emigrated from? Or the farmland along the Mississippi River south of St. Louis that they immigrated to? Was it Lawrence, Kansas, where I'd given birth to Ellie and whose streets I wandered in my dreams for years after I left, once I'd married Terry and we moved to Lawton? Was it Oklahoma, where Terry and I began our life? Was it Houston, where we now lived, that messy, sprawling, polyglot city of Latinos and Southeast Asians and Vietnamese and Chinese, of Middle Eastern Muslims and Russian Jews, of African Americans, the descendants of freed slaves—and all of their delicious food?

In Willa Cather's *My Ántonia,* that poignant love letter to the land and to Red Cloud, Nebraska, Cather's childhood home, Jim Burden is reading Virgil's *Georgics* when he comes to the beginning of the third book and discovers these lines: "'Primus ego in patriam mecum...deducam Musas,' 'For I shall be the first, if I live, to bring the Muse into my country.'" Jim remembers what his Latin tutor had explained to the class: that "'patria' here meant, not a nation or even a province, but the little rural neighborhood on the Mincio where the poet was born. This was not a boast, but a hope, at once bold and devoutly humble, that he might bring the Muse (but lately come to Italy from her cloudy Grecian mountains), not to the capital, the palatia Romana, but to his own little 'country'; to his father's fields, 'sloping down to the river and to the old beech trees with the broken tops.'" And Jim thinks, as Cather herself must have thought, of his own *patria*—the land itself and its inhabitants, the Bohemian immigrants like Ántonia, and the Danish laundry girls of his memory.

My Ántonia had been on that list of books I'd sent to Terry in Cuba. "In my mind, *My Ántonia* was so connected to you," he wrote upon finishing it, "that I could not have read it before, when we were not together." I knew why he felt that way. I felt that way too. Ántonia has a child out of wedlock, but she scorns the town that scorns her. She goes on to marry a farmer, and together they make the land fecund—an orchard and a garden—and fill their *patria* with children. This was the vision that we shared.

And yet, I have no *patria*. No fields sloping down to a river. No beech trees with broken tops to pass on to my children. I sometimes wonder if my real home is the station wagon Terry and I would pack up every summer when the girls were small, or the tent in which we all slept together, expertly set up by Terry while I cooked dinner on our portable propane stove and the girls ran around in the grass. Perhaps we carried our home, *wherever that may be,* across the country with us and placed it temporarily among the stumps of redwoods left by loggers and the alder and fern that had filled in the empty spaces between. And near the

Pacific Ocean on the coast of Oregon, and the North Rim of the Grand Canyon, and a hillside overlooking the ancient pueblos of Mesa Verde. Or in the Black Hills of South Dakota one July night. And beside Lake Pepin in Wisconsin, where the sky seemed so wide and open that I felt dizzy and thought I could sense the spinning earth beneath me. Where I had the sensation that if I stood up, I might fall off.

And yet, my heart was a homeless child. It wanted to attach itself to something permanent—*Mutterland, patria*—and take root. That's why I understood the pilgrim's sense of exile, and his quest through fields, lands, countries for an eternal home in God.

On the fourteenth of April, 1483, on the feast day of Saints Tiburtius and Valerianus, Friar Felix Fabri, dressed in his long gray gown with monk's cowl, red cross embroidered upon it by virgins, reads Mass and breaks his fast, then calls together the brethren of his convent. He tells them that he must leave them now, and he begs for a pilgrim's blessing from the prior. "He led me into the choir, wither the whole convent accompanied me," Fabri recalls, "and kneeling in the midst of the choir in the presence of the Holy Sacrament, I received a blessing from the altar, amid the exceeding bitter weeping of the Prior of the convent and all the brethren." We say *Wehmut*, Sabine Mahr had told me, pressing her hand to her chest—sick at heart, an ache in the body, a longing to be with someone, a sadness of parting.

"When I had received my blessing," Fabri recalls, "my sobs and tears made me unable to bid my brethren farewell in words, but my tears, my sorrowful face and my sobs spoke for me. I therefore embraced and kissed each of the brethren, and begged to be remembered in their prayers." He mounts his horse as the friars flock round, pleading with him to "take careful note of all the holy places I saw, and to write an account of them and bring it to them, so that they also, in mind, if not in body, might enjoy the pleasure of visiting the holy places."

Ellie and I strolled through the medieval quarter of Ulm eating gelato and talking of home and arrived at the only remnant of the Dominican priory that still exists: that same choir of the church where Fabri receives his blessing and says good-bye. I find this miraculous. Somewhere near here, forming a wall of the priory's garden, would have been a tower that housed prisoners in wooden cells, prisoners who were sometimes tortured to reveal the secrets of their hearts. From the tower, the accused would stretch out their hands through the windows and beg the friars to pray to God for them. But the tower is gone now, as are the gardens below, and the dormitory, and the refectory, and all the church but the choir. This vestige had been annexed centuries ago by a Protestant church, and the whole structure had been restored after World War II and then renamed: Haus der Begegnung, the House of Encounter. Beneath an asphalt patch outside, I'd heard, was the cemetery for the friars. Ellie and I stood in the choir, in that curvature of space with its narrow Gothic windows ascending to let in the late-day sun. We felt enclosed in a womb of light.

Afterward, we walked through a vaulted brick tunnel whose iron doors opened up onto the city walls that dropped down to the Danube. Ellie, staff photographer, took my picture standing on the Herd Bridge spanning the river. After Fabri, weeping, passes through the gates of the convent, he rides stealthily through the city as though hiding himself, perhaps unable to withstand any more painful farewells. Then he crosses the Danube by the bridge on which I would stand five hundred years later. Beyond the bridge are the pastures where flocks graze. Beyond the pastures the Alps. Beyond the Alps the sea. Beyond that, the unknown and whatever was to come.

II. ILLUSTRATIONS OF
THE UNSEEN WORLD

Venice

The kingdom of God cometh not with observation.
—Luke 17:20

IMAGO MUNDI

"EVERYTHING GOOD IS on the highway," Ralph Waldo Emerson wrote, and when we drive out west, as we did when the girls were little, as we still sometimes do, away from the strip centers and the car dealerships and the neon signs, past the Katy Prairie, which is covered by a mall, past Flatonia and Seguin and Luling, past San Antonio, I believe him. Out there somewhere, I once saw in a field of prickly pear near a barbed-wire fence a hand-painted billboard proclaiming *The Unseen is Eternal!* Then the grass-covered tors of the central Texas hill country bled into the western mesas. After that, an immense emptiness opened up where I could think about that sign.

In America, *everything good is on the highway*. Everything good is in motion toward. We're always lighting out for the territory ahead of the rest, 'cause tramps like us, baby, we were born to run. We hold tight to our romance with the open road and the freedom it implies. Train travel, with its tightly controlled schedules and finite destinations, is largely obsolete, other than for commuters between cities and suburbs along the East Coast or for cattle heading to slaughter. Traveling by train in Europe, therefore, felt quaint and slightly antiquated to me, suffused with nostalgia, though for a past I've never known. The cavernous ironwork stations with their numbered platforms and timetables and trains departing for towns and cities both nearby and far-flung. Filtered light sifting in from massive arched windows covered in a thin film of grime. Food stands and cafés near the entrance where you could drink a cappuccino in a tiny cup or sip a glass of wine. At the station in Ulm, as Ellie and I sat on a bench waiting for the train that would take us to Venice, we watched the businessmen with their quirky glasses and natty suits reading the *Süddeutsche Zeitung,* and the little schoolchildren on an outing, three or four years old, holding hands by twos and threes, wearing socks with their sandals, kerchiefs around their necks or on their heads. I loved the novelty of taking the train.

That morning back at our hotel before our departure from Ulm, Ellie and I had surreptitiously made sandwiches of cheese and salami and cucumber and tomato on sturdy brown rolls from the breakfast spread in the dining room. I went first, and Ellie watched me in mock horror, and then made one for herself. With exaggerated stealth, we wrapped them in paper napkins and stuffed them into our bags along with apples and some chocolate. If I could have figured out how to take a few hard-boiled eggs without breaking them, I would have. Now, on the train, our bags stowed in the luggage racks at the end of the cabin, my knitting and Ellie's book at hand, we pulled out our stolen feast and congratulated ourselves on our foresight and thrift.

The train that carried me and Ellie from Ulm to Venice roughly tracked Fabri's path by horseback in mid-April 1483, through deep spring mud over the Alps to the Mediterranean Sea. Fabri has set out alone and plans, somewhere in the mountains, to overtake the party of nobles with whom he'll travel as confessor and priest. In the village of Schneckenhausen, he passes the night in an inn where workers from the silver mines gamble and drink and where, in the morning, some of the guests wake to discover they have been robbed, their purses drawn from under their pillows while they slept. That day, Fabri follows winding paths up mountains and then down through green valleys until he reaches Innsbruck, where he just misses the nobles, only recently departed, who received commendatory letters from the Archduke Sigismund, addressed to the doge and the senate of Venice. But at an inn in Sterzing, he catches up with them, and they go on through the mountains together.

The pilgrims travel through Brixen hurriedly because they hear that the plague is wreaking havoc there. They find that the town of Botzen has burned entirely, save, miraculously, for the monasteries and churches. "We passed the night in this town, and saw much misery," recalls Fabri, "for many people were living among the ruins of their houses, without any roof or places of shelter, and many were leaving the town as beggars who had heretofore been rich men." Beyond the Adige River, they cross a fertile hill country full of castles and villages. While resting the horses in Neumarkt, Fabri is approached by a servant on behalf of another Dominican priest. The servant asks the friar who he is and from whence he comes, but Fabri suspects the Dominican of being a renegade priest and will not answer, "for discontented and runaway brethren both of our order and of other orders betake themselves to these parts and to the hill country, where they find the safest of hiding-places, and as everything there is very cheap, they are able to live a dissolute life, and they visit the country people, telling them about the value of Masses, so that their hearers buy Masses of them, both for themselves and their dead relatives, not knowing that the sin of simony is incurred by doing so."

Nearing Trent, they pass through the frontier between Germany and Italy, and at an inn in the city, a jongleur plays the flute while his wife sings for the pilgrims late into the night. With the common people in the marketplace in Treviso, they watch a miracle play on the life of Saint Desiderius, whose feast day it is, and then sell their horses and hire others to take them to the coast. In Mestre, they board a boat, and "when we were came to the place where the river glides into the jaws of the Mediterranean, at the edge and border of the sea, and sailed into the bitter salt water," Fabri remembers, "we began in loud and cheerful tones to sing the pilgrims' hymn, which those who are journeying to the Sepulchre of our Lord are wont to sing."

As our train passed through southern Germany, Ellie read her book of Flannery O'Connor short stories while I looked out the window, which framed fields planted and fallow, chartreuse, leaf green, black, and grasses so lush I longed to rub my hand across their surface as if along an animal's back. The fields and swaths of trees would give way now and then to the rush of a village— red-tile roofs with satellite dishes and spired steeples and onion domes and graffiti I could not understand. On the outskirts, industrial parks and *Schrebergärten*—small planted plots of vegetables and flowers with cheerfully painted sheds, tidy and hung with gardening implements. Then the green of the countryside again.

In the Austrian Tyrol, the train ran for miles and miles along a wide river and crossed valleys like abysses, steep and angular and fir-covered. Between Innsbruck and Brenner, the mountains led into lush valleys and cheery white houses with dark roofs of slate. Outside Brixen, where the plague had raged in 1483, terraced hillsides of vineyards curved in lines like waves, and rows of espaliered fruit trees furrowed the valley floor. Near Botzen, which had burned entirely, we entered the blanks of tunnels and then came out again into the world of sunlight and form. South of the Alps, near Trent, the announcements now in both German and Italian, I noticed orchards bordered by flame-shaped cypress trees, fields of solar panels, meadows of hazy golden grain.

Approaching Verona, tired of sitting, needing to stretch, I stood between train cars breathing in fresh air from an open window and looked out on the little backyard gardens, the crumbling stucco houses with their green-painted wooden shutters. I wanted to peer inside, but everything blurred as we rushed past. How unknowable all places are to pilgrims, to strangers and wayfarers, to wanderers through fields, lands, countries, to passers through, I thought. How fleeting the observable world. Only *the Unseen is Eternal!*

In her study *The Medieval Vision,* the historian Carolly Erickson argues that medieval people had a palpable sense of the unseen that is eternal. They saw into "an enchanted world in which the boundaries of imagination and factuality are constantly shifting." Though they could distinguish between the corporeal and the transcendent, medievals shared a flexibility of perception to which we moderns, inheritors of the Enlightenment who equate reality with materiality, have lost access. But reality for the medievals was in part composed of a mysterious spiritual congregation inhabiting the realm between God and man. Angels and saints who could intercede on their behalf. Demons and devils moving in the dust of light. Theirs was an animated world where the miraculous crouched within the mundane. Where the mundane could, at any moment, burst forth into the miraculous: a raven colonized by the spirit of an excommunicated soul, an apparition of a ship sailing across the firmament's black sea, the death of thousands of fish in the night preceding the death of a king.

"To a medieval man or woman," Erickson concludes, "the world of sensation was only one part of a much vaster pattern of unchanging and immortal reality that stretched out far beyond the boundaries of known time. Day-to-day experience occupied a finite plane in this infinite scheme; it was only a pause between two eternities. The visionary imagination linked the finite with the infinite, and the imminent possibility of such a link made medieval people watchful for visions."

I think what drew me to retrace Fabri's medieval journey was in part a hope that I might see briefly into that unseen, enchanted realm, like catching a glimpse into the unknowable lives of others from the window of a passing train. I was caught in this earthly *pause between two eternities*. But if I could know that this pause in which I was watching my own erasure in the growing bodies and shifting faces of my daughters—images of me—was only part of an immortal pattern of reality that did not change, this might allow me to let them go.

When Fabri and the other pilgrims with whom he travels enter the Grand Canal on April 27, 1483, the Venetian republic still controls much of the Mediterranean despite the Ottoman Empire's conquest of Constantinople thirty years before, and despite the Turks' push into the Balkans during the period in which Fabri sails. With Venetian stone forts guarding ports along the Dalmatian coast and throughout Greece and on Cyprus, pilgrims from across Europe congregate in Venice to book passage on the pilgrim galleys that sail from there to the port of Joppa on the coast of Palestine just after Ascension Day and the ceremony of the Wedding with the Sea each spring.

In their hired boat, the German pilgrims navigate the Grand Canal as far as the Rialto Bridge, where they turn off into another canal and pass the Fondaco dei Tedeschi, the warehouse of the Germans, where merchants store the goods the trading ships haul in from the ports of Beirut and Alexandria. Across mountains and fertile valleys and arid deserts, on the dusty backs of camels plodding from Persia and India, come the gums and silks and precious stones, come the pepper and the spices; to Damascus and to Cairo and then, on merchant ships, these goods sail out of the Mediterranean ports to Venice and in horse-drawn carts are carried from there to all of Europe. Venice is an epicenter of earthly delights.

Just around the corner from the Fondaco dei Tedeschi, the pilgrims disembark at the Inn of Saint George, where they are greeted by the innkeepers, Master John and Mistress Margaret, and all the manservants and maidservants, every one of whom is German. Fabri initially hopes to lodge at the nearby convent of Saint Dominic, "for it was unpleasant for me, and very distracting to my thoughts, to live entirely among secular persons." But this displeases the lords among whom the friar travels, and so they arrange with Master John to give Fabri a room of his own, where, he recalls, "I could be quite alone, and could sleep, pray, read, and write, and escape from all the noise of the inn as well as if I were in my own cell at Ulm."

Ellie and I had reserved a cell of our own, of sorts. All the hotels near the Rialto, in the heart of the tourist center of Venice, either had been booked or were too expensive, and anyway, in keeping with the spirit of our journey, it seemed more appropriate to hire a room at the convent guesthouse of the Suore Figlie di San Giuseppe del Caburlotto, the Sisters of Saint Joseph of Caburlotto, which turned out to be far from the center of anything. I had wanted desperately to stay at the hostel where Sabine Mahr and I stayed when I'd traveled those precious couple of weeks with her after finishing grad school. I still had the hand-stamped card from the convent in my notebook: Suore Canossiane, Ponte Piccolo 428, Giudecca, and the *telefono*. That was in the days before Internet reservations, and somehow, speaking no Italian, Sabine Mahr and I had found our way by *vaporetto* to the island of La Giudecca, directly south across the Giudecca Canal from Saint Mark's Square, and reserved two beds. Unfortunately, despite the years that had elapsed between that trip and this, the Sisters Canossiane didn't have much of a presence on the World Wide Web, and in my desire to have a confirmed room booked for me and Ellie, I went with the Suore Figlie di San Giuseppe del Caburlotto, who did.

As Ellie and I walked from the Santa Lucia train station toward the convent along workaday canals, our backpacks, which had been heavy enough in cool, gray Ulm, became, under the oppressive heat of Venice's late-day sun and with the thought of carrying them for nearly two more months, almost unbearably unwieldy. Trying to rally Ellie and myself I joked, "At least as we use up the shampoo, our packs will get lighter."

The guesthouse of the Suore Figlie di San Giuseppe del Caburlotto was located in the Santa Croce district of Venice on Fondamenta Rizzi, a canal, open and harshly bright, lined on either side by a flagstone street and angular buildings with green-shuttered windows, softened only here and there by the occasional flower box. But inside the guesthouse, to which we were admitted by a habited nun, tall and gaunt with thick glasses and jutting teeth, it was cool and dark and quiet, the wood-paneled walls painted a thick, creamy ivory, the floors patterned in red and white square tiles and polished terrazzo. Neither the nun nor the convent groundskeeper and handyman with her, who vaguely reminded me of Jack Black but without the crazed look in his eyes, spoke English. Nor did Ellie and I speak more than three words of Italian. They showed us silently to our room. *"Grazie,"* we said. *"Prego,"* they said. *"Ciao,"* we said, to their puzzled looks. Later we learned *ciao* was entirely too informal to use with someone you had just met, much less a nun.

Ellie and I threw our backpacks onto the narrow twin beds and closed the door and opened the shutters, illuminating our room: twin beds and an armoire and a desk of particleboard covered by faux-wood veneer; on one wall a crucifix, on another a reproduction of an icon painting of the Blessed Virgin Mary cradling the Christ Child. The bookshelf held two books: the Gospel according to Luke, translated into five languages—Italian, English, French, German, and Spanish—and a book on the founder of the convent, Luigi Caburlotto, *apostolo dell'educazione.* Our window opened onto a high brick wall, beneath which ran—or, rather, stagnated—a narrow canal of green water littered with debris and leaves. There was a vague smell of raw sewage. "The term 'miasma' comes to mind when thinking of our room," I wrote in my notebook that first night. But none of this would matter because we had three full days in Venice and about a hundred churches to see, plus the Doge's Palace and Saint Mark's Basilica, and the *last* place we'd be spending our days in one of the great cities of the world would be an austere room in a secluded convent on a backwater canal.

We're still not sure what it was. Maybe the pureed-fish dish Ellie adventurously ordered for us as we sat outside sharing a glass of Prosecco in an alleyway restaurant with a view of the Giudecca Canal. Maybe the bacteria of the *E. coli* outbreak that was sweeping through Europe that summer, carried on the cucumbers or tomatoes we tucked into the sandwiches we stole from the hotel in Ulm. Maybe the fetid waters of the miasmic canal onto which our convent cell opened. Who knows? Suffice it to say that the *main* place we spent our days in Venice was our austere room in the secluded convent on that backwater canal.

Mercifully, we became sick in turns with this twenty-four-hour plague. That first night and all the next day, it was Ellie. As she hauled her body between the bathroom and her bed, I lay in the dark wondering how to find a doctor when I could say only *Grazie,* wondering if my daydreams and nightmares from before our departure were coming true. But in the morning, though Ellie was weak and exhausted and nauseated, her body was largely purged.

When I sat on the bed beside her holding a cool cloth to her fore-head, she could even faintly joke, "Maybe one of the nuns performs miracles and can heal me."

Because the nuns spoke no English, I could not ask them to heal my daughter, and because there was no WiFi at the convent guesthouse, I could not ask Google Translate how to inquire about help. I waited until I knew Terry's alarm clock back in Houston was ringing before I called and asked him to look up how to say "My daughter is very sick!" (*Mia figlia è molto malata!*), so I could ex-plain to the nuns why we would be going nowhere that day. I failed to have him look up how to say "I'm going to buy myself a pastry and *mia figlia* a yogurt from the bakery I noticed near the station." Or "*Mia figlia* is sleeping peacefully now, so I think she'll be okay." Because when I told the gaunt nun and the groundskeeper who looked like Jack Black, "*Mia figlia è molto malata!*," they seemed concerned and asked me questions in Italian that I could not un-derstand. "She is okay. She is okay," I kept repeating in English. And then I put my hands together and laid my head upon them in the international sign meaning "sleeping." But their concern made me feel at home somehow.

All day, I sat in the convent's courtyard garden, with its wisteria-covered arbor and red and pink geraniums and its shrine to the Virgin Mary in blue and white, drinking surprisingly delicious macchiatos and cappuccinos dispensed in tiny disposable cups for forty euro cents from a vending machine in the nuns' common room. From time to time I would go in to check on Ellie and bring her a tea from the same machine. Back out in the garden, I watched the nuns hanging towels and sheets to dry on a line in the sun and, after the lunch hour, watched them come out and sit in the plas-tic chairs near me to sew. I wished I could Google Translate "Your towels are as abrasive as loofahs, but I love the needlework you are so carefully tending in this courtyard garden." I wished I could

Google Translate "I am a pilgrim, heading to the Holy Land." Instead, I crossed off nonessential churches from my list of places to visit in Venice and read the Gospel according to Luke, where Jesus speaks in parables that sound like riddles, their meanings hidden from those who have not the ears to hear, from those who have not the eyes to see.

THE BODY IS SUCH
A STRANGE HOME

AS ELLIE AWAKENED from the stupor of illness, I fell headlong into it. All that night after the day I'd sat in the convent garden, I crawled from bed to bathroom while a fluorescent light outside our window buzzed off and on above the still water. The air, too, was still, and our room too hot to close the shutters against the humming light. The fluorescent light and the stagnant air seemed to magnify my nausea. The next day I lay in bed unable to move, unable to open my eyes without the room pitching and heaving around me, my stomach clenching.

But since we were pretty sure, given the trajectory of Ellie's recovery, that I was not going to die, and since my guilt at keeping her penned up with me outweighed my worry about letting my lovely daughter, who could speak a mere three words of Italian, explore this foreign city on her own, I urged Ellie to take the guidebook and the map of Venice we had bought at the train station and go. "Are you sure?" she asked me, more out of politeness than any real commitment to stay by my bedside and minister to me, though she did bring me a plastic cup filled with tea from the vending machine before she left.

She was venturing out to Cannaregio, the northern Venetian district where the Jewish ghetto had been, neighborhood of Shakespeare's Shylock, the Jew of Venice. The Venetian republic had established the ghetto, the first in Europe, in 1516, though the lives of Jews there had already been severely circumscribed: for work, they could only run the Hebrew printing press, trade in textiles, practice medicine, or be moneylenders or pawnbrokers. The gates of the ghetto that reminded its inhabitants of these constraints were closed and locked at night; guards patrolled the surrounding canals in skiffs. During the day, if they left the ghetto, Jews were required to wear yellow scarves or circular identification badges.

Ellie planned to tour some of the remaining synagogues and visit a museum. On and off for several years now, she had considered converting to Judaism. She had a stack of books in storage she'd been collecting: *Conversion to Judaism, Choosing a Jewish Life, At the Entrance to the Garden of Eden*. "What is it about Judaism that you're drawn to?" I asked her as she headed out to the former ghetto that morning. She felt sorry for the Jews, she told me, because "everyone always hates them." And because "they never had a homeland, at least until now." And even though he was an invention of medieval Christendom, the Wandering Jew, cursed to roam the earth until the Second Coming of Jesus Christ, fascinated her. She, too, felt herself to be an exile. "What are you in exile from?" I asked her. "From other people," she replied. And I thought about Ellie's earliest memory, which she'd told me once, from the days after the birth of Mary Martha. All our relatives had driven up to Oklahoma to see the new baby. Ellie remembers a group of people encircling her newborn sister and herself on the outside of the circle, unable to get in.

Before her fascination with Judaism, she'd taken classes at the Catholic church near our house and received her First Holy Communion with a group of second-graders in their navy blue suits and ties and patent shoes and white lace dresses. She was seventeen. This all started after she went to confession once, impulsively, following the weekly Mass she was required to attend as a student at Incarnate Word Academy, the all-girls high school. In the confessional, Ellie told the priest, "who I'm pretty sure was gay," how mean she was to me and how guilty she felt about this, though "I added other stuff because I didn't want it to seem like that was the only thing I was confessing." The priest listened sympathetically and told her he could tell she was a good person. And then, though she didn't know "if I just wanted it or if it was real," Ellie felt a profound sense of peace wash over her.

Just as impulsively, after confession that day, she decided to become Catholic. But even as she attended First Communion classes, her enchantment with Catholicism quickly faded. The readings from the Gospels during Mass were too opaque. She felt nothing during the homilies. In confession now, another priest asked her, "Do you interact with people who might take you away from your faith?," which annoyed her, perhaps because, confusingly, her mother might be one of those people. She realized more and more how violently she disagreed with the exclusivity of the Church and with its doctrines on homosexuality, women in the priesthood, premarital sex. Because after all, as she said, "I was *born* outside of marriage!" Ellie wouldn't exist if I'd been a good Catholic.

For those European pilgrims of Fabri's day still determined, despite the westward conquest of the Ottoman Turks, to make the perilous journey to the Holy Land, the Venetian shipowners provide what is essentially the earliest all-inclusive package tour. A Carnival Cruise it may not be, but the fare charged by the captains takes care of transportation, food, and lodging (both at sea and in the Holy Land), as well as tolls and taxes, donkeys and packhorses, guided excursions around Jerusalem, and side trips to the Jordan River.

The two nobles whose galleys will carry pilgrims across the sea that spring of 1483 are Master Peter Lando and Master Augustine Contarini. Outside the door to Saint Mark's Basilica, their servants stand beneath white banners with red crosses upon them calling out to the pilgrims who have come to hear Mass. They try to lure the pilgrims to the galley of their master, where they will ply potential customers with Cretan wine, comfits from Alexandria, sweetmeats from the bakeries in the winding alleyways of Venice, all the while disparaging the other captain and his ship. On board Contarini's galley, anchored in the Grand Canal outside the Doge's Palace, the captain greets the pilgrims with humility, but his double-banked galley is cramped "and withal old and stinking." The Germans choose Lando's trireme, with its roomier sleeping quarters, and make their contract with him.

Once these arrangements are complete, there isn't much left to do in Venice, where the pilgrims will be stranded for more than a month before embarking for Palestine. They visit the arsenal, storehouse of the republic's war apparatus. They purchase mattresses and pillows and sheets and coverlets. As the departure date draws nearer, they will pick up a little wine, some cheese, perhaps hams or salted ox tongues, eggs, biscuits, dried figs and apples, spices and sugar, a cage for hens and millet seed with which to feed them. Aside from the markets with their fruit and vegetable boats arriving each morning, the pilgrims wander through the cobblestoned streets overflowing with the mercantile wealth of Venice — tapestries and brocades and silks, crystal vases and delicate colored glass from nearby Murano.

But the temptations of the earthly city are not Fabri's focus. Realizing it will be a while before their ship departs, the friar suggests they make a pilgrimage each day, walking the labyrinth of streets or rowing the canals to one of the great multitude of churches, where they can visit the relics of the saints. The members of his pilgrim band unanimously agree, and thus begins a dizzying tour of holy body parts scattered throughout Venice, a nonexhaustive list of which includes the head, left arm, and hand of Saint

George; the finger of Saint Andrew the apostle; the arms of Saint James and Saint Laurence the martyr; the heads of the apostle Saint James the Less and Saint Philip; the entire hand of Saint Catherine of Siena, "very large and beauteous, with all its flesh and bones, which hand I kissed many times." Also, the bodies entire of Saint Helena the Empress and countless other saints. By late May, even Fabri will grow exhausted from this enterprise. "On our return to our inn," he writes after a visit to Saint Mary of Pity, "we visited many other churches, in which we obtained indulgences; but it would weary me to write down all their names."

Back in the convent room that evening when Ellie returned, I sat propped up in bed, the nausea having finally lifted, while she detailed for me all that she had done, clearly intoxicated by the freedom she'd felt—freedom defined in part by her separation from me. She told me about the ghetto and about how, on her way back to the convent, she'd stopped in Campo Santa Margherita and watched little boys playing soccer in the middle of the plaza in the waning light and ate a piece of pizza on waxed paper, draping her legs over the brick walls of a canal, as she talked on her cell phone to her boyfriend. Then, still not quite ready to return, she read some Flannery O'Connor. Now, as she put on her pajamas and pulled out her journal and got into her own bed parallel to mine, she told me how she'd said *Buonasera*—"Good evening"—to the nuns who were watching television in the common room down the hall.

"Wandering is what we did during most of our stay in Venice," I'd written in the notebook I kept during that trip I'd taken with Sabine Mahr when Ellie was two, "and it's what we enjoyed doing the most. We would begin at some central point and walk with the crowds for awhile past tourist traps and cafés and trattorias. Then we would begin to veer off towards some interesting old basilica or down a side street with laundry strung across, row after row, and

76

sunlight shining down in shafts. And gradually the crowds would fade and then the street or alley or passageway would open up onto a small square and there would be children playing, mothers talking, a gondolier fixing his boat and singing. Very often there would be no one at all." I remember how free I felt then, in large part free from Ellie, back home in Lawrence, Kansas, with my mother, just as Ellie had been free of me in Venice that day.

Ellie noticed that I was still reading the Gospel according to Luke. "You know, I would be so bored if I was a nun," she said offhandedly. "Why's that?" I asked, looking up from the Gospel. "I mean, I like to read books a lot," she said, "but I wouldn't want to have to read the same one over and over again." Now, probably I was being oversensitive, but something about Ellie's dismissal of the nun's life of confinement, carelessly tossed out in the flush of her own newfound freedom, made me defensive for them and, inexplicably, myself.

Though I held my tongue, as we lay side by side in our room above the miasmic canal, reading and writing, I felt a strange jealousy of my daughter overtake me, knowing that she still had the liberty to make for herself the *bohemian-explorer-intellectual kind of life* that I had been forced to put aside in giving birth to her. And as she wrote in her journal about what she'd seen wandering the Cannaregio, I snippily thought to myself how variety is not always freedom. And how freedom itself can lead to its own narrowness and constraints. And I thought about how, as daughter after daughter arrived and the walls enclosed me, I had tried to tell myself to just look closer at what was right in front of me instead of wasting away longing for some unseen world beyond. Washing my daughters' faces at night, making the beds each morning—mundane repetition made up the hours of my life. A single book, read over and over again. I had tried to make it all make do because there was no other choice.

In the Gospel according to Luke, there is the sense from the beginning that something is afoot in the everyday world in this pause
between two eternities. The shepherds abiding in the field who are
given good tidings of great joy. John the Baptist, his voice crying
in the wilderness, preparing the way for the Lord, when every valley would be filled and every mountain and hill brought low, when
the crooked would be made straight and the rough ways made
smooth. And Jesus himself, in the temple in Jerusalem as a boy,
about his Father's business, sitting in the midst of the doctors, hearing them and asking them questions. Later, the healings and the
exorcisms—the blind made to see, the lame to walk, the deaf to
hear, the lepers cleansed, the dead raised. And the multitudes who
follow, reaching after the hem of his garment, hoping to be fed.

But though this new dispensation is at hand, many are skeptical. They do not know how to read Jesus. They do not properly
interpret him. "When ye see a cloud rise out of the west, straightway ye say, There cometh a shower; and so it is," he tells the
people. "And when ye see the south wind blow, ye say, There will
be heat; and it cometh to pass. Ye hypocrites, ye can discern the
face of the sky and of the earth; but how is it that ye do not discern
this time?"

With my daughters' small faces cupped in my hands, I had tried
to *discern this time,* to make them a sign unto me. I tried to pay attention to the details of that tangible and confined life I lived every
day and see in them the unseen that is eternal. They made me feel
connected to some transcendent process beyond my ken. Slowly,
my daughters began to replace God. Or, rather, they filled the void
where He was supposed to be. I adored them. If they were idols, I
did not care.

But what does it mean that that life now feels intangible to me,
as lost as if I'd never lived it? I can hardly remember the little faces
I cupped in my hands unless I look at pictures. I have no idea how

much they weighed at birth, when they began to crawl or walk, the first words they said. I can't recall which one paraded around with the duck call in her mouth, which one helped me scrub the bathroom in her rain boots and diaper. We spent our days together. Where did they go? Do they still remain as a kind of residue inside me, somewhere within the gray folds of my cerebral cortex? Are we like trees, whose years of drought and years of plenty are captured in their fluctuating bands, thickening and thinning with the rains? In the mornings now, my hips ache until I stretch. Is that from all the years of carrying babies on them, though I can't remember what it felt like to have a child nestled there? Is the ache what I've got left? Have our days together all been swallowed up by some dark eternity?

After our recovery, Ellie and I had one full day left to tour Venice. Because our time here had been shortened and we had divergent sites to see, we decided to separate for a while. She went to the Bridge of Sighs and to check e-mail at an Internet café just off Saint Mark's Square. I looked for traces of the Venice Fabri had known. I wandered through the ducal palace, center of the Venetian republic, with its dark wood-paneled walls and painted ceilings, marble floors and marble staircases with sculptures of cherubim and women bathing, masterworks in gold frames so rococo they reminded me of something we might find in the ranch house of Terry's grandmother—a Polish woman from Detroit who liked a lot of bling. From the windows of the council chamber, I could see the gray-green domes of Saint Mark's Basilica, from which I had just come, its every inch ornamented in mosaics and precious hammered metals, a thousand iron lanterns hanging from the many-domed ceiling. I'd sat in a pew next to a nun in full habit checking her iPhone. All around me, the smell of wood oil; the air humid, stultifying.

Fabri and the noblemen with whom he traveled had come to the palace after Mass at Saint Mark's to ask for an audience with the doge and senate, carrying with them the letters of introduction from the Archduke Sigismund that they'd picked up in Innsbruck. They'd been admitted into what Fabri calls "the hall of judgment," which I took to be the immense chamber with carved wooden seats for the senators lining three walls and a dais for the doge, where I stood listening to a guided audio tour on headphones. Here, the pilgrims requested commendatory letters to the governors of the islands throughout the Mediterranean, documents that could be invoked for their protection if needed. The doge, through an interpreter, offered his services to the pilgrims and, "calling each of them to him severally, gave his hand to each man, drew him towards him, and kissed him in the Italian fashion."

I left the senate chamber and found myself, to my complete surprise, in a narrow room hung with works by the Dutch painter Hieronymus Bosch, who was born around 1450 and died in 1516—which made him a nearly exact contemporary of Fabri. What was *Bosch* doing *here?* It seemed so incongruous. But the more I looked at the paintings of hell on display, the more apt it seemed. If the Doge's Palace represents the height of medieval mercantile Venice's earthly power and its glitzy outward trappings, Bosch's visions of the damned, here in a room deep in the center, reveal the terrifying interior life of the Middle Ages: its soul in doubt and torment.

I felt at home with Bosch's dark orbs descending from illuminated skies, his horizons lit by fires, his firmaments cluttered with winged creatures, neither animal nor human, nor angel either. As I watched armor metamorphosing into a misshapen dwarf, fruit sprouting a proboscis, a fiend plunging its sharpened snout into the belly of a writhing soul from whose mouth blood spouted like a fountain, I remembered how Luke's Jesus proclaims, "Woe unto you, scribes and Pharisees, hypocrites!" to those who blindly follow the rules and rituals of religion but who miss the essential love that he insists should be at its heart, "for ye are as graves which appear not, and the men that walk over them are not aware of them." Bosch's paintings pull back the fragile covering over those graves to reveal the world beneath this world where the commonplace mutates into the horrific, where the monstrous recesses of the human heart are made manifest. That restless terrifying vision, more than gold and cold marble and stylized mosaics of saints, is what spoke to me. It seemed to see into the violence that pulses just below the surface of existence, like Tennyson's Nature, "red in tooth and claw."

Back out in the Piazza San Marco, Ellie and I met up. We walked through the square along the northern arcade with its elegant facade of row upon row of stone arches, past the cafés with their violinists and white tablecloths, past the tourists taking pictures with the flocks of pigeons. In the midst of this lyrical scene, so perfect on its surface, Ellie turned to me and said, "That's disgusting! Don't they know those birds can carry influenza!"

If it is true, as Carolly Erickson argues and Bosch's paintings reveal, that the medieval cosmos was enchanted to its inhabitants, then it is also true that those inhabitants felt themselves at the mercy of enchanted forces, good and evil, that had the power to shape their lives. God was hidden in the pleats of the world, but so was the devil. And while God and His armed guard of saints might take pity, the devil and his minions were openly hostile to humans. And this hostility was not an abstraction. Famine and plague and natural disaster; medieval men and women were distressingly vulnerable. Their piety was in many respects a response to this vulnerability.

In the Gospel according to Luke, Jesus walks among the common people, and great multitudes come to hear him speak and to be healed by him of their infirmities. Near the Sea of Galilee, the crowds are so great that the friends of a man stricken by palsy must climb upon the rooftop of a house and lower him down through the clay tiles to the room where Jesus waits. "And when he saw their faith, he said unto him, Man, thy sins are forgiven thee," Luke recalls. And the palsied man rises and gathers up his bedding and leaves.

But by the Middle Ages, Jesus himself had long since departed, though the devil who tempted him in the wilderness was still here. Luckily, Jesus had not left humanity defenseless. First there were the disciples, and later the saints—intercessors, go-betweens, middlemen for vulnerable humans, individuals who could transmit the healing power of a departed God through the relics that they left behind. Diluted blood, finger bones, skulls, stones with which they'd been martyred—these remnants of the saints, gently placed in reliquaries of glass and gold or silver, encrusted with precious stones, are what Fabri and the noblemen spend their days in Venice visiting. Sometimes the pilgrims might be allowed to kiss the relics directly, but more often they would only touch them or the reliquaries that housed them with something that they carried—rings, rosary beads, crosses. Fabri explains how he himself had been asked to carry many of these "trinklets" by those back home, including a ring belonging to Master John Echinger, mayor of Ulm. This ring had been drawn from his father's finger in his final earthly moments and had belonged to his father's father before him. "I verily believe it was of more value to him than a hundred ducats," Fabri writes, "and that now"—the ring having touched the relics of countless saints—"he values it at more than two hundred."

The churches of Venice that Ellie and I visited on our whirlwind tour all blurred together. Cobblestoned streets, a glint of sunlight on water as we passed over a canal on a bridge of ironwork or stone, then the narrow streets opening up onto a bright campo, just as they had years before for me and Sabine, the church the focal point. We would enter into the dim hush and pay a few euros to wander up the nave and down the side aisles. Polished marble, gold, paintings by Titian and Tintoretto. Then we'd light a candle for another euro or two and think of those we left behind.

But in the Church of Saints John and Paul, abutting Fondamenta Mendicanti, Ellie and I stood before a pink marble altar on which reposed the reliquary holding the eternally cramped foot of Saint Catherine of Siena, set into an illuminated niche. While I had been looking at paintings by Veronese, Ellie spied the foot and pulled me excitedly to it, knowing how happy it would make me. Fabri had been to services at this church, then the chief home of the Dominicans, on May 4, 1483—Saint Catherine's feast day. He stood among the crowd waiting to kiss the relics of the saint, who had lived within her family's home in silence and solitude, suffered a mystical union with Christ, and received the stigmata visible only to herself, and who had once advised her confessor and biographer to do what she had done: "Build a cell inside your mind, from which you can never flee." Before this remnant of her, hard and veined as marble, my daughter and I now stood, taking photos.

I cannot quite explain why I found the relics of the saints so poignant. I did not believe that in these fragments some grace survived. That by touching my locket with the photos of Mary Martha and Sabine to them, I could capture that grace and bring it home. I did not believe in their healing power. I did not believe they were signs pointing me toward God. And yet there was nevertheless something touching in the foot—singular—of Saint Catherine of Siena, gnarled and a little terrifying, like a figure Bosch would have carved had he been a sculptor of marble instead of a painter. It was a memento mori, perhaps. *Remember you will die!* it said to me. *Don't get attached to the world that is passing, that has passed.*

I kept thinking, though, of a poem by Mary Cornish called "Reliquaries." "This is the mystery I adore," it ends:

> the odd
> finger. The belovèd tooth. The blood-
> soaked cheek of Saint Catherine
> after the wheel. Even a scrap of the robe
> Judas wore as he walked the rose-scented earth
> on two bare feet with Christ, and leaned
> into the kiss. The sky is so far away,
> and the body's such a strange home.

Maybe relics—scraps and bone—are all we have left to cling to in our estrangement here on earth during that pause between two eternities, as the souls inside our mortal selves yearn for the transcendent sky that relics signify.

Or maybe relics are our souvenirs of the transitory world. They are the scraps we hold tight to remind us of what we've loved, of what could otherwise be swallowed up by the dark eternity of forgetfulness that threatens. Standing before Saint Catherine's reliquary, I remembered the little pair of shoes my father had given me when, pregnant with Ellie, I told him that I would be naming the baby for his mother, Elvina. I remembered the outfit in which I'd dressed Ellie when I brought her home from the hospital, the same one I'd worn home from the hospital when I was born, which my mother had saved and given to me. I remembered the plastic hospital bands that marked each of my daughters as mine, like leg bands of a homing pigeon. And the vestiges of Sabine's blankie and the fringe from Mary Martha's. I remembered the letters Terry and I wrote, every one of which I put inside a box inside an antique trunk, a reliquary that had traveled from those villages near the Rhine with my grandmother's grandparents when they'd left that land behind to settle along the Mississippi River in Missouri.

I also remembered my grandmother's delicate gold watch, inscribed on the back by my grandfather—*Elvina, from Carl*—that my aunts had given to me, precious trinklet. And that reminded me of a folder labeled "Project: Time" that I'd found in my grandfather's basement office in St. Louis when we were cleaning out his house to sell, after my grandmother had died of cancer and he'd been diagnosed with Alzheimer's. The folder was stuffed with quotes clipped from newspapers and magazines: "We haven't the time to take our time" (Eugène Ionesco); "Time is the longest distance between two places" (Tennessee Williams). Also charts for time zones and calendars. An interview in a hospital newsletter with a cardiovascular surgeon interested in horology—the study of time, timepieces, and the art of clock making. A slip of paper from a fortune cookie: "Time is not measured by a watch, but by moments." An article from *Esquire* on the rise and fall of the digital clock, the human nostalgia for analog.

My favorite inclusion in this paper folder reliquary, though, is a table my grandfather made of the rising and setting of the sun each day from March 1985 through January 1986. In red felt-tip pen and with a ruler, he'd marked out columns, and then in black felt-tip, again in his slanting *ALL CAPS* hand, he'd written the date and then the time of sunrise and sunset. There, within these ordered lines, you can see the shifting of the light, a minute or two earlier or later each day. You can see at the summer solstice how the tide turns and time's shadow shortens. Can see, in the dark of December, the sun setting earlier and earlier until, around the twenty-first, Earth poised on that axis, the light slowly begins to return.

That evening after we'd both recovered from our illnesses, Ellie and I had dinner in a restaurant whose walls were covered with old letters in fading ink and old photos from other people's travels.

Siamo arrivati; per Milano 18 May; Desideriamo; Con amore. To save money, we ordered from the secondi section only—fish grilled with asparagus for Ellie, pork medallions for me. I was telling her about my grandparents Carl and Elvina—Venie in affection—and how they once traveled to Germany on a two-week package tour, how they'd tried to learn a little German together for this purpose. On one of my solo visits back to St. Louis when I was younger, my grandparents had taken me to New Harmony, Indiana, so that I could see the site of a former utopian community there and so that my grandfather, an industrial designer, could visit Richard Meier's Atheneum. I remember sitting on a couch in the lobby of our hotel for what seemed like hours, me in the crook of my grandmother's arm as she told me about their journey. "I have this feeling that I am somehow like her," Ellie ventured as we ate. "Well, she was fun-loving and curious and she tried to live a full life. She started taking piano lessons again in her sixties," I told Ellie. And then I remembered a strange dream I had, after cancer had claimed my grandmother. I dreamed that I was with her once more, and we were talking together. But I knew that she was dead, even as we spoke, even as she pulled me close to her chest, the chest she used to powder with the pink puff in her pink-tiled bathroom.

Once, near the end of my grandfather's life, my brother walked into my grandfather's room and found him sitting in an armchair near the window making a rowing motion with his arms. My brother, seeing that my grandfather was somewhere far away, sat quietly beside him for a while. "How long is this sea?" my grandfather asked my brother at last, and I picture my grandfather in a small rowboat on vast waters, that sun he'd charted low in the sky, the sky that was so far away, in the body that was such a strange home. My brother answered, "I don't know, Grandpa. What is it like?" "It's beautiful here," my grandfather said. A few months later he, too, was gone.

IN THE PAUSE BETWEEN
TWO ETERNITIES

VENICE, IT SEEMED to me and Ellie, had become a parody of itself, at least along the main thoroughfares over which the tourists passed; it had become some imaginary vision of what those who had to make a living here supposed travelers would expect—and pay good money—to see. On the bridges spanning the canals, musicians in berets sat on stools and played baroque music on lutes and guitars. Artists displayed their sentimental paintings of Venetian palazzi bathed in the light of the setting sun, or, more incongruously, their caricatures of American movie stars—Leonardo DiCaprio, Brad Pitt, Angelina Jolie. Graceful young Senegalese men in white T-shirts and scarves talked on their cell phones and sold knockoff Louis Vuitton and Chanel on the bridges' steps. Along the narrow cobblestoned streets, above store windows filled with garish jewel-toned opera masks and little glass animal figurines from Murano, yellow signs with arrows herded the crowds through: *Per S. Marco,* they directed, *Per Rialto, Per Academy.* In the campos at night, Middle Eastern immigrants tossed glow-in-the-dark gizmos into the air hoping to attract a sale as the waiters stood at the entrances to the outdoor restaurants calling out in English to eat their pizza, their pasta, their garlic bread.

Ellie and I both pride ourselves on our sense of direction. I like to study maps, and on this trip, I'd pore over them each evening in bed, trying to understand how the puzzle of the city we were in all fit together. Ellie's boyfriend called her GPEllie. But in Venice, it was difficult to follow the map that I'd bought when we arrived. Many of the streets were more like alleys and were marked by no discernible names. We'd wander, a little lost, usually eating a gelato to cool off, until we finally stumbled onto a landmark or a *fonda-menta* we could locate on the map. Then we'd recalibrate. As we wandered through Venice, I told Ellie about the time Sabine Mahr and I had traveled here on the night train from Vienna. How I'd been unable to sleep on the hard brown leather seats that pulled out into a bed in our compartment. "Keep your eyes open until you can't anymore," Sabine advised me, a recommendation that now seems like the moral of a parable whose meaning I can't quite perceive. We'd arrived at the train station in the morning as the shops were opening and left our bags in lockers there and had cappuccinos and pastries in a brightly lit café whose walls were tiled in blues and greens, its floor in black and white squares. We bought matching wool felt hats and cardigans at Benetton, then retrieved our backpacks and took the *vaporetto* to La Giudecca and paid for two beds with lumpy pillows and wool blankets in the dormitory of the convent there.

In the mornings at nine, the tiny nuns who spoke no English would kick us out, and we would cross by *vaporetto* over to Saint Mark's Square, briny wind in our hair. Then, as I detailed in my notebook, we would walk farther and farther from the center, the streets narrowing as the tourists thinned out until we were all alone and the lane would open onto a small plaza of sunlight and stone. We'd take photos of the laundry strung in diagonals across the streets, lines of cotton sheets and baby socks like party banners. Of gondolas and fruit and vegetable stands lining the waterfronts, the boats stacked with wooden crates. Of crumbling stucco buildings, and red-clay-tile roofs, and green shutters, and window boxes filled with geraniums. Our own idealized version of Venice. Late in the day, we would return to Saint Mark's Square, and I remembered how the pigeons had been there then, and the violins too. Walking along the colonnades, the piazza half in shadow, was, I'd written in my notebook, "one of those moments of joy mixed with sadness and longing, though longing for what I'm not quite sure."

Recalling that moment now, with Ellie walking beside me, I wondered if perhaps my younger self somehow missed not having this grown daughter with her, even then. Or perhaps the longing I felt then was actually the nostalgia I have now for my past that had evaporated. Or maybe it was both of these things at the same instant. As if—*How long is this sea?*—time did not really run forward from that moment to this, as if we were both always present, me and Ellie, always together and always alone as well, always longing for the other, always traveling side by side.

Before Ellie was born, did I dream her into being? Six months pregnant, my body growing full like the moon, I dreamed I had already given birth and that the baby was a girl. "I remember she was dressed in a pink snowsuit with little roses all over it," I wrote in my notebook—notice that verb *remember*, as if it had already happened—"and I held her up to the sky and said her name, 'Ellie.'" Then, in the logic of the dream, I found myself in a rocking chair nursing her, "and I could feel my own mother's presence, although I knew she wasn't actually there."

I remembered this dream recently, in the hospital room where I first held my brother's newborn daughter, Elodie. The crowd of grandparents and siblings and nieces had left and taken Dylan, his son, off with them, and it was just Paul and his wife, Stephanie, and the new baby and me. Night was coming on, and my brother and I were sitting on the couch and we were speaking in hushed voices as if in some holy sanctuary. "I remember after I had my accident," he said distantly, recalling us all to that terrible day a couple of years before when he'd been painting on some scaffolding a story high and fallen, he doesn't know how. Life Flight came and flew his broken body over the city to the hospital. He spent days unconscious in the ICU.

"I was driving Dylan to school one morning—this was months later—on one of those two-lane roads out by our house," he went on, and I pictured the ribbon of blacktop cutting through the pine trees near Montgomery, railroad tracks running alongside, sometimes an open field or a dance hall or a church or a shooting range. "There wasn't a whole lot of traffic, and I could just zone out. Dylan was sitting in his car seat in the back and he was holding his stuffed donkey. Steph had just sewed on a button where the heart would be. And as we were driving, these memories came back to me from that time between when I fell and when I woke up—the time I don't remember. When I was in some other world."

In the first memory, Paul is lying down—maybe in the emergency room, where I saw him strapped to a board to keep his fractured skull still, maybe in the ICU, head shaved, stent in. He is lying down and he is overcome with the sensation that the whole world is one living organism. And this organism takes a huge breath and breathes into my brother, as if resuscitating him. "And at the moment when I remembered feeling that air come into me, although it was less like a memory and more like it was actually happening to me again, Dylan said from the backseat, 'Dad, I feel my heart beating.'"

In the second memory from that morning on the two-lane road, Paul, standing in some obscure landscape, hears behind him somewhere the voice of a little girl. He knows the ground is there, but it's hazy, and he cannot feel the weight of gravity. "Daddy," the voice says, and again, "Daddy," each time clearer and at a slightly higher, more urgent pitch. He turns toward the voice and she is there, dark-haired and faint, transparent even, in a sundress. For a second, Elodie—for that is who it must be, we know that now, Paul and Steph and I, sitting in the hospital room where her body has been born years later—Elodie grows solid, like a hologram illuminated by just the right angle of light. And then the light changes, and, in the memory from that other world, she fades away again. *The sky is so far away,* after all, *and the body's such a strange home.*

Did Elodie cry out to my injured brother so that she could be born? Did she, like the organism of the earth, call him back to being? Where is the space they met? The void? The pause between two eternities? The sweet hereafter? Is it where I met my grandmother after she'd gone? Is it the place my grandfather rowed on the beautiful sea? Is it the land where I held my daughter up to the blue sky and called her "Ellie" and felt my mother's presence? In that other world, do my daughter and I still travel the open road together?

As their departure draws near, Fabri and the other pilgrims hire a boat to take them to the churches whose patron saints might be of service to them in their travels. They visit the Church of Saint Martha to pray that the hostess of Jesus provide them with good inns, or at least "the patience to bear the shortcomings of our inns during our long journey." At Saint Raphael's, they pray that the archangel will guide them as he did Tobias on his journey from Nineveh to Media. On one of the Murano islands, they visit a Camaldolese monastery and, in the church of Saint Christopher there, pray to be borne by that patron saint of mariners safely across the sea. "In that monastery is painted a very fine map of the world," Fabri notes, almost as an afterthought.

But that very fine map that Fabri sees at the Camaldolese monastery, completed in about 1459 by Fra Mauro, a lay member of the monastic community, is, as we now know, a portent of the coming world. His *mappa mundi* recalls earlier so-called T-O maps, named for the round earth encircled by the sea and divided by a T-shaped river separating the globe into the three known continents: Asia above, Europe below left, to the right Africa. At the exact center of those T-O maps, reflecting its symbolic position at the exact center of human existence, lay Jerusalem. But Mauro's *mappa mundi* is no generalized schematic representation. It is a compendium of the cosmos as it was understood in the middle of the fifteenth century and an embodiment of the transition between the age of faith and the age of discovery. Though the Americas and Antarctica aren't on the map yet, the other continents—Europe, Asia, Africa—are recognizable, and many of their countries and cities are named. Scattered across the undulating azure waves are Chinese junks, Indian dhows, European galleys and caravels. On land, in the spaces between the rivers and the place-names and the mountains, rise walled cities with their golden crenellated towers and minarets and onion domes and Gothic spires. In the deserts: conical tents, carmine and emerald and sapphire, their flaps open to the sirocco winds. All the particularities of this new world are coming into view.

Six feet in diameter and drawn on parchment with Jerusalem—radically—slightly west of center, Fra Mauro's *mappa mundi* presents the universe, says historian Angelo Cattaneo, as "an immense *liber figurarum,* a minutely 'annotated' body, full of signs and images that include all aspects of the world." What I love about Fra Mauro's *mappa mundi,* which I've seen only in reproductions in books, is the way that it embeds these stories, both real and imagined, in tidy red and sea-blue script, in legends all over the map, in landscapes and in waters, so that the observable world contains a fullness. It's pregnant with meaning. It's like the map in Sabine Mahr's mind, just written down.

Here in China, for example, the emperor, when he travels, "sits in a carriage of gold and ivory decorated with gemstones of inestimable price" drawn by a white elephant while armed men walk both before and behind. Here in India, into "these lakes, the bottom of which cannot be sounded," Brahmins throw from golden jars the ashes of burned bodies. Here in Iran come ships from India, "with their merchandise of pearls, pepper, ginger and other spices in great quantity," that then travel by way of Baghdad to the rivers Tigris and Euphrates, and then to Mesopotamia and Armenia and Cappadocia, and even to the Sea of Pontus—the Black Sea. Here in Yemen is the noble city of Thasi, "a place of great state, justice and liberty, and all kinds of foreign people live here safely." Here in Ethiopia, "there is such a great quantity of honey that they do not bother to collect it. When in the winter the great rains wash these trees, that honey flows into some nearby lakes and, thanks to the action of the sun, that water becomes like a wine." Here, somewhere in western Africa, live people with doglike faces "who are said to eat human flesh." And in the north, we are asked to please "note that in this part of Africa there are ruins of many cities, which were clearly once very great."

In our convent room on our last night in Venice, we loaded our backpacks, a ritual deeply pleasing for its promise of movement. *Everything good is on the highway,* after all. As we packed, Ellie and I thought of all the phrases we'd still like to Google Translate, though we would never actually use them on the little nuns harmlessly embroidering in the garden or watching Mass on TV: "There are ants in our room," I offered up wryly, noting a thread of them running from our trash can to the doorway and out into the hall. "There are mosquitoes in our room," countered Ellie, looking at her arms, all bitten up. "Our room still smells like raw sewage," I replied.

I was trying to finish the Gospel according to Luke before we left the next day, so after packing, I got in bed to read. Seeing me with Gospel in hand again, Ellie asked me, "Hey, Mom, do you believe in

God?" The question caught me completely off guard. And, weirdly, somehow reminded me of when Ellie had first asked about sex as I drove her to soccer practice when she was seven or eight. Maybe in both cases it was my own discomfort I was coming up against. Maybe I didn't want to usher her into that secret and intimate knowledge just yet. Should I lie, I wondered now, to protect my daughter from guessing the depths of the abyss I sometimes feel?

I tried a diversionary tactic. Thinking about Luke's Jesus and siding with the Pharisees and scribes, woe unto them, I said, "I don't necessarily believe Jesus is the son of God. Or I guess I believe Jesus is the son of God the way you and me are the daughters of God. We're all emanations of the divine." "So you *do* believe in God?" Ellie persisted. "I don't know, Ellie," I equivocated. "I don't know, so I don't know if I believe." "But believing and knowing are two different things!" she argued. "If you *know* something, you can *prove* it. But if you believe something, you just believe it. You can't *prove* God exists. You can't prove that He doesn't. Belief isn't knowing!" "But belief without knowing is what scares me," I argued back. "There's too much of that already and it causes lots of problems. People say they don't *believe* in global warming. They don't *believe* in evolution. But these things aren't a matter of *belief*."

"Do you believe in God?" All Ellie wanted me to say was that I believed in some transcendent shaping force larger than myself. "Do *you*?" I asked her. "Of course!" she replied without hesitation, and I was taken aback again by her certainty. But certainty is what Luke's Jesus wants from his followers. "Verily I say unto thee," he says to the malefactor crucified beside him who believes Jesus is the Messiah and who begs Jesus to remember him when he returns to God's kingdom, "today shalt thou be with me in paradise." That's what Luke himself wants too. He addresses his Gospel, his good news, to one Theophilus, "that thou mightest know the certainty of those things, wherein thou hast been instructed."

But though Luke and Jesus seek certainty, the Gospel as a whole is an argument against literalism. The priests and scribes and Pharisees who follow the Sabbath, who fast and tithe, who make long prayers in the temple but who do so without mercy or love, are condemned in this text. When Fabri preached to the nuns near Ulm, he must have delivered a similar message. The Pharisees demand to know when the kingdom of God will arrive, but their question suggests they are expecting an earthly ruler, an anointed king in the Davidic line, who will gather the scattered tribes of Israel together and mend the world. But Jesus's answer is an attempt to show them that they're misreading the prophesies, that they're approaching the question all wrong. He tells them, "The kingdom of God cometh not with observation: Neither shall they say, Lo here! or, lo there! for, behold, the kingdom of God is within you." But if this was true, why was it so hard to find my way there?

As Ellie waited for me to respond to her question, I thought about our origins eons ago, about the initial spark that led to me sitting at that very moment beside her in this bare convent cell beside a miasmic canal. What if the spirit of God had moved upon the face of the waters? What if He had dipped His fingers into that archaic slough and flicked life into motion? What if that movement had led to my daughters' existence? Was this a kind of fate? Was He really there behind it all, though I had not the eyes to see, had not the ears to hear the call?

Finally, I told Ellie that I believed in the mystery at the heart of human existence. That we exist and have breath and don't know why.

The parable of the woman in the convent garden: It is early morning. A woman sits in the courtyard garden of a convent. Somewhere inside, her daughter lies sleeping. The woman and the daughter are on a journey. They have stopped here only temporarily. Strangers remark on how similar they look, which makes the woman happy, but the daughter knows they are not the same. (These details are important to your interpretation of the parable.) The square of sky above the courtyard is flat gray, and across it, geese honk and moan. (These details, though they add atmosphere, are not significant.) The woman looks at maps that will guide her in her travels and drinks a cappuccino she has purchased from a vending machine. The maps make her feel that she is in control, that she knows where she is going, that the charted world has order and meaning. But through the open door of the chapel, she can hear the sisters singing hymns. Their voices tangle, then separate, then merge again, grow round and full in the echoing sanctuary. They are heavy with some profound longing to which their words give being. The longing unites them. This longing oscillates in the woman as well. But though the door to the chapel is open, a wall still separates her and the sisters singing hymns. The sisters stand together within. The woman sits alone on the other side with the maps of foreign lands she needs to guide her toward her destination. She wonders, though, if maps can take her where she wants to go. She remembers the hymns she used to sing as she held her daughter close. *Amazing Grace, how sweet the sound.* But that was years ago. Now she sits alone in the convent garden. Her daughter lies sleeping.

In late May of 1483, when the orders are finally given by the lord consuls of Venice that the captains of the galleys should depart within the week, Fabri and his fellow travelers rejoice, "because we were beginning to be exceeding weary of Venice." They make several trips out to the ship in order to situate their chests and all the provisions they'd brought from Ulm and bought in Venice. They dine with a physician, who gives them medicine and purgatives and advice for keeping in good health at sea. They settle their bill with Mistress Margaret at the Inn of Saint George. And on the first of June, they row out to the galley for good and spend the night in the harbor.

The following day, the captain, Peter Lando, embarks with his servants and household and some new passengers, including a Dutchman and his wife. All the German noblemen are displeased at the thought of this one woman dwelling alone among them during the journey, all the other women having chosen to sail on the galley of Master Augustine Contarini. She's restless and—worse—inquisitive. "She ran hither and thither incessantly about the ship," Fabri recalls, his irritation still palpable, "and was full of curiosity, wanting to hear and see everything, and made herself hated exceedingly. Her husband seemed to be a decent man, and for his sake many held their tongues; but had he not been there it would have gone hard with her. This woman was a thorn in the eyes of us all."

As day dawns, the sailors hang seven silk banners from the masts, the largest one that of the pilgrims to the Holy Sepulcher—white with a red cross. Other, smaller banners are displayed as well, that of the lords of Venice, that of the pope. The crew weighs anchor and hoists the yard aloft. The sails spread and fill with wind, "and with great rejoicing," Fabri recalls, "we sailed away from the land: for the trumpeters blew their trumpets just as though we were about to join battle, the galley-slaves shouted, and all the pilgrims sang together 'In Gottes Nahmen fahren wir'"—"in God's name we go." "We were as glad to leave it as if we had been let out of prison, for we steadfastly desired to go to Jerusalem," says Fabri, echoing Luke. Meanwhile, the galley plows through the open sea as the last of the familiar world recedes behind.

I had booked passage for myself and Ellie on a ferry that ran day-trippers back and forth between Venice and the west coast of Croatia, down which we would need to sail to follow Fabri.

That morning, we had settled our bill with the gaunt nun wearing thick glasses. The evening before, we'd waved good-bye to the circle of sisters sitting in the common room watching television and doing embroidery. *"Buonasera! Buonasera!"* we'd all cried. As the ferry threaded the canal between Venice and La Giudecca, I looked out at the passing city, risen from an ancient lagoon. *Vaporetti* and yachts and cruise ships trolled the waters and lined the docks. An enormous advertisement featuring a woman in a billowing red ball gown hung from the roof of the ducal palace. But as we sailed on, the city receded, and Venice became a narrow strip of land with its cranes and crosses and domes and spires and the campanile of Saint Mark's in silhouette between the immensity of sky above and sea below, as if we were gliding through a painting by Canaletto.

On the ferry, we were welcomed in five languages—English, German, Italian, French, and Croatian—by a beautiful Italian woman wearing a crisp white shirt, a silk scarf, and a red pencil skirt. Then her male counterpart, who wore his thick dark hair, just beginning to gray, long, and his crisp white shirt open at the neck, urged us in five languages to buy half-priced cigarettes at the duty-free shop and coffee or Prosecco or hot chocolate at the café on board. And then, in five languages, we were informed that we could write postcards to be posted in Venice. By the time the green islands of the former republic had disappeared completely, we were being given instructions, also in five languages, for surviving an emergency at sea. In front of us, a round-faced Croatian woman went through two travel-size bottles of liquor and a beer. Behind us, a couple from Northern California told me how they were following the advice of Rick Steves. The beautiful multilingual ferry attendants laughed intimately together at the counter of the shipboard café.

I looked out the window at the open Adriatic Sea and longed to write postcards to Terry, to be posted back in Venice, describing what I saw. But I could get nothing right. I might have said, *The sky was gray, and so was the water,* and that was literally true, but it flattened everything, and that's not really how it was. How could I translate into words a sky softened by shredded clouds, their undersides gray-blue, the late-day sun pulsing behind but not breaking through? How could I translate a white bird, and then another, skimming the water, far from dry land? How could I translate the relief of the open sea after narrow streets and alleys and crowds of people like a river?

I wanted to document the fleeting world, this pause between two eternities, as it existed in that moment. To read and not misinterpret. *The water is just water,* I kept telling myself, even though it looked like hammered bronze. *And the clouds aren't nearer to heaven just because a thousand painters have painted them like this, framing the saints, who lift their faces to God, Who must be the light behind them.* I did not want to see the unseen that was not there. But it was hard.

One afternoon in Venice, as Ellie and I walked toward the Academy Bridge, which we would cross to get back to the convent, we passed through a small square with a church tower whose bells were ringing. I began to film the bells and Ellie walking ahead of me, our map in her hand. In the film, the campo lies in shadow and the bells are all you can hear. As Ellie rounds the corner into a lane that becomes a bridge that crosses a canal, the sunlight absorbs her. She turns back to say something to me. She is nothing but light.

III. LANDSCAPE WITH THE FALL
OF ICARUS

Dalmatian Coast, Greece, Cyprus

The waters compassed me about, even to the soul:
the depth closed me round about,
the weeds were wrapped about my head.

—Jonah 2:5

IN THE WORLD AS AT SEA

I WAS TRYING to follow Felix Fabri's route as precisely as possible. But since the Venetian republic was no longer organizing all-inclusive excursions to the Holy Land, and since I did not have the money to charter a boat that would carry me exactly where Fabri went, I did my best to improvise. Ellie and I had taken the day-tripper ferry from Venice across the Adriatic to Rovinj, Croatia, on the west coast of the Istrian Peninsula. Like Fabri, we had seen the stone sarcophagus of Saint Euphemia, which had washed up in the harbor there, miraculously, in the year 800 and that now rested in the church at the top of the hill overlooking the town, whose red-clay-tile roofs and stucco buildings in shades of orange and ocher and ginger clambered up to meet it.

But because no ferries sailed directly from Rovinj in northern Croatia to Dubrovnik in the far south, we traveled by bus across Istria to the grimy port city of Rijeka, where the peninsula is hinged to the mainland and where we could catch a ferry that, over the course of twenty-four hours, would carry us down the length of the Dalmatian coast. From the bus windows, I looked out on small plots of land plowed and planted with rows of onions and new greens. Family vineyards and orchards with roadside stands sold grappa and olive oil. A billboard of Pope Benedict, arms open wide, advertised something I could not read. The soil was raw umber, like Oklahoma's. Here and there, sprays of red poppies lit up the green fields.

All the cabins on the Jadrolinija ferry had been booked by the time I got around to making reservations back home in Houston, and only deck passage was available for the long ride down the coast. Ellie had been having anxious sepia-tinted visions of Ellis Island immigrant ships—us in some cramped nook of a berth lying on grubby rags. But I had read somewhere that the key was to board as soon as they opened the gangway and then claim a spot in the lounge in order to be shielded from the wind, which is precisely, late one June afternoon, what we did. Scoring a booth, we stretched out in the seats, leaned against our backpacks, and looked around.

My smugness soon dissipated as I watched some Croatians setting up camp in a corner. They filled their air mattress, laid out their pillows and sleeping bags, and then began playing cards. A German couple, middle-aged and fit, pulled from their cooler apples and cherry tomatoes, which they sliced on their cutting board; salami and cheese sandwiches; glass jars of pickled vegetables; yogurt; and beer, reminding me just how woefully unprepared we were for twenty-four hours at sea with our meager pastries, purchased at the last minute onshore, flattened now, in a greasy paper bag.

The empty booths were quickly disappearing. A young couple, Australian, maybe, or British, drinking Coca-Cola and eating chips slid into the one behind Ellie, he wearing balloon pants and earrings in both ears, she in a bikini top and miniskirt. In the booth behind me, another young couple, each sporting a North Face backpack and an Ivy League sweatshirt, one Harvard and one Yale. Once all the booths had been claimed, newcomers walking in resigned themselves to the swivel chairs in the center of the lounge. "We should offer our booth to them," I told Ellie, motioning to a young Dutch family—mother and lanky father and little boy and toddler girl. Ellie wrinkled her nose. But when I did it anyway, they politely refused. As we all waited for the ferry to depart, they took turns walking around with the children or giving each other a break to smoke a cigarette outside. Late boarders, who hadn't read the tip sheet I had, entered the lounge, saw the booths and swivel chairs all taken, and reluctantly kept moving to the deck beyond.

It was early evening by the time our ferry launched. I couldn't bear to stay inside, but Ellie wanted to lie in the booth and read, out of the wind. Tucked into her abstention seemed to be a message I didn't really want to address. It felt like a rebuke, a refusal to embrace the liberty of the open sea, perhaps because it was my kind of liberty, not discovered by her. But since it was more convenient to have her there to guard our bags, I didn't push it. I sat out on deck, face to the breeze, looking at the navy water and the hills of the mainland of Croatia that receded to the vanishing point as in a perspective painting.

I missed Terry. I missed Mary Martha and Sabine. Ellie, though here beside me, often seemed in another place far away, her thoughts back at home with the boyfriend she missed and couldn't talk to or imagining the apartment in Austin in which she would live when we returned. In her notebook as we traveled, she sketched out diagrams of where she would place her furniture and made lists of all the supplies she still needed. Sometimes I wondered how much attention she was paying to the actual world we were passing through.

I missed Terry. I missed Mary Martha and Sabine. I was lonely. What was I doing here? That *bohemian-explorer-intellectual kind of life* I'd craved before I had Ellie was now making me feel adrift. I was beginning to wonder if the years for adventure had passed me by while I was wiping strained carrots off my daughters' raw cheeks. Or maybe it had happened later, one day while sitting in

Kimberly Meyer

traffic, driving them to gymnastics and ballet. Or maybe it was later still, during the nights we lay together in my bed reading *Little House on the Prairie*. It's possible I'd never really been an adventurer in the first place. And having Ellie, and then Mary Martha, and then Sabine kept me from having to confront that prospect.

Or maybe, I thought, looking out at the islands strung along the Dalmatian coast like families of turtles, my loneliness now was a function of something else. Since feeling the pull for the *bohemian-explorer-intellectual kind of life,* I had become a center out of which my children had grown. I didn't know how to conceive of myself as solitary, or even, with Ellie, only a pair. I was part of a constellation. The universe seemed off-kilter with us here and them there. I remembered that feeling from the months when Terry was in Cuba—as if our life together were already unspooling in another fold of the space-time continuum, and we just needed to arrive.

I remembered, too, the drives with Terry and the girls in the station wagon, us in the front, them in the back. Nebraska, midday, the Sandhills like dunes rolling and rising to the horizon, grasses clinging to them, cattle huddled together in one another's shade. Windmills. Round steel tubs beneath them, half filled with water. Railroad tracks, but no train. Or morning in the San Rafael Desert of Utah, earth bare of all vegetation, the two-lane highway threading its way through what looked to be massive piles of ash, past flat mesas whose bases flared out beneath them like crinoline skirts, the same matte gray. Or somewhere south of Seattle, moss-covered barns and fields of mustard plants, almost neon yellow, clusters of hydrangeas a periwinkle blue. Or on a highway heading north out of St. Augustine in the late afternoon, palm trees and saw grass and patches of water like hand mirrors reflecting the pink sky.

Terry loved the landscapes we traversed just as much as I did. We were aligned in that love in a way I wasn't sure Ellie and I could be. That's what I mean when I say that I missed him. And when I

106

say that I missed him, I also mean I missed how, as the girls would nap in the backseat or, later, read their books or stare out of the window listening to headphones, he and I would talk in that way you do on long drives, when your mind is tranquil and thoughts rise up unexpectedly, like egrets from a marsh. I missed how we'd talk and then drive on in silence. Cypress. Scrub trees. Pines.

In the Middle Ages, pilgrimages were sometimes frowned upon because in setting out, pilgrims might be tempted away from proper contemplation of their spiritual home and toward the things of the world they passed through. But sitting on the deck of the Jadrolinija ferry watching the waters grow obscure, I thought about how my own pilgrimage was keeping me in a constant state of longing for home. I wasn't crawling on my knees across stone, but this was a form of suffering for me—separated from those who were dear and from the place of familiarity where I was known. And I remembered the Irish hermits of the sixth and seventh centuries who set out on the sea, wandering with no set destination, cut off from all material comfort and human connection like the desert fathers of Egypt in the early years of Christianity, whom the hermits were emulating.

The month of June at sea in 1483, and every morning of it, at sunrise, a servant stands atop the forecastle and holds aloft a painting of the Blessed Virgin Mary with the Christ Child in her arms. All on board kneel and say the Ave Maria and pray to be brought safely to dry land. For the sea is salt and full of peril, studded with crags and sandbars, troubled by winds and by whirlpools that pull whatever sails and swims down into the abyss. In it prowl fish with beaks like augers that bore through ships. And everywhere on the sea that summer exists the possibility of Turks. Therefore the galley's prow is like a helmet, *galea,* from which the ship gets its name. It meets the waves, says Fabri, "like an armed man."

Daytime, some men play for money—dice, cards, chess. Some read. Some speak of worldly matters, while others worry beads through their fingers and pray. Some look at the sea and write. At times, music—lutes and flutes and clavichords, bagpipes and zithers. At times, the songs of mariners, one calling out orders, the others singing back in response. The astrologers watch the heavens and read the signs in the color of the sea and the smoke of the fire and the movement of dolphins and flying fish. They see omens in the flashing of oars pulled by the galley slaves as they row through the open waters. They advise the pilots, who also consult the compasses on board and a chart, an ell long and broad, whereon is drawn the coastline of the Mediterranean, with its cities and harbors, the miles between them.

Just before midday, a dry Mass is celebrated, one without the Eucharist. And then, at mealtime, a trumpeter calls everyone to the poop, and all sit together without hierarchy, poor and rich, peasant and noble, layman and doctor, workingmen and monks and priests. "The reason of this want of order and respect I imagine to be this," says Fabri, "that all pay the same money to the captain, great and small alike." There is malvoisie to begin, and a salad of lettuce and oil. Mutton and a pudding or a mess of meal or bruised wheat or barley, perhaps some cheese. On fast days, salted fish called *zebilini,* or a cake made of eggs. Fresh bread when the ship is near a harbor, twice-baked biscuits when not. The woman pilgrim takes her meals in her berth below. In stormy weather, both eating and vomiting occur.

The galley slaves, strangers and exiles caught up in the machinery of Venice's maritime empire—Macedonians, Illyrians, Achaeans, Albanians, Sclavonians, Saracens, even Turks—strain their oars beneath blows and curses. "Just as when horses are drawing loaded carts up a steep road, the harder they pull, the more they are urged on, so these wretches, when they are pulling with their utmost strength, are still beaten to make them pull harder." Fabri shudders to remember. "I have never seen beasts of burden so cruelly beaten as they are." But the galley slaves are also savvy entrepreneurs. Some are merchants who deliberately subject themselves to this brutal servitude in order to make their way from port to port to ply their wares. Others are tailors and shoemakers. Still others are washermen who clean shirts for hire. All speak several languages and have something for sale underneath their benches.

At sunset, everyone on board, great and small alike, assembles at the mainmast and kneels and sings the Salve Regina:

Hail, holy Queen, Mother of Mercy,
our life, our sweetness and our hope.
To thee do we cry, poor banished children of Eve;
to thee do we send up our sighs,
mourning and weeping in this valley of tears.

Then the painted picture of the Blessed Virgin and the Christ Child is held aloft again, and the Ave Maria repeated, and the pilgrims retire to their cabin below, where they lie with their heads against the sides of the ship, their feet toward one another, on deck beams covering the sand used for ballast just below the boards. But the clerk of the galley stands on the forecastle and begins in the Italian tongue a long chant that becomes a litany to which all the galley slaves and officers reply on bended knees while the pilgrims fall asleep below.

It was dark by the time I bought overpriced ham sandwiches and hot chocolates for me and Ellie at the snack bar on deck and returned to the brightly lit lounge. The middle-aged Germans had unrolled their camp mattresses. The Croatians were reading on theirs. The Ivy Leaguers were reading too—*The End of Poverty,* and another book whose title I could not see. Harvard was telling Yale about the youngest tenured faculty member at the university. She was arguing that college degrees from certain schools are worthless, "even if you have a four point oh." The Dutch mother and father were each holding a child and trying to sleep upright in the swivel chairs. A biker passed through the lounge, a member of that wandering nationless tribe in bandannas and black leather, his long dark hair pulled back in a ponytail, holsters of some kind strapped around his waist and thigh.

While I'd been out on deck, a young bearded guy in a concert T-shirt had settled with his laptop into the single remaining swivel chair in the lounge. Beside him sat his three-legged Siberian husky named Ska. He'd found her in a ditch, we heard him say, her leg mangled. He was a filmmaker and was making a movie about her. Ellie and I ate our sandwiches and watched as a young couple fawned over the dog. They were soon joined by the couple in bikini top and balloon pants. When, a little later, the filmmaker unplugged his laptop and Ska hopped off behind him, the two couples, having bonded over their affection for the husky, slid into the booth behind us and continued to talk. They discovered that they all lived in London, that they'd all come originally from Australia, and that in their bachelor days, both the men had lived in Brixton. They told competing stories about the gunshots they used to hear at night with a wistful bravado.

Up until this point, I had been indulging a sense of communion with our fellow travelers that existed entirely in my own mind. Here we were on the wide sea together, I thought, by chance or by some design we could not see, our various lives with all their complications and histories colliding briefly as we moved toward our destinations. But it was starting to get late. And the chatter of the Londoners was not that interesting. I had begun to resent Ska, canine film star, who had brought these couples together. So too,

I could see, did the middle-aged German woman, she of the jars of pickled vegetables, who now glared from her sleeping bag at the expat Australians who were shouting as if they were in a bar about Swansea football—meaning soccer—and about the expensive fish restaurant on the docks of Rijeka where you could choose from live specimens in a tank. The German woman and I rolled our eyes at this obscene decline in civility, and she muttered to her husband something in German that I took to mean "Is the apocalypse near?," though I could just be projecting. Finally, her husband sat up in his sleeping bag, and, evidently believing this was a gathering of old friends, he asked them in an English that wasn't quite fluent, "Would it be a big problem for you to talk your memories more slowly?" The couples looked at each other and then burst out laughing at his mistake. "If you want to sleep on this fucking boat, get a fucking cabin," said balloon pants to his compatriots but loud enough for the rest of us to hear. "You can't get mad if it's not fucking three in the morning." But I am here to tell you that you can.

It did not seem accidental that, looking over Fabri's account as we waited for the ferry to depart, I had been rereading the section entitled "How Unquiet the Sleep of Pilgrims Is on Board Ship." Aside from the mice and rats, which gnaw through larders and pillows and shoes and sometimes fall on men's faces as they sleep; aside from the vermin—fleas, gnats, flies, lice; and aside from the heat and the damp and the foul vapors, it's largely the pilgrims themselves who drive one another crazy at night. Vicious disputes arise when one traveler overlaps another's berth with his mattress and then denies it. "During these quarrels I have seen pilgrims fall upon one another with naked swords and daggers, and shout, making a horrible riot," Fabri recalls. "I have seen some throw their chamber-pot at burning lights to put them out," he goes on. Even after the lights are out and the mood calms down, some "begin to settle the affairs of the world with their neighbors, and go on talking sometimes up to midnight," and if anyone complains, they curse and shout. "During many nights I never closed my eyes."

Ellie had managed to fall asleep already. As the Londoners talked their memories more slowly, I pulled out a scarf and wrapped it around my head and lay down in the booth on my backpack, trying to block out the noise and the light.

Sunrise on the translucent waters of the Adriatic. The islands that during the night had slipped past us in silhouette, low hills like swaybacked beasts of burden, dark and isolate against a backdrop of stars, now took on definition and detail. We passed between these islands and the small harbors and rocky promontories of the coast. On deck, most people were still asleep on the coffinlike wooden cabinets storing life jackets, some in sleeping bags and on camping pads. I stood against the railing with an old man holding a cane, white hair carefully combed, pressed jeans, pressed shirt, who smoked cigarette after cigarette, both of us looking out wordlessly at the blank sky, the calm but variegated sea.

One of my favorite moments in Fabri's account of his ocean journey occurs somewhere in these waters, on one of the islands we must have passed in the night. Caught in a fierce storm, the galley had put in to a harbor surrounded on all sides by stone precipices. Fabri calls this Assaro, an island neither *National Geographic* nor Google Maps could help me locate. For three days the pilgrims are waylaid here because of poor winds. To pass the time, some of them row to shore on small boats and wander over the hills of the island. They come to fields of barley and hope this means they are near a farm where they can buy fresh bread and eggs. Walking farther, though, they come upon a miserable hut, the only one on the entire island. It's inhabited by poor Sclavonians who have nothing at all to eat except a root that they dry and grind into flour and bake into dark and tasteless loaves.

Some of the pilgrims conclude that the shore is more dull than the ship, so they return to the galley, but Fabri and a few others remain. He gives his companions the slip and tramps off on his own to climb a mountain and have a look around him. In doing so, he sees another Dominican, a brother of his own order, running his way. "Wherefore I ran to meet him, and, greeting him, inquired whence he came, and whither he was going," Fabri remembers, adding regretfully, "but this poor friar knew no tongue wherein to speak with me, neither Latin, nor Italian, nor German, for he was a pure Dalmatian or Sclavonian. He was on his way to the galley to beg."

Fabri returns to shore and finds one of the crew plucking an herb that grows in the crevices of the rock. The sailor calls it *porcella*—salty and sharply flavored, like nasturtium. Fabri collects some as well, along with boughs of the aromatic *agnus castus*, which he remembers growing in the convent garden in Basle and which promotes chastity by drying up "the substance of the seminal humors and the wind which extends the generative organs." Back on board the galley, he hangs the *agnus castus* above his berth. That evening, he does not join his company for supper but makes himself a salad of the *porcella* "on which I supped, and was content therewith."

I had wanted to try to re-create Fabri's adventures on Assaro back when we were staying in Rovinj. Ellie and I took a small ferry from the harbor there, "Pretty Woman" playing overhead, to the island of Sveti Andrija—Saint Andrew—on which sat a luxury hotel. This island, though, was connected by a man-made causeway to another island with nothing on it but dirt pathways through the shrubs. We crossed over. Out in the water, a party boat was blaring Eurotrash techno disco—I'm not sure this is an official designation—which might be tolerable in some situations, though I can't, off the top of my head, think of any.

Ellie and I began to bicker. She wanted to find some warm rocks to sit on and read and write in her journal, but these seemed to exist only on the side of the island facing the Hotel Istria and the party boat. I couldn't stand to listen to that, and anyway, I wanted to hike like Fabri. Fabri would never have listened to Eurotrash techno disco or sat still when there were hills to climb. Underneath our bickering, though, a deeper tension stretched taut between us. I was feeling myself growing increasingly resentful as we traveled. The time we would have together was already quickly fleeing. And the landscapes we were passing through—why didn't she seem all that interested in them? I had given her the gift of the thing I had renounced for her sake. Why couldn't she show a little more appreciation? While Ellie sat defiantly in the sun on the soft rocks, I, like Fabri, gave her the slip.

The sunlight shattering the water was like lighters at a concert. As I walked, I found sage and lavender and another aromatic plant I couldn't name. At the back of the island, I climbed down onto some abrasive volcanic rocks and sat watching the waves lapping them, relieved by the solitude. The wide sea, the canvas of water, gave me the space to be with my own mind. Perhaps that's what the desert fathers in Egypt and the Irish hermits had craved. *Poor Ellie,* I thought, once I had some distance between us. She didn't have the wound I did. She didn't need this cure.

After a while, Ellie found me, and we walked back across the causeway together to the ferry. On the return trip to Rovinj, I showed her the aromatic boughs I'd collected on my hike alone, which I thought smelled clean and fragrant. But she wrinkled her nose. To her they had a noxious sweetness, "like old ladies gone bad."

For breakfast on the Jadrolinija ferry to Dubrovnik, Ellie and I ate our flattened pastries and drank more hot cocoa. The Londoners and the Ivies were still sleeping. The middle-aged Germans had climbed out of their sleeping bags, the man in his underwear. The woman pulled off her shirt and put another on over her sports bra. They drew out yeasty rolls and yogurt and apples from their cooler and began to eat.

All day, we sailed down the coast of Croatia, docking in ports to let passengers off and others on. At Split, the Australians and the rumpled-looking Dutch family with little children disembarked. At Hvar, the Germans. We passed island after island that reminded me of a monk's tonsured head: rimmed by a thin band of white sand, topped with a ring of low-growing shrubs. Some passengers sat in the shade at wooden tables playing cards or reading translations of John Grisham novels. Others, smelling of coconuts, tanned. A group of Japanese tourists painted with watercolors, the rising and falling of their arms like the coordinated movements of tai chi. I stood at the stern and watched the waves arrayed in the wake of the ship, like the ribs of an enormous beast buried underwater showing through the skin of the sea.

When Terry and the girls and I traveled to the Grand Canyon one summer, years before, Mary Martha had been terrified. As we hiked, she cowered against the canyon wall as far from the edge as she could get. When we drove to various lookouts along the South Rim—Mather Point, Yaki Point, Moran Point, Lipan Point—and got out to wonder at the red striated chasm, she always wanted to stay in the car. Terry and I kept trying to get her to loosen up. "Next stop: Gravel Edge View," we would joke with her. "Next stop: Mile High Cliff." This tactic was a disaster. As we stood at one lookout, she clung to my leg and wailed, "Why can't they put a fence around this thing?"—meaning the entire Grand Canyon.

Later, along the more isolated North Rim, I walked alone out to one of the vantage points that seemed built in a less litigious era—a few iron railings defending a rocky ledge cantilevered over the canyon. As I looked down, I understood that this is how a god would see: from a great distance, and only the grand scheme of creation and destruction, unmoved by individual suffering or pleasure, incapable of witnessing the worn surface of a stone as it flakes into sand. That perspective is a little like those sixteenth-century *Weltlandschaft* paintings from the Netherlands—"world landscapes" of craggy mountains and rivers that become a sea at the horizon, all seen from an elevated point of view that dwarfs the human figures in them. *Landscape with the Flight into Egypt, Landscape with the Shepherds, Landscape with the Destruction of Sodom and Gomorrah, Landscape with Charon Crossing the Styx, Landscape with the Fall of Icarus.* What were painters like Joachim Patinir and Pieter Brueghel the Elder trying to say?

In his poem "Musée des Beaux Arts," W. H. Auden looks at these paintings and realizes that

> *About suffering they were never wrong,*
> *The Old Masters: how well they understood*
> *Its human position; how it takes place*
> *While someone else is eating or opening a window or just*
>   *walking dully along.*

And he demonstrates this obliviousness with the plowman later in the poem, too absorbed in watching the blade that slices through the turned earth to notice the white legs of Icarus kicking desperately as he drowns in the green waters below the farmer's terraced fields. But I wonder if the Old Masters were trying to say something else as well, given that expansive perspective from which we view the small figures toiling across these *Weltlandschaften*. Were they showing us that even when we feel most alone, God is watching? Or was it closer to that vision I had on the rickety vantage point in the Grand Canyon, that God has abandoned us in the welter and waste of creation against which, alone, we haven't a prayer?

On that ledge, I had felt an unsettling pull toward the emptiness before me, a yearning, almost, to jump. I wondered if that was what had frightened Mary Martha, though she couldn't have articulated it: not the height of the ledge but the terrifying desire the void called forth; the fear of annihilation and the desire to be dissolved into that vastness all at the same time. That feeling came back to me on the ferry on the Adriatic. Where did it come from? What was it? Do we sense, do the cells of our bodies sense, that we are part of that immensity? Do they long to join themselves to the matter from which they were shaped?

OUR LADY OF MEDJUGORJE

BACK IN HOUSTON before we'd left, I'd met Loreta Kovacic-Parani for a coffee. A Croatian émigré who grew up in Zagreb, Loreta is a classically trained pianist who favors white cat-eye glasses and streaks of maroon dye for her dark hair and who, despite her highbrow background, writes and performs songs for children, including my favorite, "Plywood Love Song"—an homage, perhaps, to her adopted city of Houston, which seems to be perpetually under construction. There is something darkly comic, something absurdist at the heart of her work.

Loreta gave me advice on traveling along the Dalmatian coast and where to stay in Dubrovnik, but when I told her I was also planning on traveling inland to Medjugorje, the Balkan Lourdes, where, in 1981, six children claimed to encounter the Virgin Mary on a stony hill, she scoffed. She'd heard from Croatian friends, filmmakers who went there in the early days of those apparitions, that it was all a sham, a case of mass hysteria. And that now, after thirty years as a site of international pilgrimage, it had become "like Disneyland." I tried to explain that, in following Fabri, I wanted to visit an active sacred shrine like those he would have known. Jerusalem, barnacled by centuries of tradition, would not, I worried, give me the glimpse I craved into a dynamic faith at work. Perhaps, like Venice, it would have become a parody of itself by now. But Medjugorje might be different, still in the process of its own invention. Loreta remained skeptical.

Our talk of Medjugorje, deep in the mountains of the harsh Balkan interior, turned to what feels, in retrospect, like a kind of warning. "You'll be okay in the cities on the coast," Loreta said. But in those mountain villages, she cautioned, there runs a dark Slavic undercurrent. It's a world, Loreta implied, coarse and slightly menacing that, if not overtly hostile to outsiders, was certainly not welcoming. "It's kind of like West Texas," Loreta described it. "A desolate, desperate place." When she was working on her doctorate at Rice University, she'd returned to Croatia to do research and began dating a guy—a shepherd, as it happens—from the region in Herzegovina where Medjugorje is located. One night, she'd gone to a bar to have a drink, as she did all the time in Zagreb. But here, the bar was filled entirely with men. It was eerie and threatening, the feeling that she had. One man approached her and said, "Decent women don't go out at night." Another time, Loreta was visiting with the shepherd's mother. "She lived on the earth," Loreta explained. "Vineyards, sheep. She was very poor and tiny and full of wrinkles and dressed all in black." But the mother who lived on the earth was a witch, she told Loreta, and she flew on a broomstick and met other women in secret—in the woods, in the mountains; Loreta didn't know for sure. "I wasn't drinking!" Loreta insisted. "And the mother, she might have been uneducated, but she was not crazy." After all these years, Loreta still didn't know how to explain any of this. "I was scared of it, but I was fascinated by it. I kind of believed in these stories. I felt something when I was there, something in the land itself." By which I understood her to mean some presence, haunted and haunting.

I had arranged for a driver to take us from Dubrovnik to Medjugorje, where we would spend the day with an official guide.

The driver, Zoran, a young guy with eyes the watery green of old bottles, picked us up at sunrise outside the Ploce Gate of the Old Town, whose white marble streets and baroque buildings are entirely surrounded by massive stone walls built between the thirteenth and sixteenth centuries. We drove north along the coast we'd recently sailed down, crossed through a checkpoint and went into Bosnia-Herzegovina briefly, then back to Croatia. After turning inland away from the Adriatic, we passed into Bosnia-Herzegovina again. For some time, we drove through the Neretva Valley, lush green plots and tidily harrowed fields lining the wide river that watered this basin and gave it its name. The karst mountains lay ahead, barren and sun-bleached, like West Texas, as Loreta had described.

As we drove, Zoran answered my questions about the war that had begun twenty years before and that had splintered Yugoslavia, Land of the South Slavs. He'd been a little boy when it began— six and a half, seven years old. I'd been pregnant then with Ellie, and I remember how disorienting it was at first, seeing the snipers and the bombardment of Sarajevo on the evening news. Hadn't the Olympics just been held there? It made no sense. In the early days of the war, Zoran told us in what sounded like something from a dark fairy tale, the Croatians had only one cannon, which they drove around from place to place in a flatbed truck to give the Serbs the impression that they had more. His Croatian village, which lay in the Serbs' path to Dubrovnik, had been destroyed. He remembered Saint Nicholas Day in 1991 when the Old Town had been bombarded and then went up in flames.

It seemed rude and voyeuristic to press for details that might call up some deep loss of Zoran's from those days. So we talked about the lush farmland instead. But even in the land itself was evidence of devastation and conquest. As we traveled through the Neretva Valley, Zoran explained that it was formerly named Vid

Narona and had been littered with statues of the Roman emperor Augustus. That the Ottomans, when they arrived in the fifteenth century, had built a tower to control traffic on the river. We passed mosques destroyed in the fighting. We passed road signs in both Latin and Cyrillic script, the Cyrillic of the Eastern Orthodox Serbs scratched out by the Croatian Catholics living in Herzegovina. "It hasn't been that long since the war was over," Zoran explained quietly, almost apologetically, "so it will take more time."

"Dear children, pray for strong faith. Our Lady recommends you to fast two times a week. Our Lady says those people who are sick don't have to fast on bread and water. They can simply give up something that they like the most. Our Lady recommends you to pray all three parts of the rosary. Don't just open your lips to say the words. Day by day, open your hearts. Faith is like a flower in a pot. If you put in a few drops of water each day you will see it grow. If you put a few prayers in your heart, your faith will grow like a flower. Dear children, Our Lady requires our complete conversion. She is giving us her peace, her love. You bring it to your family and your friends."

Ellie and I were standing far back in a crowd of pilgrims in a street lined with houses, some of stone, some of stucco, all with roofs shielded in terra-cotta tiles. This was in the hamlet of Bijakovici, home of the child visionaries who saw Our Lady on that fateful day in late June 1981. We'd walked here from the nearby church of Saint James in Medjugorje with our guide, Ivan Bosnjak, who stood patiently by as I furiously scribbled in my notebook the recommendations of Our Lady, spoken into a microphone by Vicka Ivankovic, one of the Medjugorje visionaries, from the aquamarine porch of her childhood home under the shade of a thick vine. Her dark hair threaded with strands of gray and pulled back tightly into a bun, her white polo shirt buttoned up all the way, Vicka spoke in Croatian, which is also the language in which the Blessed Virgin speaks to her. "She hears Our Lady in a physical way," whispered Ivan. Then she paused for the translator to relay her message in English, blowing kisses to the crowd and waving and smiling while he did. "The best weapon in our hands against Satan is the rosary. That is why Our Lady recommends us always to carry little blessed items—little medals, little crosses—a little something to resist Satan better." Conveniently, attached to Vicka's house was a shop selling just such holy souvenirs.

Actually, attached to almost every home in Bijakovici was a souvenir shop: narrow, rectangular additions jutting out from the fronts of houses lining the lane and displaying crucifixes, racks of colorful beaded rosaries, carved wooden walking sticks, straw sunhats, and infinite visions of the Virgin Mary—statues of her, framed prints, images on water bottles, baby onesies and baby bibs, pens, fans, polyester pillows, *little blessed items—little medals, little crosses*.

Our Lady, through Vicka, continued to recommend that we attend Mass and go to confession, that we pray for peace, that we pray for the Holy Father and the Holy Church, the bishops and the priests. And then Vicka shared with us the glimpse Our Lady had given to her and the other children years before of heaven, purgatory, and hell—how the ceiling opened and they found themselves in paradise, saints in gowns of green and rose and yellow, angels flying. Purgatory was fog. Hell was a great fire. Those entering the fire became wild beasts. Our Lady, it seemed to me, as I listened to her through her prophet and seer, was a little tedious and repetitive. Our Lady was rather clichéd. "There are people on earth who believe that once you die, everything is over," Vicka concluded, as if directly rebuking me for my doubt. "But this is not true."

After she finished, the pilgrims applauded. Some wiped away tears. Some tried to touch Vicka but she was spirited away by her handlers. Later, Ivan would tell us that the visionaries had to be protected—especially from the Italians—"otherwise, they'd be torn apart." But in compensation for the loss of Vicka, the translator invited us all to join together in silent prayer to Our Lady. A minute or so later he said curtly, "And then of course your Mass is at ten o'clock in the church."

Ivan and Ellie and I began to mount the Podbrdo, the Hill of the Apparitions, at the base of which sat Bijakovici. A company of Italians followed behind. The path was formed of jagged stones embedded in the red earth and lined on either side by thornbushes and pomegranate trees studded with brilliant orange buds. Ivan, tall and dark-haired and goateed, wore his official royal-blue Medjugorje polo shirt and a guide badge on a lariat around his neck. As we climbed, he narrated the story of the child visionaries, the details of which seemed long ago to have been hammered into legend or folktale or one of the accounts collected in a compendium of the *Lives of the Saints*.

It was late in the afternoon of the Feast of Saint John the Baptist. Ivanka Ivankovic had returned to Bijakovici from Mostar to spend the summer holidays with her grandparents, helping them work the vineyards and tobacco fields that they owned. Mirjana Dragicevic had likewise returned from Sarajevo for the summer. Both were sixteen. "They were sent to the country," Ivan told us, "because in the city they were in danger, shall we say, of mixed marriage." (That is, marriage to an Eastern Orthodox Serb. "Not that we're xenophobes," he added when I looked at him, slightly alarmed.) That afternoon of the Feast of Saint John, the girls headed toward the Podbrdo, stopping to collect Vicka Ivankovic—no relation—on their way. But Vicka had been sleeping, so they went on without her. It was afterward revealed that the girls had gone up the hill for a smoke.

Later, as they were returning to Bijakovici, its street then only a rutted cart track crisscrossed by wandering sheep and goats and hens, something made Ivanka look up. Off in the distance, hovering above the rocky ground, was the Madonna, luminous in gray, blue eyes, dark hair, a crown of stars above her head. Ivanka shouted for Mirjana to look, but Mirjana was too frightened. "There was a desire to look, but also religious awe and fear," Ivan explained. The girls ran back toward home. As they reached the bottom of the hill, they met Milka Pavlovic, setting out to round up her small flock of sheep grazing on the hillside. She asked Ivanka and Mirjana for help in herding them into their pen. Nearing the same spot, the Virgin Mary appeared to all three girls.

By this time, Vicka had awakened from her nap and was heading up the Podbrdo to join her friends. As she approached, the three girls motioned to her, pointing and crying out that it was the Madonna. Vicka became terrified, kicked off her slippers, and ran away. Near the village, she met two boys, Ivan Ivankovic and Ivan Dragicevic, who convinced her to turn around. But when the two Ivans and Vicka reached the spot where the others stood, Ivan the younger, terrified himself, ran off. Vicka finally looked. And then beheld. At home that evening, it is said, she cried and cried.

The following day, Ivanka and Mirjana and Vicka, having worked, as usual, gathering leaves in the tobacco fields until late in the afternoon, felt themselves inexplicably pulled to climb the Podbrdo again. Ivan the younger joined them, as did Marija, Milka's older sister, and a ten-year-old neighbor, Jakov Colo. Also a few curious neighbors from Bijakovici and other hamlets surrounding Medjugorje and the church. This time, the apparition beckoned to the children, and they ran to her through the brambles and across the sharp stones but received not a scratch. They knelt and prayed. To all of them, she said, "Go in the peace of God."

On the third day, again in the early evening, several thousand people from the surrounding hills climbed the Podbrdo behind the six children—Ivanka, Mirjana, Vicka, Ivan, Marija, Jakov. Suddenly, all six children stopped, turned their faces to the northeast, and dropped to their knees. The lovely apparition in gray told them she was the Blessed Virgin Mary, come to this obscure hill because of the faithful believers there. The people all bowed in prayer, and then the children tried to relay questions to the Blessed Virgin from the crowd and return her answers to them. Later, as the assemblage moved back down the hill, Our Lady appeared to Marija alone before a bare cross, brilliant with a spectrum of color. "Peace, peace, peace," she said. "Peace must reign between God and men, and among men themselves."

And that was how it began.

By the time Ivan finished the story of the early days of the apparitions, we had reached the site where they'd taken place, marked now by a white marble statue of a sweet-faced Madonna that had been donated by a Korean family whose son was miraculously healed in Medjugorje. The mother had traveled here with her little boy, deaf and mute, though the extended family, being Buddhists, were against it. She stayed a week, but nothing happened. So she stayed a month. "That Eastern patience," Ivan noted. But the time came when they simply had to return home. "The story goes that the mother was helping in the church kitchen," Ivan narrated. "The son was looking through a window when he suddenly noticed he could hear pilgrims saying the rosary. And he himself began to sing. After that, the whole family in Korea converted."

From the top of the Podbrdo, we could look out over the vineyards below and hear the Neretva River somewhere in the distance, a rooster nearer by. The hills reached around the valley like arms. We could see, too, the pilgrimage apparatus that has grown up over the years since those first apparitions—the cinder-block buildings in various states of construction, the cafés and the pensiones. The Italians behind us were coming up fast, puffy-faced in the heat, some with walking sticks, some carrying backpacks, some holding rosaries, some walking barefoot or in stockings. Then they all stopped at one of the many iron monuments marking the Way of the Cross and began to pray together. I thought it was beautiful, ancient words in an ancient tongue chanted in unison on stony ground beside the brambles. But under his breath, Ivan observed, "The Italians are so, shall we say, *loud*. They don't pray the Hail Mary. They *scream* it." And then, as the pilgrims—dubbed by Ivan the "Italian Invasion"—passed by, we turned to head back down the hill. Ivan declared "God is not deaf!" at their retreat. Ellie looked at me and rolled her eyes.

The anthropologists Victor and Edith Turner, who have written extensively on the phenomenon of Christian pilgrimage, argue that what pilgrims seek is something they call *communitas*. Having left dear ones behind, along with the social structures that once bound them, pilgrims occupy a liminal space—"betwixt and between," neither here nor there. Traveling alone or in small bands, they bear with them their own particular woes and personal hopes. But at the shrine, they become part of a vast throng performing the same ritual—reciting the Hail Mary, say, or walking in the footsteps of children who once encountered the divine. And by joining their small selves to this immensity, pilgrims become undifferentiated drops in an immeasurable ocean.

Communitas is "communion." It erases barriers—of class and age and gender, of religious hierarchy, of politics. It frees people and can, therefore, be dangerous, anarchic. "From the point of view of those who control and maintain the social structure," argue the Turners, "all manifestations of *communitas*, sacred or profane, are potentially subversive." And in 1981, in Catholic Medjugorje, in the Mostar Diocese, in the Socialist Republic of Bosnia and Herzegovina, in the Socialist Federal Republic of Yugoslavia, this was precisely the problem.

Actually, the problem had begun centuries before, at least according to Ivan, with the arrival of the Muslim Ottoman Turks, who reached the region in 1463, ten years after the fall of Constantinople, twenty years before Fabri passed through. The Ottomans created arbitrary borders that were maintained by the Austro-Hungarian Empire when it gained control in 1878 and, later, by Tito's Communist Partisans in 1945, the consequence of which was that the Croatian Catholics of Medjugorje and the surrounding area found themselves part of ethnically mixed Bosnia-Herzegovina, with its Muslims and Eastern Orthodox Serbs. Tito managed to keep the tensions among these factions at bay for the sake of the larger Yugoslavia. But then he died, and the apparitions began, and Yugoslavia started to splinter.

Ivan explained this history as we walked through the vineyards we'd seen from the top of the Podbrdo. Christened the Way Through the Fields, this was the pathway along which the visionaries fled when the Communists arrived to shut the whole operation down. "In the early days, the people would go to the hill every day," Ivan told us. "Very quickly, news of the apparitions came to the ears of the Communists. Even the army was sent here. Police were watching the hill and not allowing anyone to come in. They took down information and later used this against people. They declared the Podbrdo off-limits." So instead, sheltered by the Franciscans, who ran the parish of Medjugorje, the children met with Our Lady each evening at 5:40—6:40 in the summer—safe in the confines of the Church of Saint James. It was toward the church that we walked with Ivan on the Way Through the Fields, itself now flanked with open-air souvenir stalls and clotheslines hung with white linens embroidered by the women of Medjugorje.

Beside me, Ellie vibrated with a skepticism verging on anger, but I ignored her. I found myself captivated not by the events themselves but by the way Ivan had shaped them into such a cohesive narrative. Our Lady of Medjugorje, so that narrative went, was a harbinger for the fall of communism and the disintegration of Yugoslavia, which is why the authorities had at first tried to suppress news of her miraculous sightings. Then, a few years into the apparitions, they tried to co-opt her by building hotels, taking control of the tour companies, installing guides. A joke at the time went something like this: "A year ago, those who said that the Virgin Mary had appeared in Medjugorje got two months in jail; today, those who say she did not risk getting the same." But despite the imprimatur of the Communist regime in Yugoslavia, it is clear in hindsight to the people in charge here now that the Blessed Virgin came to proclaim communism's doom. She had appeared under similar circumstances—peasant children herding sheep in an arid, rocky land—in Fátima, Portugal, in 1917, ushering in, or so Ivan implied, the Russian Revolution. And years later, he pointed out, Our Lady told Marija, "What I began in Fátima I will finish in Medjugorje." But what did that mean, exactly? That the Virgin Mary had ushered in communism, hoping to level the playing field for the rich and the poor? If so, was she responsible too for the brutality and repression that followed? Did she realize her mistake and try to fix it here?

As Ellie and I sat with Ivan on a bench near the church and an immense outdoor amphitheater, nearly empty on this weekday in Ordinary Time, we watched a string of Italians waiting to receive Holy Communion from the Franciscans. Zoran would pick us up here and drive us back through the Neretva Valley to Dubrovnik. While we waited, I asked Ivan about the effect of the Yugoslav Wars on Medjugorje. He smoked a cigarette and told us tourism had plummeted during those years but that despite the fact that the front line was only six or seven miles away, Medjugorje itself was not directly affected by the fighting, because there were only Croatians here. Like Zoran, Ivan emphasized the powerlessness of the Croatians against the Serbs. "We were up against the third largest military on earth with shovels and hoes," he recalled. He drew on his cigarette. "We value the virtues of home. Material prosperity. A spiritual life. I'm not saying the Serbs don't. But this category of, shall we say, military achievement—we do not aspire to this. They might want their children to be soldiers, but not us." Despite these protestations, there was something angry and resentful in Ivan's narrative—maybe evidence of that dark Slavic undercurrent Loreta had warned me about, menacing and xenophobic. It suddenly occurred to me that Ivan, tall and dark-haired, with his goatee and paunch, looked like a medieval Slavic warrior on the downslide.

In spite of the war and the narrative Ivan was trying to impose on Medjugorje, in spite of the exhortations of Our Lady, this land remained unexorcised, rage flickering just below the surface, old grudges from the time of the Turks. And no one was innocent, I learned later, neither Croatians nor Serbs. During World War II, the Croatian Ustaše ethnically cleansed half of the Serbian population of Herzegovina. They would herd their victims, sometimes by the hundreds, into the hills and then throw them into natural pits and deep ravines of the limestone karst. Within several miles of Medjugorje lie four such mass graves—including one just on the other side of the Podbrdo. A year before the outbreak of the wars of the 1990s, the Serbian Orthodox Church orchestrated a series of exhumations and commemorations and reburials for the Serbian victims of World War II atrocities, including those from the pit near Medjugorje. Radovan Karadzic, leader of the newly founded Serb national party in Bosnia-Herzegovina, descended into that pit during the exhumation. After the war, he would be accused of war crimes against Bosnian Muslims and Croats and of ordering the

1995 Srebrenica massacre, a genocide of more than eight thousand people, mainly men and boys.

And what of the pilgrims seeking *communitas* on the Podbrdo, seeking healing or insight from Our Lady? "If the Madonna of Medjugorje did insist on peace," the historian Michael Sells writes, "one wonders why those who heard her message gave such little thought to the Muslims confined to concentration camps at Gabela, Čapljina, Dretelj, Ljubuški, and Rodoč," all quite near Medjugorje. "Did those buses full of pilgrims, filled with inner light and joy, hear the screams from the other side of the Medjugorje hills?"

In our rented apartment near the music conservatory within the medieval walls of the Old Town of Dubrovnik, Ellie threw herself on the bed. The silence she'd forced herself to maintain all day long with Ivan broke like a storm. "I don't see how they can believe any of this," she declared with a quaver in her voice. She seemed on the verge of tears. "I'm sure there's a scientific explanation for everything that happened. And anyway, how they presented the visionaries, it's like they're flawless."

Ellie was right. It had all felt so hokey, *like Disneyland,* as Loreta's filmmaker friends said. Ivan had mentioned Our Lady was revealing ten apocalyptic secrets little by little to the visionaries. And when the time came for the visionaries to make known these secrets to everyone else, the apparitions would stop and God would leave a sign, "something visible, something eternal, something only He can make," Ivan explained. But if, for the believer, these secrets pointed toward religious mystery, for Ellie, Medjugorje felt totally contrived.

Even worse, it was banal. "It's not like this is a holy place like Jerusalem—like this is where Jesus actually lived and died," she went on. "But the places in Jerusalem that are holy now weren't holy yet when Jesus was alive." I, playing the devil's advocate, pushed back. "The holy places weren't holy until his followers made them that way." "But Jesus started something new!" Ellie argued. "He didn't repeat these old messages that anyone could come up with: say the rosary, go to Mass, fast, read the Bible." As for the miraculous healings, they seemed to offend Ellie's sense of justice, to call into question the essential fairness she assumed of God. "I mean, why would God heal a little deaf boy and not someone else just because he came to this place? What if you couldn't afford to travel all this way?" "But that happens all over the Gospels," I countered.

Why was I tormenting my daughter? She was traveling now in a liminal space, *betwixt and between*. Dislocated from friends and from the social structures in which her life made sense, she didn't need an argument with the devil's advocate. She needed to feel joined together with me, her fellow pilgrim, in *communitas*. But all day at Medjugorje while she'd wanted to argue with Ivan, she'd had to tolerate me looking upon everything he said with anthropological curiosity and detachment, trying to understand how the thirty-seven million people who had traveled to Medjugorje since the apparitions began were not entirely deluded.

Still, Ivan's xenophobia had deeply disturbed me—his complaints about the Italians, his barely concealed hatred of the Serbs. At one point, in recounting the days when the Communists had taken over the tourism industry in Medjugorje, he'd declared, indignant, "Some of the guides were not even Catholic! How can a Muslim explain a Marian shrine?"—a blinkered position that seemed allied with the factionalism that led to war: "How can a Muslim understand a Catholic?" "How can a Croat understand a Serb?" "How can a Serb understand a Muslim?"

Anyway, the whole place—the souvenir village of Bijakovici, the Podbrdo, the Way Through the Fields, the Church of Saint James—this Medjugorje complex, holy land and prophets alike, had a kind of pathos about it. I sensed that, though pilgrims continued to travel to these forbidding hills of Herzegovina en masse, the moment for Medjugorje had passed. The Church has never officially sanctioned the site. And the child visionaries are all middle-aged now, most married with children of their own. Half have stopped receiving daily visions. Mirjana receives them once a month and on her birthday; Ivanka only annually on June 25. Jakov had his last apparition on September 11, 1998. He says that date was not a coincidence. Marija and Ivan and Vicka still see Our Lady every day, but usually in the privacy of their own homes, where no one else can witness.

Somewhere on the hillside above the white marble Stradun, Dubrovnik's main thoroughfare, Ellie and I made dinner. It was the first home-cooked meal we'd had since we left Sabine and Martin's apartment in Frankfurt. That afternoon on the drive back to the city through the Neretva Valley, we'd stopped at a roadside stand overlooking the river and the fields and bought cantaloupe and tomatoes and onions and zucchini, dried figs and grapes, from a farmer and his wife. He had *Ivana* tattooed on his forearm. The beloved Ivana herself gave us a bottle of pear liquor. That evening as we chopped the vegetables and cooked pasta in *communitas*, we could hear through the open windows a waltz for piano and violin, played a little off-key by students at the music school, and the sound of forks scraping plates from houses nearby. After we ate, we stood and looked out at the tops of fruit trees just visible behind neighboring walls, and at the late light on the limestone facades, and at the shadows. A skinny cat was digging her paw into a heap of trash.

I felt sorry for Ellie, tagging along, trying so hard to be patient with my obsessions. This wasn't what she'd had in mind that day in the spring when I'd called her in the library and asked her if she wanted to come with me. How could I explain to her that in going to Medjugorje, I was hoping to strip away all the politics, religious and civil, to dig beneath ancient and bitter resentments, to try to find out what exactly those children had seen on the Podbrdo in the late days of June 1981? Was there anything, I needed to know, other than human longing at the center?

Do the visionaries wonder in their hearts, or at night when they dream, why, if they have access to those with the power to ease suffering and to bring peace, nothing ever really changes? Do they worry, as they wait for all the secrets to be revealed, that they have invented all of this? That they've mistaken an inner voice for the voice of God? (Is that voice like the one that spoke to me when I was pregnant with Ellie?) Was there really here, in this obscure village in a haunted land, a tear in the veil separating this vanishing life and the eternal? And those seers whom Our Lady has abandoned, do they wonder why she has left them? How do they ease back into their existence on this side? Do they wander the barren hills hoping every bush that stirs will again call out their names?

LANDSCAPE WITHOUT DIVINITY

AFTER DUBROVNIK, WE quickened our pace through the Mediterranean. We needed to get to Methoni, on the western coast of the Peloponnese, but there were no ferries that could carry us southeast from Croatia along the coast of Albania to Greece, and, even if there had been, none that ran between the northernmost Greek island of Corfu and Methoni. But the flights from Dubrovnik to anywhere in Greece were too expensive, and the trains too far off course. I wanted to stay on the water as long as we could, but the only possible sea route to Greece required an overnight passage across the Adriatic, from Dubrovnik to Bari, at the heel of the boot of Italy, and then another overnight crossing from Bari to Patras, in the northern Peloponnese. From Patras, we could conceivably take a bus to Methoni. I say *conceivably* because timetables posted online seemed vague and incomplete.

Fabri hardly writes about his travels through the Mediterranean. His pilgrim galley passes city after city without stopping: Shkodër, Durrës, Vlorë, which by this point have all been captured by the Turks; Corfu, where the plague is raging. So between the impossibility of traveling by boat directly along his route and the expense of traveling any other way, I felt justified in straying from Fabri's path to crisscross the Adriatic.

I had succeeded in booking a cabin for us this time, several floors below deck in the front of the ship. All night, waves lashed the hull. The boat rose and fell like a carousel horse. For hours, I threw up every bit of the lovely Dubrovnik fish dinner that we'd splurged on that evening in an outdoor café and listened to vomiting from the men's bathroom down the corridor. Ellie managed to escape our cabin and crawl upstairs and lie down in a carpeted hallway, but I was too sick to even turn my head. I thought of Fabri, in the midst of a storm somewhere in these same waters, remembering aphorisms of the Greek philosopher Anacharsis, who said that those who are at sea cannot be counted among either the living or the dead. "Moreover," Fabri recalls, "he said that they were only removed from death by the space of four fingers, four fingers being the thickness of the sides of a ship. Also, when asked which ships were the safest, he replied, 'Those which lie on dry ground, and not in the sea.'"

Did the Greek bus system have it in for us? Were the ticket sellers and bus drivers contemporary incarnations of Homer's capricious gods? Because when we arrived at the northern port city of Patras at midday, we found that there were no buses that traveled from there directly to Methoni at the southern end of the Peloponnese and that we would need to go first to Kalamata, where we could catch a transfer. What time would buses run from Kalamata to Methoni that day? "Here is a number to the bus station in Kalamata," the woman behind the window said as she wrote, not even looking at me.

But when I called that number, it turned out I was calling someone's house, and this someone did not speak English but passed me on to his daughter, who did, and she explained to me, kindly, my mistake. To the exquisite annoyance of the woman behind the window, I returned. When she realized she had written down the wrong number, she wrote down another. This time, on the other end was a recorded message, all in Greek.

Back to the window I went, feeling ashamed and desperate. I begged the woman to listen to the message for me, which she grudgingly did. But it gave no information on Methoni, which probably meant, she explained, already motioning to the person behind me in line, that the buses that ran between there and Kalamata were run by a different company. And there was no way to call and talk with someone in person? She shook her head. "Next!" Were there any other numbers she could suggest? She looked at me severely, then flipped through her binder to a blurry and mottled page with lists of numbers that looked like they had been photocopied hundreds of times twenty-five years before. But when I called the number she gave me, it just rang and rang.

I went back to the little camp in the corner of the station where Ellie and I had piled our backpacks, and I did what I always do when I need help and feel like crying: I called Terry. Within about ten minutes and from across continents and oceans, he managed to find the bus schedules from Kalamata to Methoni. But we would not arrive in Kalamata in time to catch any of them. So he booked us a hotel room in Kalamata and canceled our reservation in Methoni for that night. We were going to be okay.

A few hours later, we boarded the bus that followed the western coastline south for a while, the blue Ionian sea coming in and out of view. The air vibrated with Greek pop music from over the loudspeaker, and the constant ringing of cell phones. I'm pretty sure we were the only tourists on board. The landscape of the northern Peloponnese was flat, and the towns we passed through—Pyrgos, Anemochori, Zacharo—cheerfully haphazard. Rosebushes—reds and pinks, fuchsias and peaches—grew in the yards of whitewashed houses of cinder block and stone. Men sat outside the storefronts on straight-backed chairs. Geese ambled by a river, and scrappy goats perked their ears and stared. The small cemeteries were all slab and monument, bleached stone, no green grass in sight. In between the red-roofed towns grew olive trees and oleanders, reeds in swaths of marshes, fields of what looked like corn.

After a couple of hours, we turned inland. As the bright sun sank and got tangled in the trees, the shadows stretched out on the face of the earth. The land grew hillier. The towns disappeared. The songs on the radio changed to traditional music—tambouras and clarinets. Something about the songs, plaintive and mournful, something about the shifting light. The passengers seemed to grow pensive. Ellie fell asleep. But I was trying to write down all of it as it passed by—Kalo Nero, Kopanaki, Kallirroi. Stone aqueduct. Cypress. Flock of chickens trailing a woman in a cotton dress. Wooden pallets and plastic crates in a yard.

The Peloponnese was the home of the ancient Spartans, who defeated the Athenians and their allies and brought an end to the golden age of classical Greece. Before that, Sparta was the home of Queen Helen and her husband, Menelaus. Then Paris, prince of Troy, seduced her and carried her away across the Aegean, launching the Trojan War. The stronghold of Argos had also been here, and after the war, when King Agamemnon returned to his palace, he was slaughtered by his wife, Clytemnestra, as he took a bath. Meligalas. Tsoukaleika. Agios Floros. Wooden shutters, blue and green. It would all go on existing, I thought to myself, whether or not I wrote it down. And then I wrote down anyway: "Old couple tending their gardens. Fields of straw-colored grain."

Methoni and Koroni, both at the southwestern end of the Peloponnese, were said to be the *oculi capitales Communis Veneciarum*, the Eyes of Venice, for the careful watch they kept over this region of the Mediterranean. Methoni had been fortified and used by the Venetians in the Middle Ages for hundreds of years as their main port of call, a place for merchant ships and pilgrim galleys to rest and take in supplies. On the morning of the fifteenth day of June in 1483, because there is no fair wind by which to sail, the galley slaves must heave Master Peter Lando's ship through the water and into the harbor here. The pilgrims enter the enormous walled city and hear High Mass at the Dominican church, then visit the bakery where biscuits are made for seafarers, and there they dine. Afterward they walk around on the walls of the town and admire these "impregnable fortifications," surrounded on three sides by the searing blue Ionian waters and on the fourth by a moat, all necessary because by this point, the entire Peloponnese, save a few coastal cities that Venice still controls, is in the hands of the Ottoman Turks. From these walls, punctuated by gates and drawbridges and towers, the pilgrims are able to look down and see the city's timber houses and stone buildings and cathedral, its narrow paved streets, its market square. In the harbor, the galley of Master Augustine Contarini also lies anchored, and though the captains despise each other and think that their passengers should share that animosity, the pilgrims from both ships make "a happy and merry fellowship," eating and drinking together until vespers, when the patrons blow their horns and call the pilgrims to board again.

Except for the unassailable walls, almost none of what Fabri would have seen that day in June was visible to Ellie and me. Inside the former Eye of Venice, dirt thoroughfares, which must once have been its paved streets, cut through the grass like ant trails. Under clear skies, with the sound of the sea all around us, we walked these deserted roads past mounds that must once have been human structures but that were now covered by the earth. Fig trees grew up in front of crumbling stone walls. Queen Anne's lace and red poppies, nettles, berry brambles, wild gourds, onions, and some kind of sage concealed everything else. Even the walls themselves, though still punctuated here and there with stone reliefs of the winged lion of Saint Mark, symbol of the patron saint of Venice, sprouted clumping green shrubs, as if deep within the stone were planted the seeds of the thing that would one day overtake them.

One of the few standing structures was a humble, double-domed Turkish bath, its ceiling perforated with circular holes bored in through stucco and brick like a constellation, like the cupola of heaven. The bath was a clue to what had happened here just a few years after Fabri's departure, in 1500: Sultan Bayezid II had laid siege to these "impregnable fortifications," slaughtered its citizens, and repopulated the city with the conquered from other areas of the Peloponnese.

It had taken some ingenuity for me and Ellie to get from Kalamata to Methoni, whose town of white stucco houses and buildings and churches now existed beyond the fortified walls, along the curve of the harbor and up the slope of a hill. We'd been tested again by the Greek transportation system. The driver of the bus traveling to Pylos, eleven kilometers north of Methoni, waved me away when I asked, in English, "This bus goes to Methoni?" "No Methoni. Just wait," he told me. So we sat on a bench in front of that bus and I stared at the bus driver and waited. But five minutes before the bus to Methoni was supposed to leave, I was getting nervous because the Pylos bus was the only one around. I asked a young man at the information booth from which track the bus to Methoni would leave. He pointed to the bus I'd been staring at for the last half hour. So I returned to the bus and asked again, "This bus goes to Methoni?" and showed the driver our tickets. This time, annoyed, he waved us on.

But this bus did not go to Methoni. And we were saved from finding this out the hard way in Pylos, as the bus was emptying. A young woman with cropped black hair and wearing sunglasses said, almost beneath her breath as she passed by, "Come with me. You go to Methoni? Come with me." So we came with her and she told us we had to change buses to get to Methoni. She was from

Bulgaria, working down the road in a tourist bar in Foinikounta, and she couldn't stand the Greeks, especially the bus drivers, who, she said, would have let us stay on the bus and driven us back to where we came from rather than tell us we needed to change buses to get to where we needed to go.

Her name was Plamena, "a fire name," she said, and as we rode the Methoni-Foinikounta line, she told us that she spoke five languages and had recently begun tackling her sixth. She had come to this country that was in deep financial crisis because bad as it was here, it was worse back home. She couldn't stay in Bulgaria because she couldn't afford to pay for university studies and she couldn't find a job. Bulgaria, she said, was a beautiful country, full of forests and no stones. Sometimes when she talked with her friends and her family, her heart would cry out for her to return. But then her brain would tell her that she must stay in Greece with the tourists and the deceitful bus drivers because, despite her five-going-on-six languages, there was nothing in Bulgaria for her to do. When our bus finally did reach Methoni and we were parting, I told Plamena, meaning "flame," meaning "fire," how grateful I was that she had saved us, and she told me, "I have this feeling that when we need it, someone is always there to help."

Perhaps Plamena was right, because after Ellie and I had walked the windswept grounds of the abandoned fortress of Methoni and returned to our room in the Hotel Castello, with its window that opened out onto the street toward the sea, I had Ellie confirm what I feared was true, given the insatiable itching at the nape of my neck and behind my ears: I had lice. This had not been contemplated under any of the various contingency plans I'd made in my mind, though perhaps I should have known to be prepared for the possibility. "Finally, there is among all the occupations of seafarers one which, albeit loathsome, is yet very common, daily, and necessary—I mean the hunting and catching of lice and vermin,"

Fabri wrote. "Unless a man spends several hours in this work when he is on a pilgrimage, he will have but unquiet slumbers."

Luckily, sleepy Methoni with its two or three bougainvillea-draped tavernas and its bakery and its grocery store did have a pharmacy, whose sign I discerned via common sense and a vague recollection of the Greek letters on the frat houses I used to walk past in Lawrence, Kansas. When I realized the pharmacist, a mousy young woman with pale blond hair and glasses, could not speak English, I performed the international sign for *lice:* a violent scratching of the head. She kindly pointed us in the right direction and I bought two doses of spray, and then plastic wrap at the grocery store, since there were no shower caps to be had. And because when we need it, someone is always there to help, all afternoon, as the waves crashed on the sand and the walls of the fortress nearby, Ellie picked nits from the shafts of my hair, her own head wrapped up in a scarf for protection.

I was sending postcard dispatches to everyone back home, where our familiar mode of existence appeared to be churning on without me. Somehow, it seemed, my daughters were being fed and driven from activity to activity. My husband surely was arising from our bed every morning after snoozing the alarm six or seven times. But on the sea, I felt myself among neither the living nor the dead. I was *betwixt and between,* in that liminal space beyond time and the tangible world. But in that space, I did not feel my self dissolved into *communitas* with God. For me, it was a landscape without divinity. And nevertheless, I'd been swallowed up, if not in mystic oblivion, then in still another immensity that was like the sea we were always looking out upon: the sweep of historical time, the rising and falling of empires.

I'd felt that sweep listening to Ivan talk about the capture of the Balkans by the Turks. I felt it standing on the beach in Methoni that evening we were there, looking at the abandoned Venetian fortress against the darkening waters, my head no longer itching. And I felt it again looking at another Venetian fortress in the busy harbor of Heraklion on the island of Crete. The fortress here was closed for renovation, as was the Dominican convent—or rather its ruins—that Fabri had visited. Ellie and I could see both the ruins and the limestone citadel from the rooftop of our hotel. Impossible to determine was where the house of ill-fame had been located, a warren of chambers kept by a German woman who'd cleared out the prostitutes and their customers to make room for the nobles and monks and priests. "She was a well-mannered, respectful, and discreet woman," Fabri remembers without irony, "and obtained all that we needed in great quantity, and we had a glorious supper, with Cretan wine, which we called malvoisie."

Methoni could be traced back through the Ottomans and Venetians to the Romans and Greeks and Homer's ancient Achaeans. But Crete's history stretched back even further into the mythic past. On our one full day there, Ellie and I took a bus from Heraklion through the suburbs into the interior of the island to the Minoan archaeological site of the palace complex of Knossos, partly reconstructed. Under the hot midday sun, our guide recounted the story of King Minos and the labyrinth of the Minotaur, which she claimed these ruins to be. Marinella was short and curvaceous with tiny feet; her shape reminded me of the Neolithic female fertility figurines we'd seen in the archaeological museum that morning.

The myths Marinella told were those I'd read to my daughters at night, just as I'd read them obsessively when I was a little girl, in my room in the house on Echo Street. The myth of the wife of King Minos of Crete who falls in love with the snow-white bull sent by Poseidon and who then bears the Minotaur, half man, half beast. The myth of the labyrinth designed to pen in the Minotaur by the craftsman Daedalus with the help of his doomed son, Icarus. The myth of the Minotaur, who must be fed seven Athenian boys and seven Athenian girls each year. The myth of Ariadne, daughter of King Minos, who gives to Theseus, prince of Athens, a ball of string so he can enter the labyrinth, slay the monster, and then retrace his path. The myth of Daedalus, who gives the ball of string to Ariadne to give to Theseus and who is imprisoned for this crime but then fashions wings out of feathers and wax for his son and himself so they can escape. The myth of Icarus, who flies too close to the sun and falls into the green waters of the sea below, the sun's heat having melted the wax.

The whole palace complex of Knossos, Marinella claimed, is a labyrinth—"easy to come in, but hard to get out." And this site, she implied, was the historical source for all those myths I'd always loved. She even directed our attention to a symbol carved into the stone here and there, a sort of sideways pitchfork, three-pronged, which she claimed showed the route of escape. From our vantage point, standing on the central limestone courtyard, looking into the warren of rooms below, walls eroded down to a foot or two, alabaster floors mostly rubbed away, it did look something like a maze for rats or mice, easy to come in, but hard to get out. But it also looked, to my untrained eye, almost exactly like the ruins of the Dominican convent by the sea in Heraklion, which looked like ruins everywhere. Marinella could place any narrative upon these stones and say it was true. No one would refute her. We needed the myths to still be alive.

Felix Fabri's ship arrives at the port of Rhodes on June 22, 1483. Master Lando obtains leave from the grand master of the Knights Hospitallers of Saint John to enter the city, and so the pilgrims leave their galley and walk up the honey-colored cobblestoned Avenue of the Knights to the Palace of the Grand Master with its Church of Saint John. After Mass, some of the German knights of Rhodes approach the lords with whom Fabri is traveling, greet them with deference and with pleasure, and invite them all to dine "in a respectable house." But after dinner, Master Augustine departs, so Lando, not wanting to lose ground, blows his trumpet and recalls his crew and passengers, and they board in haste, not even spending the night.

Fabri's first visit to Rhodes had been more eventful. After Constantinople had fallen in 1453, the Turks set their sights on Rhodes, stronghold of the Knights Hospitallers. The Hospitallers, a militant religious order, had originally been protectors of pilgrims to the Holy Land, then, after the First Crusade, defenders of it. They had built the cavernous Hospital of Saint John beside the Holy Sepulcher in Jerusalem, where Fabri's secular travel mates would soon be staying. But in the years after the final defeat of the short-lived kingdom of Jerusalem, when Acre fell and the Christians were expelled from the Holy Land in 1291 for good, the Knights Hospitallers of Saint John had turned to Rhodes, conquered it, and set up shop. By 1480, the Ottoman Empire wanted Rhodes for itself.

So as Fabri sailed through the Mediterranean on his first journey to the Holy Land, his galley nearly turned back for Venice in Corcyra because of reports that the sea was crowded with Turks. Some forty pilgrims did hire a ship to return them and then let it be known that those who went on had been taken captive. "In consequence of this, requiem Masses were said for my soul in several places in Suabia," Fabri recalls, not amused. On they sailed. In Crete, they met some Turkish merchants from Constantinople who said the ship would be lost if it went any farther. But it went on anyway, avoiding Rhodes, which was at that moment under siege. The pilgrims made it to the Holy Land, where they spent nine days perfunctorily visiting the sacred sites, and then set sail again.

Somewhere past Cyprus, another Venetian galley drew near and gave them news of the defeat of the Turks, who had raised the siege of Rhodes and retired in confusion. A few nights later, as the pilgrims approached the island and attempted to enter the harbor, the defenders of Rhodes, nerves still on edge, fired a cannon. The sailors and the pilgrims on board the galley lit candles and lanterns and called out to the people onshore until the guards heard them and unstrung their bows. When the pilgrims passed into the city the next morning, they had to avoid the bodies of dead Turks, cast up by the sea and littering the shore. The city itself was in tatters, the streets and lanes scattered with cannonballs, the towers and walls ruined. Everything was dear because it was so scarce. Fabri himself suffered from dysentery.

For us, Rhodes was too hot and too bright, the narrow beachfront near the harbor too packed with tourists, many of the museums and archaeological sites I wanted to visit closed because of strikes. Our cheap room in a white stucco pensione near the back of the Old Town smelled like raw sewage and our towels like cat urine, which the toast and jam and fresh fruit and coffee served outside on the balcony every morning didn't quite make up for.

And the lice were back. So I repeated the violent scratching of the head for the benefit of the pharmacist, and Ellie repeated the picking of the nits in our dark and dank room, and we tried to make the best of things. We paid fifteen euros apiece to have our laundry cleaned and folded and tidily put into plastic bags by the Turkish family who ran the laundromat. We shopped at H&M. We ate spanakopita and drank fresh-squeezed orange juice at a little stand off a plaza near an abandoned graffiti-covered mosque, which the posted sign noted was the first mosque built on Rhodes after the Turks finally did win control of the island in 1522. At night we strolled through the Old Town past tavernas lit by strings of light, the soft Mediterranean air in the trees made wistful by traditional Greek music played on lute and guitar. It could have been worse.

But one afternoon, we heard that the Palace of the Grand Master of the Knights of Rhodes would open up for a few hours, despite the strikes. So Ellie and I made our way through the Roma children playing plastic accordions for the cruise-ship tourists on Sophocles Street and walked up the Avenue of the Knights. The cobbled street was lined like a canyon with those imposing stone edifices wherein once lived the Knights Hospitallers, divided into their various tongues according to their places of origin—England, France, Germany, Italy, Aragon, Auvergne, Provence, Castile—each group responsible for defending a sector of the walls of Rhodes.

Inside the cavernous, crenellated palace, now a museum, was an exhibit on medieval Rhodes. Ellie dashed through and then waited for me in the flagstone courtyard of the palace, reading, while I carefully regarded the material culture of the Rhodes Fabri would have known. That Rhodes, beyond the reach of the Venetian republic, was a nodal point linking Syria to Constantinople, linking Venice to Alexandria in Egypt. What remained of this nodal point of empire: needles and bronze thimbles and straight pins. Bone dice. Lead spoons, glass drinking cups, amphorae. Glazed tiles in yellow and blue and green. Cannonballs and clay grenades once filled with naphtha and sulfur and quicklime and then lit with a fuse and flung by a sling. Pilgrim unguentaria—small, spindle-shaped clay vessels stamped at the base with figures of animals or the names of bishops or the Virgin, probably filled with oil from a martyr's tomb or water from the river Jordan.

When the Greek Orthodox Byzantines overcame the pagan Romans here, they etched over the faces on the statues of matrons and patricians with the symbol of the cross, the way the Cyrillic road signs of the Eastern Orthodox Serbs in Herzegovina had been scratched out by the Croatian Catholics. Then the Knights Hospitallers conquered the Byzantines, and the Ottomans conquered the Knights. Churches became mosques, their frescoes painted over.

Later, Italy seized Rhodes from the Turks, and the minarets of the mosques were hacked off, a torch with no flame. Mussolini used the Palace of the Grand Master as a holiday retreat. Today, it's Greek again.

For millennia, empires have swept over the lands of the Mediterranean like tidal waves, leaving the dead and the bitterness of the living like wrack along the shore. The histories of these places were too large, the hatred and division too old and intractable. What was my little life, my sweet little faraway life, the one with the green teakettle and the Sunday paper and my daughters' messy rooms, against those immensities?

Just before we left Rhodes, Ellie and I stumbled into the tiny Church of Saint Trinity, built in the fifteenth century of local square-cut limestone, its confusion of low domes and arched roofs shielded by curved red-clay tiles. The church seemed shrived of all excess ornamentation. The altar was a simple table laid with a white lace tablecloth and two silver candlesticks. Along the floor beneath a transept wall hung with small icons in a hodgepodge of frames were vases filled with daisies. In the doorway, an ancient woman with a bent back wearing a kerchief and apron and sandals and stockings was performing her ancient rites, waving incense, sweet-smelling and thick, which she carried in an aluminum contraption like a Jiffy Pop pan. She crossed herself and whispered prayers before ghostly frescoes nearly scoured from the plaster walls by the passage of time or the conquerors of the island. Watching her with our backs to the wall, I wanted a ritual, too, to face the void, one that would remind me how small I was. I wanted words with which to plead for some connection.

A few hours later, on the plane to Cyprus, Ellie read José Saramago's *Death with Interruptions,* which imagines a country where no one ever dies. Maybe it was the book, maybe it was the shrived church, maybe it was the sea below, the sea Icarus fell into when he flew too close to the sun, and us somewhere between earth and sky, like Fabri on the pilgrim galley, neither living nor dead. But "I can't stand the thought of dying, Mom," Ellie turned to me and said, clearly distraught. "I mean, how does anyone accept it? Even if you believe in this heaven where God exists and there's eternal life, how can you not want to stay with those you love and have built a life with? It seems cruel—our most cruel enemy. To give life, then take it away." She was quiet for a moment, looking out the blank window of the plane. Then more to herself than to me she said, "Maybe that's why we need God and heaven. We're all scared. Maybe the idea of life after death brings people comfort if they know they'll be reunited with their loved ones. Maybe believing in heaven is more about people wanting to return to the arms of their husband or mother or child or friend than the arms of God."

I had been thinking, as we ascended over the harbor of Rhodes while the sun set behind us, of Fabri's departure that day in June of 1483. "There remained behind also the one woman who was with us, because she had strayed away to some church outside the town, not supposing that the galley would sail that day," Fabri recounted. "Except her husband, no one was sorry at the absence of this woman, because she had rendered herself odious beyond measure by her silly talk and her inquisitive prying into unprofitable matters."

But I was sorry for this curious woman. I imagined her there all alone on the shore, among the ghosts of the slaughtered Turks who had died three years before and been churned up by the sea. And I kept imagining her as I listened to Ellie talk about her fear of death, which reminded me of the fear of death I'd experienced in those summer nights after she was born, when, *betwixt and between*, I had been opened up to a vision of that abyss, the oblivion that is the ultimate abandonment, like the abandonment in the mountains Ellie had dreamed of years ago, an eternity in which we are cut off from all union with others and left entirely alone.

We were flying now over the inky waters of the Mediterranean. In my mind, Fabri, dead five hundred years, sailed below, on the eve of the feast of Saint John the Baptist—Midsummer Eve. In 1981, 498 years and a day after Fabri was here, on the feast day of Saint John, the Virgin Mary appeared to children on a rocky hillside urging peace while the bones of their fathers' enemies whitened in a pit in a nearby forest.

But in 1483, as the sun sets and it grows dark, the sailors on board the galley prepare to light Saint John's fire to protect themselves against the evil spirits who roam abroad freely at this moment of the sun's shifting, as the light from each day forward will begin to wane. "They took many more than forty lanterns made of wood and transparent horn, and hung them one above the other on a long rope, and then, when the lamps were lighted, they hoisted them up aloft to the maintop as far as the rowing-benches, and lighted up the whole galley," describes Fabri. The passengers and crew all gather on deck to see this spectacle, and the trumpeters blow their trumpets and the galley slaves sing and dance and clap their hands. Fabri has never before beheld the practice of clapping hands for joy. "Nor could I have believed that the general clapping of many men's hands at the same time, when done out of gladness, would have such great power to move the human mind to joy. So we rejoiced greatly on board of the galley until about midnight, sailing along all the while swiftly and quietly on our way."

I liked imagining this small, flickering ship sailing below on the vast ocean that could swallow it whole, as it did the beloved body of a boy with wings. I thought of my grandfather, who'd once charted the same shifting light that brought out the evil spirits and who now rowed on the long, beautiful sea somewhere, the sky so far away. Did he have a lantern of horn to protect him?

And Ellie: What lamp could I give her to cleave the darkness?

Would it only illuminate the fact that she was alone? In the story of Icarus, it's the father himself who hands to the child the wings that will carry him away forever. But what can Daedalus do? They've been imprisoned in the tower. The shroud of sea surrounds them, and the sky with its torch of sun. This is no life, even if they're together. But when he stitches the feathers with cords of wax, supple and pliant, he thinks of Icarus, and his love becomes confused with trepidation. He knows what can happen. He's felt that longing to see the curvature of the earth from great heights too, from the vantage point of the gods. But he hands his son the wings anyway, because he must, because without risk there can be no salvation.

PUTTING THE LEAVES IN ORDER

I LEFT MY guidebook to Cyprus on the plane. This may or may not have been an omen for our guided tour to Salamis and Famagusta. Or perhaps our guided tour to Salamis and Famagusta was an omen for our time in Cyprus. Or perhaps our time in Cyprus was a metaphor for our travels through the entire Mediterranean—no official narrative we could trust, only the pull of stories told to us by parties with a vested interest in their own versions of events.

Since Ellie and I would be in Cyprus three nights—because the flights from Cyprus to Israel were limited and there were no longer any ferries running between the two countries due to the political situation—I had, as the guidebook I'd left on the plane suggested, rented a traditional home in the village of Skarinou, a little inland from the port city of Larnaca. I had visions of the two of us waking in the morning and making our way to the village café, of spending evenings drinking wine and looking at the dry hills. After all, "in this small village, where architectural structure blends in with nature and modernization co-exists with tradition, culture and customs have survived through time," the agrotourism website had insisted. "A walk through the village will ensure that as you may see women embroidering or knitting in their courtyards or even making the traditional halloumi (Cypriot cheese). You should not be surprised if you are called in by these hospitable people to be treated to a homemade sweet or a cup of coffee as this is considered natural and normal."

It's not that our house was not lovely. Built of limestone into the side of a hill, it was part of a whole complex of old structures that had been renovated into luxury tourist apartments, each with its own flagstone porch leading to a shared pool surrounded by cactus and oleander and bougainvillea in the central courtyard. Inside our studio were heavy wooden beams and the same stone walls, and a four-poster bed that Ellie and I shared, though I wrapped my hair each night in a scarf to try to keep whatever lice might still be hatching away from Ellie's miraculously nit-free head.

So the house was lovely, as was the cultivated valley below, and the distant low hills. But the village itself seemed strangely deserted. There was no café. There were no women in black embroidering or knitting. No one was making halloumi. No invitations to share a sweet or a cup of coffee were extended. I wondered if perhaps the entire village had sold out and decamped for life in the city, leaving all the empty houses to be converted into agrotourism luxury apartments like ours. Each day, Ellie and I would walk the two-lane road leading out of the village to the supermarket near the highway to purchase groceries—ingredients for a Greek salad, some baklava for dessert, bougatsa pastries for the mornings. Connected to the supermarket was a McDonald's.

Though Fabri had never traveled there, since we had the time, I arranged to join a guided tour of Famagusta and Salamis in the north of this partitioned island. That is, in the Turkish Republic of Northern Cyprus, a state recognized by no nation other than Turkey, from which it is separated by a narrow expanse of the Mediterranean Sea. Our instructions specified we were to meet the tour bus at the Olive Park in Skarinou, which I assumed was the quaint, traditional name for the grove of olive trees we passed on our way to the supermarket. Turns out, the Olive Park in Skarinou was several kilometers away. Eventually, for reasons that were never made clear to me by the excursion company, we were picked up at the McDonald's by a white SUV driven frantically by a middle-aged Russian man accompanied by his much younger Russian girlfriend, neither of whom spoke English but who, nevertheless, deposited us in a beachside resort beside the tour bus we had missed. On the bus: a Russian tour group, pasty and plump, and Maria, a squat Greek guide who lifted her Terminator glasses to reveal eyes green as the shallow waters of the sea and who scolded us in perfect English for being late as we took our places in the plush, velveteen seats.

Apparently, we would be assigned an English guide once we crossed the border into the north. Until then, the tour would be conducted entirely in Russian, and we would not complain. But every once in a while, Maria, miked and sitting on a jump seat next to the driver, would take pity on us and condense the history she was giving into a few curt English sentences. In 1571, the Ottoman Turks invaded Cyprus. They were here until 1878, when the British took control. In 1960, Cyprus was granted independence, and the struggle was on to reunite with Greece. In 1974, the Turkish army invaded the island, a violation that eventually led to partition. "We are about to enter *our* land," Maria said bitterly. "The Turks have brought in tens of thousands of people to settle here. No photos. This is occupied territory, like Palestine. I am speaking history, not propaganda."

At the checkpoint between the Republic of Cyprus, which existed, and the Turkish Republic of Northern Cyprus, which did not, our English-speaking guide, Kazim, boarded the bus wearing an orange polo shirt and stylishly cut, dark-rinse blue jeans. He could not, in fact, speak English. Or not enough, anyway. At the archaeological site of Salamis, he handed us a brochure, told us to be back at the bus in two hours, and walked off. Later, we saw him smoking and drinking a coffee at the open-air snack shop overlooking the sea.

Ellie and I wandered beneath the oppressive sun, trying to follow the spare brochure. We stood in the half-moon Roman amphitheater, the carved stone seats still largely intact. We made our way to the gymnasium with its now-useless columns supporting nothing. We viewed the ruins of baths and sweating rooms and swimming pools, now dry and bleak and filled with grass. We took our photos with the headless marble statues of women draped in tunics and *stolae,* but we had no idea who they were.

It was the same story in Famagusta. The bus driver deposited us at another fortress marked by the Venetian lion of Saint Mark's over whose ramparts we climbed listlessly for a few minutes before heading into the streets of the city to find something to drink. There was Kazim again, at a café, enjoying another coffee and smoking another cigarette. He waved cheerfully as we passed by. We peeked into the Lala Mustafa Pasha Mosque, formerly Saint Nikolas Cathedral, with its appended minaret rising above the ruined Gothic towers. We saw the hollowed-out relics of other churches—Saint George of the Latins, Saint Peter and Saint Paul—just a few walls and empty arched windows. We bought freshly squeezed orange juice from a cart and I watched as a teenage girl elaborately greeted an elderly man in the doorway of a shop, kissing his hands and bowing down to touch them with her forehead. I wondered what they meant, her delicate, graceful gestures. But without a guide, we'd never know.

All that day in Salamis and Famagusta, I kept thinking of the Sibyl of Cumae, who appears in Virgil's *Aeneid* and leads the hero Aeneas through the underworld, interpreting as they go. She was a prophetess of Apollo, and people seeking her guidance traveled to the deep cave where she sang of human destiny and wrote out the stories of people's lives on leaves. She placed each leaf in order on the cold stone floor, but when someone pried open the door of the cave to gain wisdom and understanding, the faint breeze stirred the leaves and scattered them all around. In Medjugorje, the leaves had been forcibly joined together, and a story imposed on the landscape. But in Salamis and Famagusta, the landscape had no meaning. It was a series of pictures without a narrative that made them make sense. The leaves were all out of order and we had no guide.

On our way back to the border, we drove past the green zone, a no-man's-land of shells of buildings and houses and churches, dust coating the leaves of the abandoned fig trees. We passed through the outskirts of Famagusta where the imported Turks lived, like the refuse of empire everywhere, among piles of concrete and trash and corded wood, and little gardens of squash and cucumbers and melons, grape arbors of rusted rebar.

As soon as the galley pulls into the eastern harbor of Larnaca, which Fabri calls Salinae, named for the saltworks there, the captain and his servants hire horses and ride to Nicosia to the court of Queen Catherine, a Venetian. She will be deposed in 1489 by the Venetians themselves, who in 1517 will lose control of the island to the Ottoman Turks. But at the moment, Lando's wife is a lady of the queen's bedchamber, and Lando is riding inland to see her. Fabri, knowing the captain will not be returning before the evening of the following day, at the earliest, organizes an impromptu pilgrimage to the Mount of the Holy Cross, the highest peak in Cyprus, on whose top is a monastery church wherein hangs the cross of the Good Thief. His small band of eight hires mules and sets out in the dark beneath the light of the moon, glad at heart. "The weather was fine, the country beautiful, the road good," Fabri remembers, "and besides all this the shrubs of the land breathed forth the sweetest fragrance, for almost all the herbs of that isle are spices of divers sorts, which smell by far sweetest in the night time, when they are moist with dew." They reach the base of the Holy Mount in the early morning, tie their mules to trees, rest briefly, and begin to climb.

I left Ellie reading, poolside, at the luxury agrotourist apartment and got a ride in a taxi to the Eastern Orthodox Monastery of the Holy Cross, which still stands. The day before, we'd gone in to Larnaca to see some churches and relics, including those of Lazarus from when he'd died the second time, forever. Afterward, we'd stopped in at an English-language used-books store. Ellie was tearing through her list of reading material at a much faster pace than the book-per-week strategy had allowed for, and she needed reinforcements. I wasn't in the market myself, *East of Eden* having waylaid me, but I took comfort anyway just looking at the familiar titles in the literature section. After a while, though, as Ellie continued to scour the shelves, I went outside to call Terry. I was stressing about money, how much everything was costing—and not just the luxury agrotourist apartment in the abandoned traditional village or the wasted trip to Famagusta and Salamis. "You're there now in the middle of it, and there's nothing you can do," Terry said sympathetically. "Try not to worry. You're *supposed* to be doing this." His words, his voice in my ear, calmed me. He knew what I needed to hear. I knew he would say it. It was our routine—a call-and-response ritual in the common country that we'd founded. Then I saw Ellie motioning to me through the window of the bookstore. "Look!" she whispered confidentially when I went in. Fellow citizen of the homeland of my heart, she had *Moby-Dick* in her hands—one of my favorites.

So the next morning I left Ellie reading by the pool and headed up the mountain. Every website, as well as the guidebook I lost, had warned me that no women were allowed inside the monastery, and I held out no real hope that an exception would be made for me, an agnostic American following after a medieval Latin priest. But the cabdriver, Mr. Dimos, tall and lanky with a thick head of white hair combed back, told me as we drove the winding road up the mountain and past a military installation that he'd find a way to get me in. Out of bravado, perhaps, or in the belief that anything could be had here if you talked to the right person, or in hopes of a bigger tip, he said, "Mayer"—perhaps not realizing this was my last name, not my first, and a mispronunciation of it at that—"we'll tell them you're from a university. We'll have a coffee. You'll see."

Entrance beyond the bookshop is permitted only to male pilgrims, said the sign posted on the massive, firmly closed gate, above which, I could see, the monastery rose like a jeweled crown from the top of the mountain. The air up here was clear and cool and dry, the sky blue—*the country beautiful, the road good*, as Fabri had said. The terraced hills below were mottled green with clumps of olive trees; the farther hills rolled on like successive shallow breakers until they met the sea. *Female pilgrims remaining here, inside the monastery's premises, may visit the All Saints of Cyprus Church and the bookshop. In the same place there are confession rooms.*

In the bookshop, Mr. Dimos spoke confidentially in Greek with an Eastern Orthodox monk in a black cassock and chimney-pot hat, black hair pulled back in a small bun. I stood beside them trying to look as humble and unthreatening as possible, for of course the reason women could not be allowed to enter was the temptation we would pose to the men inside. But the monk's position was absolute and unyielding. He was not hostile. He asked me my religion ("Catholic," I lied, thinking any religion was better than doubt), and he asked me what I was studying. And though I told him about Fabri and the ride on the mules through the night air scented by herbs, it was clear he was not budging. He did, however, hand me a book on the history of the monastery for free.

The legend, recounted by Fabri and included in the book the monk gave me, is that Saint Helena, mother of the Roman emperor Constantine and convert to Christianity, traveled to Palestine in 326 to scout out holy sites connected to the Lord's life and death and resurrection and mark those sites with churches and basilicas. While there, she discovered the three crosses of Our Lord—those of the two thieves as well as that upon which Christ had been crucified. On Helena's return journey to Constantinople, a tempest waylaid her ship and she sought refuge in Cyprus. There, an angel of the Lord appeared to her and told her to erect churches on the island as she had done throughout the Holy Land, including one upon the highest mountain. On the mountaintop, a temple of Zeus was razed and a church built wherein was placed the Cross of Dysmas, the Good Thief, as well as a fragment of the True Cross of Jesus Christ. The irony that a woman had brought these holy relics to Cyprus and built a church to house them that no woman was allowed to enter seemed lost on everyone.

Fabri says Mass for his brigand band of pilgrims, and they examine the cross, which seems to hang wondrously, without any means of fastening. They stroll the brow of the mountain and find the remains of a temple, and in whatever direction they look they can see the sea. But they are hungry and thirsty and the place seems strangely deserted. So the pilgrims hurry back down the mount to where their beasts stand waiting and ride to the village of Holy Cross and sup at an inn. In this village are two churches— Eastern Orthodox and Latin—but only one priest between them. On Sundays, "he first celebrated Mass in the Latin church, and consummated it in the Western fashion with unleavened bread; and when this office was finished he crossed over to the Greek church, and consummated in the Eastern fashion with leavened bread." I find this flexibility charming, but it horrifies Fabri, who notes, "I held that priest to be a heretic of the worst kind, leading the people astray hither and thither: for the two rites cannot be performed by one and the same person; nay, hardly in the same city."

The following evening, back on the ship, the captain still had not returned from his conjugal visit in Nicosia, but the curious woman left behind in Rhodes is rowed by boat to the galley. At her miraculous restoration, "there was but little joy; yet I pitied the poor creature," admits Fabri, "because of the straits to which she had been put by the sailing of the vessel."

On the way back to Skarinou, Mr. Dimos stopped in the village of Psevdas at the base of the mountain and treated me to a coffee at an open-air café run by an old woman, bowlegged and wearing a black dress and faded green floral apron. She moved a backgammon set on the Formica table out of the way and, unsmiling, motioned for us to sit down. Mr. Dimos spoke to her in Greek and she brought out the coffees, along with *haritaki,* a strange black fruit preserve, hard and rubbery, on small white plates. Watching us the entire time, unsmiling as well and flicking his prayer beads, was the husband of the proprietress. I kind of liked how unfriendly they were. There was something honest in their unwillingness to become part of the tourist machinery of the Western world. Beside me, Mr. Dimos chain-smoked and lamented what he called the occupation of Cyprus for what it had done to villages like this all over the island, where, he claimed, Turkish Cypriots and Greek Cypriots had lived peacefully for centuries side by side.

"They don't even know their own history!" Sevgi exclaimed when I mentioned this complaint of Mr. Dimos the following day, our last in Cyprus. Sevgi and her husband, Mehmet, were Turkish Cypriots living in Nicosia—or Lefkosia, as it is known in the north. "It was only thirty years ago," she said indignantly, "and I remember." Sevgi and Mehmet were friends of my friend Iain, a philosopher with whom I teach. Mehmet and Iain had studied together at the University of Texas, and Iain had been in Cyprus visiting the week before me. Knowing I was following on his heels, he helped arrange a meeting.

On the Greek side of the divided city, Ellie and I walked the green line demarcating north from south for a while, the shells of buildings in between, windows broken or missing altogether, paint wearing off, tagged with graffiti. Everywhere, signs warned us not to take photographs. Then we crossed over to the Turkish side at a border on Ledra Street, and Mehmet and Sevgi collected us in their sleek SUV outside the Buyuk Han, an Ottoman caravansary, a two-story walled courtyard inn lined with stalls shielded from the sun by arched arcades. Formerly for medieval merchants catering to travelers and their beasts of burden, it now served tourists, what few there were, the open square scattered with umbrellaed tables and chairs.

Iain had told me Mehmet's story, which sounded like some ancient Greek tragedy: Mehmet had been born into one of the most powerful families in the Turkish Republic of Northern Cyprus, but he'd been disowned after he'd married a divorcée with a young daughter, an older woman with whom he would not be able to have children to carry on the male line. Iain described Mehmet's wife, Sevgi, as the classic Mediterranean woman: strong-willed, hot-blooded, and fiercely independent. And with her onyx hair and enormous designer sunglasses and sleeveless linen dress and heels, she looked the part as well. Mehmet, tall and well built, wearing chic jeans and gold-rimmed aviator glasses, kept brushing the hair from Sevgi's shoulders as she spoke. Their families, they told us as we drove, had been in Cyprus since the time of the Ottoman Empire. It suddenly occurred to me: *they* were the Turks—or at least the descendants of those Turks who'd posed such an existential threat to Fabri and his companions.

Mehmet and Sevgi drove us out of Lefkosia to the ruins of Bellapais Abbey, where, in 1187, the canons regular, custodians of the

Church of the Holy Sepulcher, had fled from Jerusalem after its fall to Salah al-Din. Over strong Turkish coffee in a café on the grounds of the former abbey overlooking the sea, Mehmet and Sevgi recounted the years leading up to the Turkish invasion, when the right-wing nationalist enosis movement for union between Greece and Cyprus was on the rise, and many Turkish Cypriots were forced to live in enclaves. Sevgi's father was from Paphos and when they visited his family there, the Greek paramilitary checked their documents and rifled through their bags. That same paramilitary was later behind the coup d'état of 1974, which brought on the Turkish invasion, which sent Greek refugees from the north southward into the Republic of Cyprus and Turkish refugees from the south into the Turkish Republic of Northern Cyprus and that established that green line of demarcation Ellie and I had walked along. Recalling what Mr. Dimos said about Greeks and Turks peacefully living side by side in some kind of Eden before the Fall, Sevgi scoffed. "They're not honest," she insisted. "But I admire them for it. They made a story and they're sticking to it."

As the edge of the harsh sun wore off, and Mehmet and Sevgi drove us back to Lefkosia, from where we would take a cab to the airport in Larnaca and then fly over the black waters to Tel Aviv, Sevgi told us about the day in 2004 when the border between north and south opened for the first time. "Let's take a walk," Sevgi had said to her daughter. "This is history."

Thousands of Greeks were streaming into the north that day, looking for the homes they'd been forced to abandon thirty years before. "I felt so sad looking at them," Sevgi remembered. "They were so desperate, these poor people." One woman in particular caught Sevgi's attention. Sevgi approached her and asked her where she wanted to go and she took the woman to the address she gave. The Turks living in the home invited the woman in. Even the furniture was the same as she remembered. "For four or five years we did this, and we became friends," Sevgi told us. "And then one day, we were at my house, and this woman got a phone call. I heard her say, 'I'm in the occupied area.' I told her, 'I would appreciate if you would not use that phrase.'" But in that moment, some abyss had opened up between Sevgi and the woman. And even though this woman's husband later verified Sevgi's version of history, "that was the last time I ever saw her," Sevgi said. "She was my only Greek friend."

As Ellie and I moved over the surface of the Mediterranean, we seemed to be two small figures in a *Weltlandschaft,* dwarfed by the immensity around us: *Landscape with Mother and Daughter Following a Dominican Friar.* The sea was wide, boats small upon it. The waters compassed us about. Medjugorje, the fortress of Methoni, the palace at Knossos, Rhodes, Cyprus—what did they really mean? To what empire in whose imagination did they belong? The leaves had all been scattered out of order and there was no Sibyl of Cumae to restore them, even if she would.

Ellie was trying to join the leaves together, though. Ever since we'd wandered around the ruined Venetian fortress at Methoni on the Peloponnese, as I'd been trying to take dictation from the people we encountered and from the land and sea, Ellie had been at work on a story set in that ancient place—or at Icarus Castle, as she renamed it. She was her own sibyl. In the story, it seemed to me when Ellie let me read it later, she gives order to her past and to her present yearning—the circumstances of her birth, the birth of Mary Martha, her love for the realm of the imagination, her desire for the world beyond and for some lasting connection, my brother's fall when the earth breathed into him, her newfound sense that death is always present in us.

The story is this:

In a village by the sea, a boy and a girl are born to separate families; the girl is held first by her sister, who is four years old. Together the boy and the girl are baptized on the feast day of Saint Mary Magdalene—a woman who was witness to the risen Christ and who was perhaps a harlot. "Some say it was the holy water" that bound them together. When they are young, the boy and the girl and the other village children spend their days at the abandoned castle, where "mint, sage, and burnt yellow thistle flowers grew amid the wild ochre-colored grass," and where "moss spread out of the cracks of the fort's walls," and where they are transported away "from the place that had nothing to offer but the sea."

In their youth, the boy and the girl discover that they love each other. But the boy must leave. He ships out to sea. The girl reads books in the castle by the water—*Anna Karenina, Don Quixote, Jane Eyre*. She longs to see the places he describes in letters to her, which she reads over and over again. The boy longs for home. One day he returns, and in the castle, surrounded by her books and by the sea, they reunite. Then—the tragic turn—walking on the stone wall of the castle fortress, the boy falls, though the falling feels like flying. "Some say that you can't feel yourself dying. The truth is, he felt his last breath leave him and he heaved with the loss of it. The cerulean water rushed around."

But in autumn, "when the leaves on the trees had begun to change," the girl's belly begins to swell. And in the spring, the girl holds the hand of her sister, the one who first held her when she was born, and she gives birth to a child, whose fingers she marvels over while knowing that one day, "a day that merely seemed far away," the skin on those fingers would be lined with years.

Reading Ellie's story, written as we traveled, written when I thought she hadn't been paying attention, I realized that she had been, just in her own way. Same material, different arrangement. Which reminds me now of how, as we wandered the duty-free stores in the Cyprus airport waiting for our flight to Tel Aviv, Ellie and I had stopped at a perfume stand. We took the caps off the bottles to test the scents, and we came to Trésor, which I had worn for years, in part because I wanted to be like Isabella Rossellini, daughter of Ingrid Bergman and the face of Lancôme. As we inhaled together, Ellie exclaimed, "Oh, it's you! I remember this from when I was little!" And what I remembered, what I always remember when I smell that perfume, is standing before the mirror in the hospital bathroom in a black dress with coral flowers as, just beyond, my newborn daughter lies in a clear plastic bassinet. I have showered and changed out of the hospital gown I wore while in labor and in the days after as Ellie, because of a slight case of jaundice, lay under blue bili lights with a white mask over her eyes like a little blind mouse. But now, the bilirubin levels having decreased and the all-clear given, I have dressed her in the peach outfit embroidered with pale blue and green flowers that was once mine and that my mother has saved all these years. And I spritz on Trésor as I look at myself in the mirror. It's time to go home and begin this new life for which I've been waiting.

IV. OMPHALOS

Holy Land

For the letter killeth.

—2 Corinthians 3:6

IN THE COURTYARD OF THE CHURCH
OF THE HOLY SEPULCHER

WITH OUR PACKS on our backs and clutching our purses to our chests, Ellie and I entered the walled Old City of Jerusalem in late afternoon through the northern Damascus Gate and made our way, top-heavy and off balance, through the narrow lanes of the Muslim Quarter. At this hour, it was crowded with people shopping for the evening meal at the produce stands set up like stones in the midst of this human river. Men leaned against the limestone walls, smoking or talking in small groups. The guttural sound of Arabic was harsh in our ears. Outside the gate, we could still hear the cars and buses honking and braking and stuttering. Inside, church bells were ringing. Strands of children wove through the crowd like stitching. From the roofs of the shops hung merchandise jutting out over the streets—T-shirts of President Obama wearing a black-and-white kaffiyeh in the manner of Yasir Arafat; the long black *jilbab* cloaks that covered so many of the women; sequined bras and lace panties.

We were staying at the Ecce Homo guesthouse for pilgrims, run by the Convent of the Sisters of Zion and situated along the Via Dolorosa, the Way of Sorrow, in the heart of the Muslim Quarter. The Via marks the path Jesus took through Jerusalem, cross on his back, to the site of his crucifixion and burial. Golgotha and the empty tomb are now enshrined inside the Church of the Holy

Sepulcher, end point of the Via. Ecce Homo Arch, spanning the limestone street outside the heavy wooden door of the convent, is the beginning. Here, they say, Pontius Pilate presented Jesus Christ, bound humiliatingly and crowned with thorns, to the crowd below, saying, *Et dicit eis ecce homo.* "And Pilate saith unto them, Behold the man!" In actuality, the remnant stone arch was part of the entrance to the forum of Aelia Capitolina, the city that the Roman emperor Hadrian built more than a hundred years after the death of Christ on top of the ruins of a Jerusalem destroyed by Rome to quell the Jewish uprising. Jerusalem is built of stones such as these marking poignant moments in an imagined history. They are a way of claiming territory.

We had arrived at the omphalos: Jerusalem's Old City, fragmented into sectors—Christian, Muslim, Jewish—though the lines of demarcation weren't always clear to Ellie and me. From the communal terrace outside our rooftop room, we could see the golden Dome of the Rock built on what was once the Temple Mount of ancient Israel, sacred center of the Jewish faith. We could see the gold crosses crowning the Church of the Holy Sepulcher, and the minarets topped by crescent moons, and the copper steeples. During the day, from the terrace above, we watched Arab shopkeepers calling out to tourists who mostly ignored their propositions, and Orthodox Jewish men in kippoth and tefillin making their way to the Western Wall to pray, and groups of Christian pilgrims bearing crosses and singing hymns and snapping photos as cars got stuck behind them. In the evening, we ate at communal tables with the other pilgrims and checked e-mail in the lounge. In the darkness we were awakened by the muezzin's plaintive call to prayer, which sounded like a lamentation.

Something compelled me, that first morning in Jerusalem, to travel the deserted lanes of pale limestone and enter the Church of the

Holy Sepulcher in the hushed hours before the tourists came. Perhaps it was that call to prayer, or the early sunrise at 5:30, or the austere twin bed in the guesthouse, perhaps it was something greater, but while Ellie slept, I rose and dressed in the indistinct light, then shut the heavy door of the convent behind me and passed through the empty streets, the stores closed up, their metal doors in pale blue and turquoise like rows of lockers in a high school. A young man was wheeling a cart piled high with *baygeleh*, elongated oval loops of dough encrusted with sesame seeds. A few policemen nodded. I caught the eye of a veiled woman as we passed each other and I smiled at her but couldn't tell if she returned the smile.

I don't know what compelled me to go to the Church of the Holy Sepulcher, the epicenter of the medieval Christian world, that first morning in the Holy City. I don't think I really expected to be moved. And yet, after I found my way through the dark lanes, descended the stone steps to the open courtyard, and entered into the thick opacity of the church, the massive and austere stone columns, the flagstone floors polished smooth by a ceaseless procession of pilgrims, the countless crusader crosses carved by medieval knights into the walls, the quiet, the absence of any kind of numinous light, only the common gray morning sky that dissolved the darkness coating the windows far above—all this pierced me unexpectedly.

For a while, I wandered through the church with its various alcoves and shrines and chapels, the voice of a priest somewhere above, the responses of the people muffled and echoing. Three old men cleaved together on a bench chanting prayers. A young woman in hiking boots sat in the dark alone, leaning her head against a pillar. An ancient woman in black, black shawl covering her head, lit candles and kissed the stones.

Eventually I found myself descending a flight of stairs to the cavernous Chapel of Saint Helena. Beyond one of the closed doors near the altar must have been the cistern where, in 326, legend has it, the mother of Emperor Constantine found the True Cross and the crosses of the two thieves, one of which hung at the Monastery of the Holy Cross in Cyprus. She'd also found the nails and the crown of thorns, the lance with which Christ's side was pierced, the reed with the sponge by which he was offered vinegar. How had Helena seen what others could not? Didn't this make anyone suspicious? Or were they just desperate to have some concrete proof for that which they'd staked their faith upon?

In Saint Helena's chapel below, I sat in a pew in the oblique light. From this spot, I could hear the knot of women I'd passed a few moments before, some standing, some kneeling in a small alcove beneath a painting of the Virgin Mary. They were saying the rosary. Over and over again they prayed: *Hail Mary, full of grace, the Lord is with thee. Blessed art thou among women, and blessed is the fruit of thy womb, Jesus. Holy Mary, Mother of God, pray for us sinners, now and at the hour of our death. Amen.* Like sediment stirred up from the bottom of a creek, the words called forth some vague memory of catechism classes at Sacred Heart Church in Conroe, Texas, where my mother would collect me in the early evening, in fall, the sky already dark because of daylight saving time. I would sit in the backseat on the drive home to the Woodlands, the new utopia of nowhere, and say the Hail Mary to myself, over and over, moon through the pine trees, trying to memorize it so I could get a gold star. The *Lord* and *Mary* and the *fruit of thy womb, Jesus,* were just words, remote and abstract and unquestioningly there, like gravity, and the prayer just words too, and it offered no comfort, though I wasn't fully aware then that any was needed.

Though maybe that's the moment when I was becoming aware—after we'd moved from Missouri and left the family behind, when I told my father that growing up "is painful," when I ran my hand across the pattern of sunlight and shadow cast by the leaves outside the window onto the carpeted floor of my bedroom in the house on Echo Street, when I felt weary for the first time in my life. *Human generations are like leaves in their seasons.* When I sensed in some inarticulate way that what was fleeting was beautiful, beautiful because it would pass. But I had no one to whom I could unburden myself about the heartache that this gave me, least of all God in my prayers.

Holy Mary, Mother of God, pray for us sinners, now and at the hour of our death, said the women at the top of the stairs. And I found myself thinking ahead to that fearful hour and longing for myself to have someone in it, husband or daughters, blessed fruit of my womb, to pray for my departing soul. It came to me then with a sort of tangible clarity that the prayer I was hearing and the church in which it was uttered were both attempts to come to terms with the unalterable fact of our mortality. And I felt a deep pathos for all my kin, meaning other human beings.

Where do I want my body to lie? Where, being from nowhere—*Holy Mary, Mother of God*—would I want my ashes spread? If I were more rooted to a particular place on earth, would I have felt less compelled to wander? A few years before, one winter, Ellie and I had driven up to Lawrence, Kansas, place of her birth, and spent a weekend seeking out the spots holy to us there—the apartment in student-family housing, the library on campus, Clinton Lake. It was bitter cold that weekend, and the water had frozen, I remember, into low purls. We could hear, from far off, the bleak caw of a blackbird from across the ice. Tramping around through the grasses near the lake where I'd once carried her on my hip, Ellie had asked me, "Mom, didn't you say you wanted to be cremated when you die?" I told her that I supposed I probably did because I didn't feel that I really belonged anywhere. "Would you want your ashes to be spread here?" "Definitely I would want some of my ashes spread here," I told Ellie. "And maybe some in other places I've loved. And hopefully there are still places I'll love that I haven't even seen." She was quiet for a moment, and then she continued, "Did you know that dust from Africa can blow all the way to Florida?" "I didn't know that, Ellie," I replied. "That way," she went on, "if you have your ashes scattered after you die, your spirit can visit places that your body has never been before."

Alone in the Chapel of Saint Helena in the Church of the Holy Sepulcher listening to the voices of the women praying the Hail Mary, I understood that those words were not just words for them. I saw how prayer could be a talisman, a torch to fend off the dark that is always threatening. Prayer uttered in *communitas* constructs a kind of homeland, a space of belonging for those repeating the words. And though the words had meant nothing to me in my childhood, hearing them now, their familiarity in this foreign city, they felt oddly like a kind of home to me too. Or if not a home, a lean-to, a temporary shelter.

Before leaving the Holy Sepulcher, I passed by the gaudy Tomb of Christ in the rotunda, a larger-than-life reliquary like those we'd seen in Venice, adorned with gems and gilt in gold and silver and built around the stone crypt that, they say, once held the body of Jesus. In the wooden pews arrayed before the tomb were a few Franciscan friars in their brown cassocks and a nun of the order of Mother Teresa's Missionaries of Charity with her blue-striped white linen sari. I stood to the side for a while and watched as pilgrims entered the tomb one by one, then emerged again. But I myself did not once feel called to go inside.

In the hill country of Judea, somewhere between Rama and Jerusalem, Fabri's pilgrim band sets up camp for the night in a stony field on the side of a mountain near a village. Their escorts on horses and donkeys arrange themselves around the pilgrims so that they are protected on all sides. They have traveled inland from the coast, from the port of Joppa (today's Jaffa), where they had anchored for several days as they awaited permission to enter this land held tenuously for the moment by Muslim Mamelukes, whose sultan, Qa'it Bay, rules his empire from Cairo. Word had been sent forth of the pilgrims' arrival, and days later, a host of armed men on horses and mules arrived and pitched their tents and pavilions upon the shore of the Mediterranean: the governors of Jerusalem and Gazara and Ramatha, as well as the father guardian of Mount Sion, himself a Franciscan, and other Saracens and Eastern Christians, all of whom would provide the pilgrims safe conduct through this troubled land. Beyond the bright encampment, the city of Joppa lay in ruins, the walls that the crusaders had built thrown down by the Mamelukes, who left only two towers to guard the way to the sea.

On the day they were to leave the harbor and travel overland to the Holy City, the pilgrims were each assigned an ass and driver who would attend to him throughout his stay. Fabri had been overjoyed to be reunited with Cassa, the slave of a "kinglike Saracen noble" and the same man who had served him on his first pilgrimage to Palestine. As soon as Cassa spotted Fabri amid the tumult, "he recognized me, and I him, and he ran to kiss me after the fashion of the Saracens, and greeted me with a most joyous countenance, rejoicing and marveling much at my return." Fabri recalled then how faithfully and well Cassa always took care of him. "He often changed my asses that I might have one which pleased me better," he says, and "when the ass was climbing a hill he supported me; when going down steep and rough roads he held me that I might not fall; gave me drink from his water-skin, and shared his biscuits with me: he would climb over the stone walls of gardens and bring me figs, grapes, and other fruits out of them."

With their armed defenders like a membrane around the cell of pilgrims, the foreigners are protected for the moment on that stony hillside somewhere near Jerusalem from the plague of Bedouin who roam the desert spaces between the towns and cities. Villagers bring the pilgrims loaves of bread and fruit and water. The moon rises. But though the pilgrims are weary, in their impatience to see the place for which they've thirsted, they cannot sleep.

On that Judean hill beneath the moon, Fabri says, "We embraced the rock itself, as Job...nay, I know some pilgrims who so loved the Holy Land, that both by day and by night they would constantly bow themselves to the earth and caress it with the sweetest kisses, and would venerate the stones themselves as relics." For Fabri and these pilgrims, the stones are signs of the land beneath the land. Touching them is the nearest they will come in this life to God. "These stones Christ chose to aid Him in the work of our redemption," Fabri points out, "for He was conceived in a stony cavern, born beneath the rock and the stone, laid upon a stone when born; He preached standing upon a stone, thrice prayed in a cave in a stony rock, was scourged beside a pillar of stone, stood upon a stone to receive His crown, stood upon a stone before Pilate His judge, was crucified over a stone, anointed on a stone, buried in a stone, and ascended into heaven from a stone." Such stones along with thorns like those of Christ's crown are the only souvenirs that Fabri records collecting during his travels.

The next day, the pilgrims reach the Holy City of Jerusalem. They dismount from their asses beside a castle built by the sultan, and, taking their scrips, which hold their few belongings, they walk two by two toward the Gate of David, singing the Te Deum with the voices of their minds alone so as not to offend their Muslim guides. Some of the pilgrims throw off their shoes. They will go barefoot the rest of their journey. In the courtyard of the Church of the Holy Sepulcher, they fling themselves down and kiss the ground. Many are utterly overcome by feelings of devotion. Some wander the courtyard beating their chests. Some kneel with bare knees and hold their arms out to their sides as if nailed to a cross. The women shriek as in childbirth and cry aloud and weep. Other pilgrims cannot hold themselves up and are forced to sit down and cradle their heads in their hands in order to endure the sobs racking their breasts. Still others lay prostrate such a long time that it seems they are dead.

And yet, not all are so affected. Recalls Fabri, "I have seen during the aforesaid devotions of the pilgrims some dull and unprofitable pilgrims, nay rather brute beasts, not having the spirit of God, who stood and smiled mockingly at the prayers, tears, prostrations, beating of breasts, and the like, which were done by the rest. What is even more damnable is that these brutish men, blind to all piety, void of all religious feeling, full of all uncleanness, held such devout people to be fools, hypocrites, vain-glorious, deceivers and brain-sick, and ever thereafter treated them with scorn."

Years ago, when Terry and I stood in the doorway to the sacristy at Chimayó, I had longed, like the pilgrims there, to see miracles in the dirt. And now I had made my way here, seeking some kind of healing, perhaps, for those wounds meted out at Ellie's conception, and those long before, seeking a homeland in which to plant my feet against the void. But everywhere we went in the Holy Land, I found myself still staring at the pious from the other side of belief, like those unprofitable pilgrims in the courtyard of the Church of the Holy Sepulcher whom Fabri abhors. Aside from that first morning in Jerusalem in the Chapel of Saint Helena, as we retraced the temptation of Christ in the desert, and his death and resurrection in the Holy City, and his birth in Bethlehem, my heart, like the land, was a stone.

ON THE JERICHO ROAD

BECAUSE ISRAELIS GENERALLY aren't allowed in Jericho, which is part of the Palestinian West Bank, Carol Ann Bernheim took off her official Israeli guide badge as we approached the checkpoint and stowed it in the glove box of our rental car, one with Palestinian tags because Israeli insurance companies will not cover cars going into the territories. Tall and auburn-haired with manicured nails, Carol Ann dressed in white tunics and loose white pants and Birkenstocks. She is my mother's age. We had been paired up with her by Steve Langfur, who helped found the Great Books program in which I teach before emigrating to Israel in the 1970s. He now led guided tours through the Holy Land. Because Steve had been booked already by an evangelical church from Cincinnati, he recommended Carol Ann. During the days Ellie and I spent with her, I noticed the way she carried herself, striding ahead of us without hesitation as we followed falteringly in her wake, meeting those we encountered with a directness that often flustered them. She was a woman among men, a Jew among Muslims, a secular among orthodox, an Israeli among Palestinians. Her boldness I came to think of as a necessary shield when she entered the terrain of others.

Arriving at the checkpoint in Jericho, she breezily told the Palestinian guard we were all Americans, and he believed her and waved us through. This declaration wasn't entirely untrue. Carol Ann was raised Jewish in Irvington, New Jersey, and her family tree includes both Italian Catholics and Eastern European Jews who went to America to escape the pogroms of some czar's army. A great-grandfather was a Talmudic scholar. One of her grandmothers became a wrestler in vaudeville after her husband, a window washer, fell to his death. The story of how Carol Ann arrived in Jerusalem and made a home there seems born of that conflicted lineage, though perhaps the seekings of the scholar and the vaudeville traveler, wanderings internal and external, are not all that different in the end.

Though her brothers abandoned Judaism after their bar mitzvahs, after her own bat mitzvah, Carol Ann stubbornly kept on with Hebrew school. She went to synagogue out of defiance. "I was going to go despite the fact that I didn't quite get it," she told me. "It was the 1960s and the whole Jewish community was either smelly old Eastern European men or the wealthy Jewish relatives up the hill who were all climbing social ladders." Eventually, she thought, she might become a Unitarian instead, but first she decided she needed to go to Jerusalem to see if there was anything authentic about the faith into which she'd been born.

By then it was 1967. The Six-Day War had just ended and Israel had decisively taken the Gaza Strip and the Sinai Peninsula from Egypt, the West Bank from Jordan, and the Golan Heights from Syria. Back in the United States, the Newark race riots had broken out and the Vietnam War was in full swing. The threat of nuclear war lingered. Israel seemed like a place to escape all that turmoil. Carol Ann was accepted into an institute in Jerusalem for the training of Hebrew teachers in the Diaspora. When she arrived in Israel, she was twenty—a little older than Ellie now, a little younger than me when I'd felt the pull toward a *bohemian-explorer-intellectual kind of life*. As she walked along King David Street, still shot up from the recent fighting, she glimpsed the walls of the Old City between buildings. It was, she says, like looking across a crowded room and seeing the person with whom you're fated to be. She fell in love.

The Old City in those years seemed like a small town, with one discotheque, one boutique. At the teaching institute, Carol Ann's instructors included the novelist Aharon Appelfeld and the poet Yehuda Amichai. Amichai once wrote a poem about the director of the institute, who traveled from Israel to New York to commit suicide because, the poem went, in Jerusalem the buildings were too low, and besides, everybody knew him there. Something like that. She lived in the Armenian Quarter, a walled city within the walled city, one of clean bright lanes and small open courtyards and breezy doorways, where thousands of Armenians lived, many refugees from the genocide in Turkey. The Armenian *mukhtar* adopted her because she had no family, and on Sundays she would eat lunch at his home. His daughters and sons had married Arab Christians and Greek Christians and other Armenians. Around the table flowed a babel of Arabic, English, French, Armenian, Greek, even Yiddish, which the *mukhtar* knew from before the war in '48, the war that had established the State of Israel. Anything seemed possible those first four or five years she was in Jerusalem.

But in 1971, Carol Ann left Jerusalem and went to Greece with a man, another American, who'd once plotted to rob Saint Catherine's Monastery at the base of Mount Sinai and who had walked the Sinai for twelve days stashing food along the way so that he could survive during his escape back to Israel. He was arrested before he could carry out his plans. "I liked the way he looked at the desert and I wanted to learn how to survive a nuclear holocaust," Carol Ann said by way of explanation for her moving to Greece with him. "You mean you liked his descriptions of the desert? Or the metaphysical way he viewed it?" I asked. "No. I simply liked the way he looked at the desert," she clarified. Like, literally. Like, how he regarded it with his eyes.

So she went with this man to Greece, to the island of Sifnos, an island they chose because nobody ever went there. It was a place, unlike New Jersey, that was on no one's list of targets in case of a nuclear war. They lived in a house near a village on a few acres by the sea. They had a cistern but no electricity. For all of this they paid $13.50 per month. But eventually, Greece became too expensive and the man who looked at the desert was drinking too much. He became abusive. Carol Ann had to run for her life. She returned to an Israel different from the one she had left. "I came back after a few years in Greece and hope was gone," she told me. "The world was transformed. Everything had changed after the Yom Kippur War."

Our destinations with Carol Ann were the Jordan River, where, tradition has it, Jesus was baptized by John, and Mount Quarantal, where Jesus was tempted by Satan for forty days and forty nights in a cave on a mountain in the wilderness above Jericho. To get there, we drove east for about an hour through the Judean Desert, within whose folds lay hundreds of monasteries or, more frequently, their ruins. In these hills, too, Bedouin encampments sprawled along the side of the highway: corrugated steel, plywood, burlap, blue plastic tarps, satellite dishes, water pipes, wooden pallets. Dusty children. Dusty camels. Dusty asses. "The Bedouin call themselves *il Arab,* the true Arabs," Carol Ann told us as we drove past, and I thought of the "fierce Arabs," as he called them, that ruled the desert places Fabri traversed. "But they are no longer allowed to live as nomads, herding sheep and goats," explained Carol Ann, "because they could wander into the military training camps. They aren't Israeli. The Palestinians don't want them. The Bedouin have fallen into the cracks."

Somewhere between Jerusalem and Jericho, as the highway sloped gently down toward the Dead Sea, we passed the Sea Level sign, tethered to which was a camel, all decked out in colorful woven blankets and fringed and tasseled headgear. Beside the camel sat a Bedouin, who would allow you to take a photograph with his bedecked camel for a small fee. We didn't stop there, but farther on, at an overlook where we got out to gaze down at Saint George's Monastery, built into a wall of stone, Bedouin rushed toward us holding rayon kaffiyehs for sale and offering us donkey rides. From one young man we bought water frozen in used plastic bottles. The monks at the monastery had let him use their freezer. He had stored the bottles in a canvas bag handed out by the UN. All these I took to be examples of the cracks into which the Bedouin had fallen.

I liked the way Carol Ann looked at the desert. She helped me to read it. Once in a while, as we drove, she would point out an acacia tree or a tamarisk, once in a while a saltbush plant growing within some crevice that received a trickle of water. The hills, bone-colored, were traced with fine lines, like the thumbprint of God. Carol Ann told us these lines were goat tracks. And though it seemed so utterly barren, she pointed out, "If you can see tracks, then even though it's a desert, you know that there is the possibility of sustaining life."

I liked the way Carol Ann looked at the desert. And it reminds me now of something else she told me, about a time on that remote Greek island when she confronted the idea of survival in the most elemental of ways. The man who looked at the desert had gone to a village on the other side of the island for supplies, as they both took turns doing every other week. "And the sun started to disappear," she recalled. *That's okay,* she told herself. *It's an eclipse of the sun. I know what an eclipse of the sun is.* "And the sun was disappearing. And I thought, *Gee, I wonder if they know up on the top of the mountain that the sun is disappearing in Vathi. And I wonder if they know on the next island that the sun is disappearing in Vathi.* And the sun was disappearing. And something so strange started to happen. It became such a primal thing that took over. Because the sun was disappearing. I realized that I was going into a certain mind state where I would sacrifice something or somebody to get the sun back. And I was having this battle with myself. *Come on, brain, this is an eclipse of the sun.* But the other part was saying, *The sun is disappearing in Vathi. How do I get the sun back?*" Carol Ann said then, "I understood, this is how it begins. I understood how religious ritual evolves."

The Venetian captains don't want to go down to the Jordan or to Jericho—because of the Bedouin lying in wait, because there's no church and therefore no indulgences to be gained, because water and bread and a place to rest are not easy to find in the desert they'll have to traverse. But the journey is part of the contract they signed back in Venice, and for two hours the pilgrims argue until the captains finally relent.

After leaving Jerusalem, they pass through Bethany and into the Judean Desert. They try, with night coming on, to stop at an old caravansary, "an inn of the Eastern fashion," with stables below and chambers above, but after they have eaten their supper and put out their lights, as they lay their heads upon their scrips and begin to fall asleep, they are attacked by Saracens. So they move on, under the light of the moon, their asses navigating the rocky terrain in the dark. "There was a Saracen woman who rode with us as far as Jericho," Fabri remembers of that journey through the desert, "young and well dressed after their fashion; but no one could see her face, because her face was covered with a black cloth, which was transparent, so that nevertheless she could see us." Fabri marvels, too, at the old women who accompany the pilgrims, "that they should ride so boldly, seeing that a woman is timid by nature." Later he recalls something a knight said to him on his first pilgrimage: "Lo! my brother, I don't believe these old creatures to be women at all, but devils, for women, especially old women, are frail, tender, and delicate, whereas these women are made of iron, and are stronger than all of us knights."

All around the holy river is wilderness where already, in July of 1483, the monasteries and dwellings of religious persons hidden in it are mainly ruins. And in this wilderness roam many wild beasts—lions, bears, foxes, roebucks, deer, hares, wild asses— "and at eventide they come down to the water to drink like flocks of sheep," says Fabri, "but during the heat of the day they lie in caves in the rocks." When the group arrives at the Jordan, some knights plunge into the water fully clothed. They will keep these garments like treasures and wear them when going forth into battle, believing no harm can then befall them. Other pilgrims dip bells into the river, bells that will later, if rung in times of tempest, save them from lightning and thunder and hail. Still others believe reports that the Jordan is a kind of Fountain of Youth, and, says Fabri, praising the modesty and silence and devotion of the female pilgrims as they bathe among the reeds, "I could have wished, in the case of these old women, that the common report might prove true....But our women comrades would have needed a bath of sixty years to restore their youth, for they were women of eighty years of age and upwards."

On the outskirts of Jericho, they pass dry stone walls and gardens of fruit trees and grapevines and roses watered by the Fountain of Elisha. Fabri notes the place where children mocked that bald prophet; he cursed the children, who were then devoured by bears. "Hence it is clear that it is a perilous thing to mock at old and bald men," Fabri says, perhaps a little oversensitive, "seeing that old gray-haired and bald men ought rather to be held in honour." At which point in my edition, the humorless Victorian translator notes, "A dissertation on baldness and the ecclesiastical tonsure is here omitted."

At midday, beneath the searing sun, the pilgrims begin to climb Mount Quarantal, the path so narrow that they are forced to walk sideways, backs to a wall of stone, faces turned toward the abyss below. At the entrance of the cave where Jesus contested with the devil, a Bedouin stands with a club demanding a toll. Fabri seems moved less by the consecrated chapel here with its altars and paintings than by the other caves nearby. "In them Christian saints used to dwell in the days of old, for then the whole mountain was full of religious persons who passed their time there with the Lord in penitential mortifications," he remembers. "I could trace in those caves distinct places for prayer, for sleep, for the dressing of food, for the keeping of necessaries, and in the walls square recesses to place books in." But these caves have become again the dens of wild beasts.

The truth is that Ellie and I weren't all that interested in the river Jordan, mired and brackish and lined with reeds, where the gift shop sold Coca-Cola and cotton baptismal shifts with a quote from the Gospel according to Matthew: "Jesus when he was baptized saw the Spirit of God descending like a dove, and lighting upon him." Nor in Quarantal Monastery, clinging like the cars of a train to the ledge of the mountain above Jericho. The monastery wasn't even here in Fabri's day. But we made the climb, as Fabri had, though now the path was safe and wide. A man—*il Arab,* perhaps—still stood before the entrance collecting money and making sure our shoulders were covered, and a boy sold plastic-bead necklaces that he draped in display from his arm. The walls of the cave where Satan tempted Jesus were plastered with Eastern Orthodox icons and covered with soot from fires, and there were rolling wooden altars, and a bench for the three or four monks who live there now. A passage from scripture recounting the forty-day struggle of Jesus in the wilderness, translated into English, Greek, Arabic, German,

French, and Spanish, was tacked inside a Plexiglas case in an alcove above.

Looking down from the ledge into the abyss, Ellie and I could see the greens and blues of discarded plastic bottles. Beyond that was Jericho, one of the oldest cities on earth, a lush oasis fed by springs like the Fountain of Elisha. Nearby was a Palestinian refugee camp of cinder block we'd driven through with Carol Ann on our way to Quarantal, the streets lined with garbage like gray plowed snow. Though once teeming, it now seemed a little desolate. From behind the cinder-block walls we had seen satellite dishes and the tops of fruit trees planted in courtyards—citrus, mulberry, banana, papaya, date palm, fig. But this land, Carol Ann pointed out, belonged to the UN, not to the refugees who had planted those trees.

On the way back to Jerusalem across the Judean Desert, Carol Ann drove along the old Jericho Road where Jesus sets his parable of the Good Samaritan, the story in which a traveler, presumably a Jew, is savagely beaten by thieves and stripped and left for dead in these barren stone hills etched with the tracks of goats. Fabri never mentions this story. No road sign explains to tourists how the priest and the Levite, Jewish holy men, both see the victim lying there, abandoned, and go out of their way to avoid him. But then the Samaritan comes upon him. We forget now because the name has become synonymous for someone who helps others in need, but in those days, Samaritans, who claimed descent from the Hebrews who had remained in the land during the Babylonian captivity, were regarded by Jews as pretenders to the true religion of the ancient Israelites, one forged in exile. But on the Jericho Road, that one Samaritan has pity on the broken and abandoned man, and he binds his wounds, and sets him on his own ass, and carries him to the nearest caravansary, where he pays the innkeepers to care for a man his tribe says he should hate.

This parable is Jesus's answer to a lawyer who questions him, trying to trip him up. "What must I do to win eternal life?" asks the lawyer. "What does scripture say?" asks Jesus. "To love God with all my heart and to love my neighbor as myself." "Go then and do thou likewise," Jesus commands. But the lawyer keeps testing him. "Who is my neighbor?" he asks Jesus. Our neighbor, answers Jesus by way of the story, is the abandoned man in the desert on the side of the road.

Carol Ann recalled that parable as we drove along the road from Jericho to Jerusalem. And she pointed out that one explanation for the actions of the priest and the Levite might be that they had probably spent time ritually purifying themselves for the journey to the Temple in Jerusalem and knew they would defile themselves if they touched another human body, so they passed the beaten traveler by. The story for her was about the danger of getting caught up in rules, in following religious law too literally, for as Paul says in his Second Epistle to the Corinthians, "The letter killeth, but the spirit giveth life."

I love Martin Luther King Jr.'s reading of this parable, which comes from his "I've Been to the Mountaintop" speech that he gave during the sanitation workers' strike in Memphis on April 3, 1968 — the day before he was assassinated. King begins by imagining that God has asked him in which age he'd like to live, and after envisioning all the kingdoms of the world in an instant of time — Egypt and Athens and Rome, Europe in the Renaissance and at the beginning of the Protestant Reformation, America during the Civil War when Lincoln signed the Emancipation Proclamation — King concludes that he would still choose to live in his own age, when God is at work among the people who are rising up across the world, crying out to be free.

Late in his speech, King recalls the story of the Samaritan on the Jericho Road, this isolated and meandering thoroughfare so conducive to ambushes, a road he himself had driven on a trip to Jerusalem with his wife, Coretta. King imagines that the priest and the Levite see the man left for dead and wonder if the thieves are still around or if the man is faking his injuries in order to lure them over so he can rob them. "And so the first question that the priest asked, the first question that the Levite asked was, 'If I stop to help this man, what will happen to *me?*'" King says to the audience of sanitation workers, *crying out to be free.* "But then the Good Samaritan came by, and he reversed the question: 'If I do not stop to help this man, what will happen to *him?*' That's the question before you tonight."

We drove back along the Jericho Road, detouring in Bethany, part of Palestinian East Jerusalem, to see the dingy tomb of Lazarus—where he was placed when he died the first time and from which he was raised by Jesus—with some pilgrims from Bombay. We could not, like Fabri and his cohorts, continue from Bethany on to the Old City directly because of the huge concrete-slab separation wall that Israel was building between itself and the West Bank. The wall would run seven hundred kilometers upon completion, but it was already making the lives of ordinary Palestinians inordinately difficult, cutting off the towns and villages of the West Bank from each other and from Israel and thus the inhabitants from their livelihoods and family and friends. "This is a vital, viable suburb of Jerusalem and has been for centuries," Carol Ann explained as we drove through the city of low-slung buildings, its haphazard streets lined with piles of watermelons and stacks of carpets, rows of bicycles and plastic chairs and plastic tubing. "But because of this wall, what had been a five-minute trip is now forty-five minutes. And Palestinians can only come into Jerusalem if they have an Israeli work permit or residency card. The discrimination is hard to understand. It's so distressing."

We went into a souvenir store to buy carved olive-wood crucifix necklaces for my nieces and a woven hemp slingshot for my nephew. My purchases felt like a wholly inadequate attempt to be a good neighbor and to ask, "If I do not stop to help this man, what will happen to *him?*" Even worse, when the shopkeepers put the hard sell on us to buy more, Ellie and I got flustered and fled after Carol Ann in her desert whites, who walked assuredly before us toward the rental car, greeting the dark-eyed Arab children in the streets with *"As-salamu alaykum"* (Peace be upon you). They just stared at her, then turned and ran.

After Carol Ann left Greece, she returned to an Israel transformed by the Yom Kippur War, a conflict in which those countries humiliated by the rout of 1967 — Syria, Egypt, Jordan — banded together and attacked on Judaism's holiest day. Though the war ended in a cease-fire, Israel was shaken. Whereas before, its citizens had felt secure in their military might, they now understood their vulnerability, and hope for peace was gone.

Though I was fascinated by Carol Ann's stories, Ellie struggled against her brusqueness. On one occasion, for instance, Carol Ann asked Ellie to take off her sunglasses because she didn't like to talk to people when she couldn't see their eyes. On another, she'd pointed out to Ellie how often she inserted *like* into her sentences and how juvenile this made her sound. I felt sorry for Ellie and slightly defensive. The *like* was a tic, almost a stutter, and Ellie herself was embarrassed by it and working hard to cut it out, but when she was nervous, as she was with Carol Ann, it only got worse. About the sunglasses, however, I totally agreed.

But besides all this, for me, Carol Ann was a sign of the road not taken. Never marrying, never having children, living on Sifnos, living in Jerusalem. She'd followed a man because she liked the way that he looked at the desert. She found a homeland far away with people who spoke in a babel of tongues. I once thought I might be the kind of person who would live a gypsy life like that. I had grown up a child of the suburbs, bored with that life, embarrassed by it, because it was *u-topia,* "no place." Being from no place said something about me. It said I was without history, meaning depth and richness, meaning a past connected to larger forces that could give meaning and substance to my life. It said I was sheltered and naive. I thirsted for what I did not have, even the tragic, especially the tragic, because of course it was only in suffering that we actually lived. So I dreamed of leaving. And of spending weeks at a time on an island surrounded by the sea. I dreamed of running off with a man because of the way that he looked at the desert. Now, I remembered only that I once was someone who dreamed of those things. The dreams themselves, their particularities, evaporated as I tried to recall them. And in my waking life, their residue remained as a craving for something I couldn't quite name. Which explained in part, I suppose, why I was now here.

A BRIEF FOR THE DEFENSE

IN THE STREETS of the Muslim Quarter where we were staying, though the white stone magnified the heat from the sun, Ellie and I kept putting on more clothes every day. Alongside the women whose heads were all covered and whose curves were hidden by those long black *jilbab* cloaks despite the heat ("Like a mode of torture," decided Ellie), we felt too exposed, even in our modest long-sleeved linen shirts and cargo pants and sandals. But regardless of the head scarves we draped over our long hair and the jackets we added to our ensembles, we'd still get stern looks from the women and men standing in the doorways, and the Arab teens outside the rug store near Ecce Homo would mock us, offering to marry Ellie in exchange for a few camels. In her humiliation and frustration and perhaps overdeveloped sense of injustice, one day Ellie blurted out to them, "Would you talk to your mothers that way?" I tried to shush her but the boys only jeered louder, and after that we tried not to even look at them when we passed the shop. In fact, we avoided eye contact with just about everyone and mainly stared straight ahead or down. "My eyes have definitely come to know the stones of Jerusalem," Ellie said.

But Basti's, where we stopped nearly every day for a minty limonana or some falafel, was different. We often caught the owner, Anwar, always wearing a black T-shirt and jeans, in the slow hours between the rush of lunch and dinner, and he would take our order and chat with us—small talk, this and that. "Feel at home," he would tell us. "This is your place." One afternoon he invited us to return to the restaurant that evening for a special meal being prepared for a group of pilgrims from Ecce Homo. He called it *maqluba,* an "upside-down" dinner, layers of chicken and rice and eggplant and cauliflower and tomatoes baked in a pot and then inverted onto a platter. Ellie had planned a phone call with her father and was looking forward to a quiet evening in the convent, so she declined, but I resolved immediately not to turn down this or any other invitation. It wasn't running off with a man because I liked the way he looked at the desert, but it was probably as close as I was going to get to recklessness. I went alone.

Anwar, whose name means "light," seated me at a table away from the crowd while he and another older gentleman, grim and silent with a trim mustache and a face creased like the Judean mountains crisscrossed with goat tracks, served us. I had been intrigued by the many framed black-and-white photos of the Old City that hung on the walls, and I asked Anwar about them when I was waiting for the main course. "You like old photos?" he asked me. "They're fascinating," I replied—shorthand for *Tell me the story behind each one. I've got all night.* "I have something to show you," he said then, and he pulled down an album from a shelf and handed it to me. "Four hundred years, my family has been in Jerusalem. My grandfather was *mukhtar* here." Then, as he left me to go dish up the *maqluba,* he said, "Feel at home. This is your place."

All through the upside-down dinner I looked at those pictures of Jerusalem in what must have been the early twentieth century, during the period of the British Mandate—after World War I and the collapse of the Ottoman Empire—when Jerusalem, still entirely contained by the walls of the Old City, was a provincial, unornamented place. Here were women in dark linen dresses with white cotton scarves wrapped round their heads threshing grain near the gates. Here was the Dome of the Rock, here was the Al-Aqsa Mosque, and small, isolated figures walking across the barren expanse of the former Temple Mount, now the Haram al-Sharif. Here was a shepherd in white kaffiyeh and black band herding horned rams. Here was a ceremony in front of the Holy Sepulcher, the courtyard full of people: kerchiefed women and men in fedoras and fezzes, Greek Orthodox priests on a platform, Turkish merchants with their wares spread out on the cobblestones. And here, in one of the only close-ups, was a Bedouin couple. Wearing a dark-striped robe over a pale linen shift, a turban on his head, prayer beads in his hand, the husband looks sternly at his wife. She stares ambivalently into the distance, a veil covering her hair, her body weighed down by layers upon layers of fabric, bracelets on both wrists, a headdress hung with chains and disks of hammered metals—*young and well dressed after their fashion,* as Fabri had said of the Saracen woman who accompanied the pilgrims across the desert to Jericho.

These old pictures, however, even that last one of the Bedouin husband and wife, did not strike me as being family photos. Rather, they were an argument, a brief for the defense. *Four hundred years, my family has been in Jerusalem. My grandfather was* mukhtar *here.* That's what Anwar said. That's what the photos of the Old City said. Like the crusader crosses carved into the walls of the Church of the Holy Sepulcher by medieval knights, they said, *We were here.* But what he did not say is that his family is no longer in charge. He did not say that for the Arabs in the photographs and for descendants of them like himself, Jerusalem has become another paradise lost, and they were now uprooted exiles from it, as had been Jews and Christians before. I saw then that the omphalos is not a center. It is a void of yearning. All those who want to claim it are united at least in that.

After the upside-down dinner was over and the Ecce Homo party had left, Anwar sat with me and we drank cardamom coffee and he told me how he didn't go to college because the Second Intifada had made it too difficult. So he'd gone into the restaurant business instead. But he was good at this, he realized. He respects people, can speak with them. He enjoys helping the travelers who come here, especially when they are trying to understand the lives of other people. His wife had been studying accounting, but he made her quit to stay home with their two little boys. "But she will go back, *Insha'Allah*." "*Insha'Allah*," I repeated, a little clumsily.

As I was preparing to leave, the grim man with the face lined like the hills came up to me, a cistern of resentment in his voice and in his eyes. Perhaps because he sensed I was trying to understand the lives of others, or perhaps because he thought of me, an American, as an ally to those Israelis with whom he would not speak, he told me in disjointed and bitter English that the Jews had been in the Holy Land for only the time of a pebble—a period he indicated by pinching together his thumb and forefinger—versus all the stones in Jerusalem, which was how long his family had been in this land. I stood there staring into his dark eyes, not knowing what to say, wanting both to show compassion for he who was my neighbor, abandoned in the desert, and argue with him at the same time. But I didn't have the facts at hand to do either. I did not have to decide how to respond, though, because at that moment he turned abruptly from me and left to pray as he had been called to do by the muezzin over the loudspeaker in the minaret lit by green neon lights.

In his book *Confession from a Jericho Jail*, Steve Langfur, the guide who had introduced me to Carol Ann, writes of one of the routine detentions he endured for refusing to follow orders when his army reserve unit was called up to guard Jewish settlements in the occupied West Bank. But the book is also a meditation on the suffering on both sides of the conflict, and an examination of what it means to be a Jew. Steve traces his return to Judaism back to the revelation he had one winter break in college when he read in a book by an obscure German Jewish philosopher that exile was his inheritance and his birthright as a Jew, that "unrootedness was my rootedness." "Who is born a Jew bears witness to his faith by multiplying the eternal people," this philosopher, Franz Rosenzweig, wrote. "He does not believe in something, he himself is belief."

Growing up in a suburb of Long Island, Steve had seen Judaism as "so much nonsense, wishful thinking easily disproved." And he had felt he had no roots, no place. But he began to understand, that winter break reading Rosenzweig, that by remaining a community, despite centuries of persecution and exile, by marrying within it and giving birth to more Jews, the Jewish people, himself included, were bearing witness by their very existence to the faith in God's promise to Abraham and Isaac and Jacob that those Chosen People would be many as the stars and the desert sand. Steve saw that he was part of a roving tribe who did not belong to any land, only to one another. And suddenly, Steve realized he "had grown up on Long Island of all places, among family and neighbors newly arrived, because I belonged to an ancient, wandering people. It made sense! My life made sense." It was his destiny to be placeless, and what he was seeking, in those years after his return to Judaism and in his emigration to Israel, was a community "rooted in one another," as Rosenzweig says, and bound together by the Book.

And now, after centuries of persecution and exile that had culminated in the Holocaust, members of that community, *rooted in one another*, had shaped Eretz Yisrael, the Land of Israel, with their own hands. Those Jewish settlers, whose presence in the West Bank Steve had been protesting, conceive, he believes, of the righteousness of what they are doing thus: "Out of the Diaspora, in which by dint of blood and word and practice God preserved His scattered sheep as one community for two thousand years, they have been brought back, by the miracle of the Six-Day War, to the very same biblical places, with the mission of fulfilling in the present generation that for which the previous generations had prayed three times a day: the renewal of the age-old community upon its original land."

One afternoon, Ellie and I made our way to Yad Vashem, the Holocaust Memorial, whose name comes from the book of Isaiah: "I will give in my house and within my walls *a monument and a name* better than sons and daughters; I will give them an everlasting name that will not be cut off." Perhaps because of her pull toward this nation of exiles, Yad Vashem was the place in all of Israel that Ellie most wanted to see. Back in Frankfurt, Sabine and Martin had told us about their experience here a few years before—how they'd been guided through the memorial by a Polish survivor of the concentration camps, who'd initially hesitated to lead two Germans, and how they'd all ended up weeping together.

So we wandered the halls of Yad Vashem, which marked out in concrete and claustrophobic detail the attempted obliteration of the Jewish people. Wearing a kelly-green cotton scarf draped around her head and a black print dress of mine that she'd borrowed for the day, Ellie made frantic lists in her notebook of what had been saved from this *holocaust,* this burnt offering—"personal touches," as she called the sacred relics to which she was most drawn. We emerged from Yad Vashem, as all visitors must, onto a terrace in the open air with an exalted view of the cypress-covered hills of Eretz Yisrael beyond, and stood quietly together, because anything we might say would be too trifling. But looking out over the green hills, I felt as if God were sweeping His hand across the land that He had returned to His own forsaken and outcast remnant, those abandoned in the desert, saying, "Here," saying hopefully, in the words of His prophet Isaiah, "For you shall go out in joy, and be led forth in peace; the mountains and the hills before you shall break forth into singing, and all the trees of the field shall clap their hands." This vision, too, like the photos at Basti's, was another argument, another brief for another defense.

"God was on our side" was how Carol Ann explained that hopefulness she sensed when she first arrived in Jerusalem in 1967, as America was exploding in race riots behind her, and Martin Luther King Jr. was on the verge of being assassinated, and all hell was breaking loose. But after the Yom Kippur War, the Israelis began to rethink the myths they'd been raised on and that had shaped them in the early years of the formation of their state. That was the moment she had returned from Greece, the moment after everything had changed and all hope was gone. Because by then, Israelis were being forced to confront the fact that what had been, for them, the miracle of the establishment of the Jewish state out of the fires of the Holocaust was, for Arabs, the *nakbah,* the catastrophe.

That evening, because we had lingered so long at Yad Vashem, Ellie and I missed the communal dinner at Ecce Homo, so we walked down to Basti's. El-Wad Street, which led south through the Muslim Quarter toward the Western Wall, was lit up with festive strings of lights and seemed more crowded than usual with the Haredi, ultra-Orthodox Jews whose name comes from the Hebrew for that fear and trembling one experiences before God—kind of like the American Shakers. As we sat outside and ate slices of thin-crust pizza, we noticed many more Israeli soldiers than usual, and more police in body armor carrying heavy weaponry.

We had been shocked and fascinated a day or two before when we'd driven with Carol Ann through the Mea Shearim neighborhood just outside the Old City where many of the Haredi live: the broadsides plastering the walls of buildings with pronouncements from the local rabbis; the men all in black or else in enormous fur hats and white stockings and what looked to us like silk bathrobes, their long side curls framing their faces; the women covered head to toe. And everywhere, the signs directed, it seemed, at us: *To women and girls who pass through our neighborhood we beg you with all our hearts: Please do not pass through our neighborhood in immodest clothes. Please do not disturb the sanctity of our neighborhood, and our way of life as Jews committed to G-d and his Torah.* It wasn't just us in our immodest clothing, though, that the neighborhood seemed intent on keeping out. It was modernity in general, anything that might threaten the cohesion of the community, anything that might keep them from remaining *rooted in one another.*

Sitting at the next table over from us at Basti's, smoking a cigarette, Anwar looked exhausted. He'd hardly greeted us when we arrived. In the street outside, beneath the strings of lights, the Israeli police also seemed on edge as they regarded the Haredi families heading toward the Western Wall and the Arab shopkeepers standing in their doorways staring resentfully. I felt protective of my neighbors in the Muslim Quarter, and when Anwar had brought our pizzas, I'd asked him, "What's going on around here tonight?" "Nothing. Nothing. Absolutely nothing" was his weary reply. But in that *nothing* was something I couldn't quite discern. Maybe it was only the ordinary *nakbah*, the ordinary catastrophe of despair.

THE WAY

THE FRANCISCAN FRIARS, mostly young and trim, their heads close-shaven, were lined up against the courtyard wall of the Madrasa El-Omariyya in their long brown wool cassocks tied with white rope and their flat leather sandals and Tevas and Birkenstocks. They looked like a sports team preparing to take the field. Some had rolled the sleeves of their vestments up to their elbows, and they all stood planted, legs apart, on the limestone plaza staring straight ahead. As they did every Friday, they were awaiting the appointed time of three o'clock, crucifixion hour, when they would lead those pilgrims who wished to follow—Ellie and me among them on this blistering day—along the Via Dolorosa, Jesus's path through the city to his execution on Golgotha, meaning Place of the Skull, and his burial in the tomb of Joseph of Arimathea nearby. I must admit that, compared to the priests I had known in the comfortable suburban churches of my youth or in the beautiful old cathedrals of dying cities of the Midwest, these Franciscans looked kind of badass. They seemed aware of the hushed awe with which the crowd regarded them and at the same time scornful of that reverence. Their aloofness made them even more alluring.

I had gained a reputation with Ellie back in Venice for being a stalker of friars when I returned from a brief outing to San Francesco del Deserto, the island where Saint Francis landed after his journey to the Holy Land and founded a hermitage, with photo after photo of an unsuspecting mendicant in the same brown cassock and Birkenstocks as the Franciscans here. At the monastery in Venice, I'd tried to talk with that friar, but we didn't have enough words between us to really communicate. I told him in my almost nonexistent Latin that I was on my way to the Holy Land, to "Terra Sancta." I said I was a *peregrinus,* a pilgrim. He said something in Italian about a *croce,* a cross. Something about a sword. When I got back to the convent beside the miasmic canal, I showed Ellie the photos I'd taken of him while pretending to focus on the cypress trees in the garden. She looked at me askance.

In the courtyard of the Madrasa El-Omariyya, a boys' school, I felt giddy, like some groupie at a concert of her favorite band, the band whose songs she's learned by heart, whose lyrics say exactly what she feels. Because the Franciscans are still, as they were in Fabri's day, the official Custodians of the Holy Land, a right granted to them by Pope Clement in 1342. They watch over the holy places and welcome the pilgrims who travel to them. They run guesthouses and lead tours, like this one every Friday afternoon. They are a living link to an otherwise vanished world.

At 3:00 sharp, we set out, the friars leading the way.

One morning a few days before Ellie and I walked the Via Dolorosa with the Franciscans, I tagged along with Steve Langfur as he led the evangelicals from Cincinnati in their sunglasses and floppy hats and fanny packs more or less elaborately outfitted with water bottles along the Palm Sunday route from the top of the Mount of Olives overlooking the Holy City down to the Garden of Gethsemane near the Kidron Valley below. This was the route, tradition has it, of Jesus's triumphal entry into Jerusalem, riding on a donkey—prelude to his bitter labor along the Way of Sorrow bearing a cross toward Golgotha.

In the story, it is Passover. Up in the tower of the Antonia Fortress, Pontius Pilate, with the might of Rome behind him, is on the lookout as upwards of four hundred thousand pilgrims stream into Herod's magnificent Temple, sheathed in gold. They have made the ascent to their Holy City to offer sacrifice in the largest structure ever built with human hands. They'll purchase animals in the Temple and give them to the priests, themselves ritually purified, who will present the sacrifices to God. But Jesus will "cast out them that sold therein and them that bought," and he'll warn against the scribes and priests who "walk in long robes, and love greetings in the markets, and the highest seats in the synagogues, and the chief rooms at feasts but who devour the widows' houses, and for a show make long prayers," those who do not ask of the abandoned neighbor on the side of the road to Jericho, *If I do not stop to help this man, what will happen to* him? After that, Judas Iscariot will betray him to the Romans in the Garden of Gethsemane, and Pontius Pilate will display him in his crown of thorns to the crowd below. *Behold the man!*

"As he came down the Mount of Olives, he probably recited Psalm One Hundred and Twenty-Two, praying for the peace of Jerusalem the way all Jewish pilgrims did as they approached the Temple," Steve explained at a lookout where we'd paused. Then he read from the psalm, almost conducting with his right hand to convey the rhythm. "On that day living water will flow out from Jerusalem," he began in English, and then he finished the verse in Hebrew, reciting from memory. "A later mystical Jewish reply to this passage says that God has been broken into pieces and will only be made whole again when the people of Israel all return," he finished. We walked on.

When we reached the walled-off Garden of Gethsemane—from the Aramaic *gat shemanei,* "oil press"—Steve sat down on the ground and propped himself against an ancient hollow of an olive tree and took off his safari hat and ran his fingers through his thick white hair. The evangelicals spread out around him like disciples. Beyond this enclosure, the sloping hillside of the Mount of Olives was paved almost entirely with Jewish graves, a city of the dead. For a while, everyone sat in quiet contemplation. Soon, though, a man in a Lockheed Martin backpack held up his hands, eyes closed, and began to sing a psalm, while another pilgrim called out the coming verse to the others. One woman wept. Looking off into the distance, a man sipped from his camel pack. Another man in a striped golf shirt hung his head, his hat waving in his hand as he bent over. Some women clasped their hands in prayer.

But then Steve began to speak in a gruff voice suffused with a quality I couldn't quite decipher—weariness, perhaps, but with a penetrating force as well. He read from the Gospel according to Matthew the prayer Jesus offers up to God in this garden, surrounded by the nearby graves of all the Jewish dead, his face pressed to the earth in which they lie. "'O my Father, if it be possible, let this cup pass from me; nevertheless not as I will, but as Thou wilt,' he prays three times while his followers drift off to sleep." Here Steve paused. "I think this is the moment of decision," he went on. "*Decision* is related to the word for *scissors*. It's the moment of the cutting away of options. Jesus could have prayed to be saved from this fate, but instead he hands himself to his Father. *Not as I will, but as You will.* Paul calls Jesus the second Adam, or the last Adam, who has come to redeem the sin of the first Adam, who ate the fruit of the Tree of Knowledge. That eating is like saying, 'As *I* will.' But here in *this* garden, Jesus redeems the sin of the first Adam: Not as *I* will, but as *You* will. So from the Garden of Eden to the Garden of Gethsemane, the circle is complete."

Steve spoke then about how this notion unites all three monotheistic religions, how the word *Islam* itself means submission, how Christians praying the Our Father say, "Thy will be done." "We say it, and we want to mean it," he went on, "but there's always a little bit of 'I will.' We want to be fully present with God, but there is always the tug of 'I will.' But with Jesus we have a perfect human being who can say this prayer with his whole being. Luke portrays this by having his sweat turn to blood." Steve broke off, and into the fissure of silence rushed the sound of the wind in the leaves of the olive trees, and of birds I couldn't name, and of the cars on the highway separating the Mount of Olives from Jerusalem. "The question becomes," he continued, "How can Jesus's prayer here help us to be more fully present? How can we, too, be released from the sin of Adam? What is the Way?"

A little later, as I continued on down the Mount of Olives and through Saint Stephen's Gate toward Ecce Homo Convent along the Via Dolorosa and to Ellie waiting for me so we could go eat lunch, I thought about what Steve had said, his readings of these stories. *Not as I will, but as You will.* God, it seemed to me, could be another name for the mechanism of the world whose purpose—if purpose even exists—cannot be fathomed but that will have its way nevertheless. We can, like Adam and Eve, try to kick against this will. We can eat the fruit that's been forbidden to us. But that only leads to exile from God in an inhospitable land. And in the meantime, God still has His way. Or we can try to align ourselves with this mechanism, this dark, unfathomable machinery. We can try to listen, to be alert to what the universe wants, and in that way be fully present, as Steve had put it, with God.

All those years ago, when I found myself pregnant and unmarried, a year still to go before completing a college degree, I did not turn to God as I conceived Him from my childhood—abstract and remote. And yet neither was I listening only to my own desire. By the time I chose to have the child growing in my womb, I was trying, it seems clear to me now, to make my will the will of the universe, to be fully present with what Steve Langfur called God.

And this dark machinery of the world, perhaps in its mercy—if mercy exists—placed Ellie, then Mary Martha, then Sabine in my arms for their protection.

The Via Dolorosa cuts through the Muslim Quarter like a sword. As we processed from station to station, marked by Roman numerals painted on the stone walls or on plaques, one friar balanced on top of his head a loudspeaker housed in a vintage black leather carrying case that amplified the voice of another friar chanting the Our Father in Latin.

Here, the Franciscans told us, near the Ecce Homo Arch spanning the entrance to the convent where we were staying, Jesus took up his cross. And then they sang, as we walked on behind them, *"Pater noster, qui es in caelis: sanctificetur Nomen Tuum"*— "Our Father, Who art in heaven, hallowed be Thy name." Then we paused at the next station. Here, they said, on some ancient paving stones that still exist, Jesus fell for the first time. *Pater noster, qui es in caelis: sanctificetur Nomen Tuum.* And so it went. Here, where the veiled Arab woman was always begging with her child, a little girl Carol Ann suspected had been drugged to make her lie still for hours in that heat, Jesus encountered his mother, Mary. Here, just down El-Wad Street from Basti's, Simon the Cyrene helped Jesus carry his cross. Here, near the fruit stand with the beautiful guavas, Veronica wiped his face. Here, in a narrow alleyway called Souk Khan el-Zeit, where today the square wooden boxes of the spice sellers were filled with cumin and saffron and *zaatar* and paprika but where the gates of the Roman city once stood, he fell again. Here, outside the gates, he met the women of Jerusalem and told them not to weep for him but for their children and themselves, "for behold, the days are coming, in the which they shall say, Blessed are the barren, and the wombs that never bare, and the paps which never gave suck," so horrific would be the coming destruction of the city. Here, beside a green door that led to another courtyard that led to a back entrance of the Holy Sepulcher above which was taped a mimeographed sheet of paper telling pilgrims *Please mind your head* in six languages, Jesus fell a third time. *"Fiat voluntas Tua,"* sang the Franciscans. "Thy will be done."

The route of the Via Dolorosa has changed over the centuries depending on which parts of the city the Franciscans controlled at the time. When Fabri walked the streets of Jerusalem with the friars and the dragoman, who slashed through the crowd with his staff and chased off little boys throwing stones at the pilgrims, they traveled in the opposite direction and to sites that have been dropped from the route Ellie and I now walked. In fact, the route of the Via Dolorosa was shaped in the Middle Ages by the commerce of pilgrims traveling to Jerusalem and by their Franciscan guides. The friars, Custodians of the Holy Land, had developed a walking tour of eight stations for visiting pilgrims. The pilgrims carried this understanding home with them and ritualized the walk within the confines of their parish churches. Eventually, the eight stations became fourteen in churches across Europe, and when new pilgrims arrived in the Holy City, they expected to see fourteen there as well. The Franciscans felt compelled to add extra stations to the Via so as not to disappoint or confuse the faithful.

The poignant chanting of the Pater Noster pulled me along in the wake of the Franciscans, now dripping with sweat in the afternoon heat. But as the crowds of tourists respectfully pressed their backs against the limestone walls of the narrow streets of the Muslim Quarter to let us through and looked at us the way we'd looked at the Franciscans standing in the courtyard of the Madrasa El-Omariyya, I felt like an impostor. When the young Palestinian men in tight shirts and acid-washed jeans—men like Anwar at Basti's—cranked the Arabic music on their boom boxes to drown out the Latin hymn, I kept wanting to leave the procession to explain to them, "We're not really *those* kind of pilgrims! We're not with *them!*"

My panic increased in the Church of the Holy Sepulcher, where the final stations of the cross are housed. Our small group became absorbed in the press of hundreds of other pilgrims, who tried to push us out of the way so they could climb the worn stone stairs to Golgotha, Place of the Skull, now housed in an alcove above lit by dim lanterns of red and blue glass and divided into separate rival chapels for the Latins and the Greek Orthodox, both of whom were vying to be heard. I felt like I couldn't breathe, and it wasn't because of all the incense. I kept grasping for Ellie's elbow so that I wouldn't lose her. When we got to the socket where Jesus's cross had stood, we leaned down and stuck our hands into the cool dark void as we'd seen the other pilgrims do and then quickly stood up again. The Greek Orthodox priest watching suspiciously over these proceedings offered us candles for sale. We declined and fled back down, past the Chapel of Adam, where Adam's smooth skull was, miraculously, discovered at the base of the cross of Jesus's crucifixion, signifying, as Steve had pointed out, our eternal redemption from original sin.

At the Stone of Unction, where Jesus's body had been laid out and anointed before being wrapped in a shroud, an elderly woman poured oil on the stone and wiped it up with a handkerchief that she then dropped in a plastic baggie; a stylish Russian woman in heels, her hair barely tucked into a flowing silk scarf, laid down three gilded wooden icons and bent to kiss the slab. "I wonder if they let people kiss the stones if there's an outbreak of swine flu?" Ellie whispered to me in an attempt to lighten the mood in this house of mirrors from which we were beginning to feel we'd find no escape. In front of the Holy Sepulcher, we listened as the Franciscans sang a song of hallelujah. But we didn't wait in the crowd with the other pilgrims to enter the empty tomb.

*   *   *

I like to think that, after traveling over land and by the wide and empty sea, after narrowly escaping the advancing Turks, after confronting the Bedouin tribes in the Judean hills, and after arriving finally in the Holy City he longed for, in the end, before the tomb to which he'd hinged his faith, Fabri too is, perhaps, dismayed.

On the evening of July 14, 1483, as the setting sun washes its nostalgic light over the city of Jerusalem, the pilgrims pass two by two between the Saracen lords sitting on benches of polished marble on either side of the door. They regard the pilgrims keenly. "They were men of a fine presence," recalls Fabri, "well stricken in years, handsome, wearing long beards, and solemn manners, dressed in linen clothes, and with their heads wrapped round and round with countless folds of very fine linen." These Saracens are reputed to be skilled in the art of physiognomy and can read a man's station in life, his disposition, his desires, merely by looking at him. Perhaps, too, they can read the bitterness to which Fabri confesses: "We went by them with shame and blushing, because it is a great confusion that Christ's faithful worshippers should be let into Christ's church by Christ's blasphemers." Once the pilgrims are all inside, the guards bolt the doors. They will be alone with their Franciscan guides until morning.

With lit tapers purchased from merchants inside the vestibule, they process through the church chanting the Salve Regina. They enter the chapels of all the competing sects—the Latins and Greek Orthodox, Georgians, Jacobites, Abyssinians, Syrians, Armenians, to name a few—and sing a hymn. But after they have fallen down and wept and prayed and pressed their faces against the earth and made their lamentations at the socket hole in the rock that held the cross, after they kiss the holy bier, the pilgrim band disperses a little before midnight and they all drift off to eat the food they'd bought in the courtyard of the Holy Sepulcher before they'd entered, and to lay down and rest.

But Fabri can't sleep. And so he wanders. "In these solitary visits to the holy places men feel greater devotion and abstraction from the world than when they do so in the general procession, in which there is much pushing and disorder, and disturbance, and singing, and weeping, whereas in the other case there is silence and peace," he says.

He pokes around the Holy Sepulcher, trying to determine for himself whether or not it is authentic. Holding his taper near the walls, he discerns a portion not covered over by marble and with the marks of iron tools upon it. He notes a fracture, mended by stones and cement. "From this it appeared to me that the Lord's sepulchre had once been destroyed," Fabri deduces, "but never completely rooted up; that what is now there is a restoration, and that it has stood for more than two hundred years as it appears this day, save that it is now more carefully encased with marble, lest the pilgrims should pick off pieces from the walls for relics." Still, though, Fabri concludes, perhaps trying to convince himself, "Whether the cave as it stands at the present day be the true and entire monument of Christ, or whether a part of it be there, or whether none of it be there, matters very little either one way or the other, because the main fact connected with the place abides there, and cannot by any means be carried away or demolished."

Maybe those walking the Way with us felt God's spirit inhabiting the Stone of Unction, or the rocky socket of Golgotha, or the cold marble of the Holy Sepulcher. Maybe by traveling in the footsteps of Jesus they'd been able to re-create within themselves his *passion,* that suffering endurance. I understood intellectually that the pilgrims were attempting to fathom the agony Christ felt. The point was to be vulnerable—from the Latin *vulnerare,* "to wound." It was to be wounded as Christ was, to feel that one has been left bleeding and abandoned like the man in the Judean Desert whom the Samaritan alone attempts to save. "My God, my God, why hast thou forsaken me?" Jesus cries out in the Gospel according to Matthew. Perhaps in re-creating this wounding within, perhaps in that act of imaginative sympathy, pilgrims hope they can be transformed morally. Or that they can reach through the veil of stone that separates this world from another and be fully present with God.

So I understood, intellectually, what the pilgrims were trying to do. But I myself didn't feel any connection to the Via Dolorosa in Jerusalem. For me, there was no veil. There was only lifeless stone pressing back against my hand. Because in truth, I was starting to see that, though I had followed Fabri to the Holy Land, this wasn't my omphalos. My spiritual homeland was not Jerusalem. I might have felt, growing up, an unrootedness similar to that of Steve Langfur and a similar desire for some ground in which to plant myself. But it wasn't going to be here.

And then I remembered one afternoon in Lawrence, Kansas, with Ellie—it must have been about a week after her birth. In the apartment I was renting in the old house on Tennessee Street, I had laid her on my bed, beneath a window, swaddled tightly in a soft white blanket. She was sleeping. We were entirely alone. I laid my head down next to hers and just stared and stared. The feeling I had for her at that moment contained in it, I'm sure, whatever we call God. God was not the dark mechanism of the will of the universe to which we must submit. He was the gravitational pull between my child and me. And what I realized walking the wrong way along the Via Dolorosa, from the tomb back to Ecce Homo with that same daughter, nearly grown and gone, was that the only place to which I had ever felt rooted, umbilically, wasn't a place at all.

*   *   *

That memory came back to me the evening after we followed the Franciscans on the Via Dolorosa when Ellie and I shared the communal dinner at Ecce Homo Convent with a French nun and a professor of German philosophy originally from South Korea and now teaching in Nebraska. Each evening we would sit with different guests at the tables laid for *Pilgrims:* a Baptist preacher from Kentucky and his wife who had been traveling to Israel every summer for years to participate in an ongoing archaeological dig in the Galilee; a musician from Paris who, herself an atheist, had nevertheless become obsessed with the ethical teachings of Jesus. A group of nurses from California and a woman working on her master's in theology. I would inevitably talk about my own preoccupation with Fabri, and the hour would pass pleasantly enough, and then we'd part.

That evening as we handed around the platters—baba ghanoush, hummus kawarma, pita, a chopped salad of cucumbers and tomatoes and peppers and parsley—we asked and answered the usual questions: Where are you from? What do you do? But when we'd finished those introductions, the professor of German philosophy prodded us further. "What are your hobbies?" he asked. Ellie told them that I spin yarn and knit and that she likes to read. The French nun, who had studied architecture, said she liked to draw. The professor told us he visited hot springs. "What is the strangest thing you've ever eaten?" someone suggested as a topic. "I once ate live octopus with sesame oil," said the professor of German philosophy. "Why?" I asked. "What is the reason for this?" "Aesthetics," he answered. "What is your object in life?" he asked. And by way of answering, I told them the story of Miss Rumphius, from a children's book I used to read to my girls.

A little girl named Alice Rumphius listens to her seafaring

grandfather's tales of travel and resolves to travel to faraway places and live beside the sea. "That is all very well, little Alice," her grandfather tells her, "but there is a third thing you must do." "What is that?" Alice asks him. "You must do something to make the world more beautiful," he replies. When Alice grows up, she does indeed travel to faraway places, and when she grows older, she lives beside the sea. But she knows she must still do something to make the world more beautiful, though she does not know what that could be. Then one spring, she notices that the lupines she planted in her garden the year before have spread to a nearby hillside, their seeds carried by the wind, by the birds. Inspired, she sends off for bushels of lupine seeds. All summer long she wanders over the fields and headlands, scattering seeds along the highways and down country lanes, into hollows, along stone walls. The following spring, lupines bloom everywhere. She has made the world more beautiful. At the dinner table in Ecce Homo Convent, I told my fellow pilgrims this story. "So to answer your question," I said, turning to the professor of German philosophy, "I think that my object in life is to make the world more beautiful, and I am trying to do that by raising my daughters to be good people and then sending these beautiful daughters out into the world to do good things."

"What is your faith, if I may ask?" the professor asked me in response to my story. "I was raised Catholic," I replied, "but now I am mainly just seeking. I'm fascinated by belief, but I don't believe myself." "You believe in the humanistic approach, rather than the religious?" he suggested. And that seemed exactly right. Dinner had officially ended by now and the student volunteers interning at Ecce Homo in exchange for room and board were attempting to clear our plates, but none of us was quite ready to end the conversation. So we made coffee with the Nescafé packets in the lounge and moved out to the rooftop terrace, the lights of the Old

City below us and the lights from the stars above. In that dark middle ground between, we talked and talked, me and the professor of German philosophy trying to speak in broken French to the nun, because she spoke almost no English, and Ellie trying to speak Spanish to her because they both spoke some, and then me and Ellie and the professor of German philosophy translating into English for each other what had been said.

The professor told us then how he had walked through the streets of the Holy City that day watching the aggressive merchants, the pushy tourists with their cameras. "I have Jerusalem in my heart," he said, echoing the Gospel according to Luke: *The Kingdom of God is within you.* "But I did not feel that this was a city of peace." I admitted how disconnected I'd felt walking the Via Dolorosa and in the Church of the Holy Sepulcher. And Ellie recalled her shock at the Church of the Ascension where we'd gone during our first full day in Jerusalem. We'd entered into a dusty courtyard, bare and unpaved. In the center was a small domed church made of stone the same color as the dust of the courtyard. In the center of the church was a rock with an indention—the footprint of the risen Jesus Christ, pushing off to heaven. "It's just like any other indention!" she'd said to me, incredulous, as we stood looking down at the depression in the stone. And then she went on a tear, almost personally offended. "Like, literally, there is nothing there. It looks like any other hole in any other rock. This doesn't even look like a footprint. If Jesus is perfect, he should have a perfect footprint! We haven't evolved that much in two thousand years!"

That night at Ecce Homo, she spoke with more equanimity. "It's all so exact," she observed to the French nun and the professor of German philosophy. "'This is the stone where Jesus was betrayed.' 'This is the stone where he wept.' 'This is where he ascended into heaven.' I guess I want a little more mystery. I'm trying to find room for some kind of "—she paused and chose her words carefully—

"some kind of *imaginative spirituality* amid all the concrete statements." Ellie was right. *Imaginative spirituality*—that was what was largely missing here. That deeply imagined sympathy for the passion of Christ, which I envisioned pilgrims trying to re-create inside themselves, seemed more often to have hardened into a literalism that naively insisted on the tangible. The mystery had been drained away, leaving only lifeless stones—*for the letter killeth*—to mark the Way.

"Today, walking the Via Dolorosa, I felt disconnected, separate from the stones," I told them. "But here, talking to you, I feel that something is alive," I confessed. And the French nun replied, "You feel *relation*. And when we are *in relation* with others, we feel God." I supposed this feeling of being in relation is similar to what Steve Langfur, quoting Franz Rosenzweig, had called being *rooted in one another*. Maybe it was what the Turners' called *communitas*. At any rate, I liked this idea of God as the movement between people. God as the invisible suturing. God as the fluidity between what exists and what cannot always be observed. God as activity. God not as the finite Samaritan but as his act of binding the wounds of the man abandoned on the Jericho Road. God as the swaddling of my child and the staring at her. God as Ellie walking with me along the Via Dolorosa. The Via not as a stone path but as the act of traveling on it. The Way.

LOOKING FOR THE FIELD OF
DAMASCUS

TOWARD THE END of our stay in Israel, we traveled again into the West Bank, this time with a Palestinian guide, Hijazi Eid, a friend and colleague of Carol Ann and Steve's. Hijazi picked us up on the other side of a checkpoint, with its turnstiles and Israeli guards, between the southern outskirts of Jerusalem and Bethlehem—*Bet Lehem,* House of Bread, in Hebrew; *Bayt Lahm,* House of Meat, in Arabic—a fertile land. Hijazi was waiting for us beneath the concrete separation wall, another section of which we'd glimpsed in Bethany when we came in from the Judean Desert with Carol Ann on the Jericho Road. He was long-limbed, his thinning hair cropped close. He wore his gold-rimmed aviator glasses on the top of his head when we weren't driving. There was an elegance about him, a graciousness. I'd heard that, because he once directed a medical clinic funded by Hamas, he could never leave the West Bank. "Thank you for meeting us on such short notice," I greeted him, Carol Ann having made these arrangements only days before. He placed his hand on his heart. "It will be my pleasure," he replied. He would repeat this gesture a number of times.

As we walked to Hijazi's car, Ellie and I regarded the separation wall, tagged with graffiti: a painting of the view of the city of Jerusalem that would be visible if only the wall weren't there, a dove of peace flying above the Dome of the Rock. *Once a Human*

Rights Teacher Was Born in Bethlehem, one writer ruefully reminded us. *Palestinians Must Live at Home!* Ellie walked over to the wall to take photos of a stencil by the British street artist Banksy of a soldier being frisked by a Palestinian girl in a pink dress. Ellie's boyfriend was a Banksy fan. "It's like the Berlin Wall," she whispered to me afterward. Seeing the wall, she told me later, was when she began to understand in more concrete terms the Israeli-Palestinian conflict.

Bethlehem wasn't really our destination with Hijazi that day, though I knew I had to see it because of Fabri. So we drove to the Shepherds' Fields just beyond Bethlehem and stood that bright morning where once the angel of the Lord appeared and the glory of the Lord shone round about and the shepherds with their flocks were sore afraid, as Luke says, when they heard of the coming birth of the Savior.

"We went down hill, through olive-yards, and came into a wide valley full of ploughed fields and meadows," Fabri remembers of this same spot, one of my favorite descriptions in his entire *Book of Wanderings.* "In the midst of this valley we saw great ruined walls, and the remnants of ancient buildings, towards which we turned ourselves. When we came to the place, we found a church, ruined and cast down, yet with its front part still remaining." And the pilgrims sang the angels' hymn: "Glory to God in the highest, and on earth peace, good will towards men."

The olive groves and meadows and ruins were still there—remnants of a Byzantine monastery—and we walked among them too. And into a cave in which, tradition has it, the shepherds had taken refuge and in whose rough-hewn niches Ellie and I now noted a fake electric-log fire and a crèche scene with hay-filled manger and plastic golden angels and shepherd figures that looked vaguely like German Hummel collectibles. On that day, the cave was filled with Sri Lankan pilgrims wearing royal-blue collapsible nylon cowboy hats. Back outside in the sunlight, Hijazi pointed in the distance to Har Homa, an Israeli settlement inside the West Bank, a raised scar of white buildings on the land.

They say the heavenly host along with the angel of the Lord sang out somewhere above these fields, now owned by the Franciscans. Or perhaps it was down the road at the Greek Orthodox site. Or even the Protestant shrine farther on. Because of this wrangling, though, because of Har Homa, their song of peace and goodwill seemed to me ironic and sad. And in the Church of the Nativity in Bethlehem itself, Greek Orthodox priests trying to bless an icon hurried us irritably through the underground grotto where Mary gave birth to her firstborn son and wrapped him in swaddling clothes and laid him in a humble manger because there was no place for them in the inn, a grotto now hung with silken brocade and gold and silver lanterns.

But Bethlehem hadn't really been the point of our journey into the territories that day. What I had crossed the border to try to find was the Field of Damascus, somewhere, according to Fabri's account, near Hebron, in the hills south of Bethlehem and Jerusalem. Like Adam's skull buried at the base of the cross of Jesus, the Field of Damascus was layered with meaning, like a metaphysical archaeological dig. I'd been strangely drawn to it.

In late August of 1483, the pilgrims have traveled south out of Bethlehem and entered the city of Hebron encircled by curious residents, who have seen no Westerners there for many years. After situating their belongings at an empty caravansary, they set out with their dragoman and some of the Saracens of the city to see the sites. Traveling along the main thoroughfare, passing workers in glass and other crafts, they leave the city gate and, somewhere along the highway, come to the Field of Damascus, named for

Abraham's servant Eliezer of Damascus. The pilgrims begin to climb the wall around the field so they might kiss the earth and say their prayers, but a fierce Saracen meets them on the other side, shouting and throwing stones. To the pilgrims this is holy ground. To the Saracen, this is his plowed land. But through the dragoman and the men from Hebron, the man is appeased with four *madini,* and then he himself reaches his hand down to the pilgrims to pull them over the wall.

Hebron means "friend" in Hebrew. The city is called Al-Khalil in Arabic, referring to Abraham, *Khalil al-Rahman,* Friend of God. In this Field of Damascus, named for the servant of the Friend of God, Fabri recalls, Abraham had sat in his tent in the heat of the day and seen three strangers coming toward him. He offered them bread and meat and washed their feet, not knowing they were servants of the Lord. Here, too, dwelt Isaac and Jacob, his son and grandson. But long before all of that, God reached down His hands into this field, says Fabri, and shaped Adam from the tough red clay, the *adamah,* lying just below the coarse brown crust of the earth. And then, after Adam and Eve had been driven out of Eden in the east, they returned here, and their son Cain rose up against his brother, Abel, and slew him amid thorny bushes, and "the earth opened its mouth and received that holy blood from the hands of the fratricide."

But we couldn't find the Field of Damascus. Because Fabri mentions that in the field is a "mosque" where Adam and Eve offered sacrifices and prayers, Hijazi thought we might be looking for the forlorn hilltop Maqam an-Nabi Yakin, the Shrine of the Truthful Prophet, southeast of Hebron. Surrounded by a stone wall, the shrine was bare except for a coffin-shaped indention in the dirt floor enclosed by iron fencing painted Palestinian green. Within the indention in the earth were two footprints—those, Hijazi explained, of Abraham as he looked east toward the Dead Sea and saw the rising smoke of Sodom and Gomorrah as the cities lay in ruins. On the top of the hill, through the cool air we could hear the calls of a vegetable seller in the nearby village of Bani Na'im. But the stone enclosure was too small, given Fabri's description, to be the Field of Damascus, and anyway, the dirt was a dingy beige.

Nor did the Field of Damascus appear to be the traditional site of Mamre north of town. Herod had built a great wall around the site, and Constantine a church, but that's all gone now, as is the oak tree that once offered shade. Only the stone foundations remain, beside a new apartment building, and the field is overrun with thistles and poisonous arum. As we walked through this forlorn place, Hijazi said, "The stones are talking here"—like the voice of Abel's blood crying up to God from the ground—"but nobody listens."

I wanted to find the Field of Damascus but it was at least as important to Hijazi, I think, that we see Hebron itself. He wanted to show us the *nakbah,* the catastrophe, of the Israeli occupation and what he called the "demographic war against the Palestinians," evident everywhere we went. We drove through the Palestinian-controlled Area H1, in the heart of Hebron, cars and taxis pressing close and loud, merchandise spilling from the fronts of flat-roofed buildings with their signs in Arabic. Within the city itself is Area H2, controlled by Israel. This is where the settlers live. Palestinians cannot approach this sector without special permits from the Israeli Defense Forces, the IDF. Theoretically, the converse is also true. "The Israeli army is not allowed to be here," Hijazi explained. "Nevertheless, they do not respect this rule."

Almost as if to illustrate his point, a few minutes later, we saw members of the Israeli police, weapons drawn, helmets on, entering a building. Hijazi pulled over and jumped out to ask some Arab men on the sidewalk what was going on. "Did they want to arrest someone?" he wondered out loud to us. But it was only a new captain of the police introducing himself. "Captain Tariq," Hijazi said. "They use Arabic nicknames so they can be understood." But as we drove on, Hijazi remained indignant. "Imagine you are sitting in your home in Houston and the Mexican police arrive and take your daughter in for questioning," he said, gesturing toward Ellie in the backseat. "If this is an independent area, what are they doing here? And yet this happens all the time."

If Hebron is a divided city, the symbol for this division sits squarely at its center: in a building constructed above the Cave of Machpelah, which Abraham bought of Ephron the Hittite, who owned the field in which the cave was situated. In the cave Abraham would bury his wife Sarah. And in it he himself would be buried, as would his son Isaac and Isaac's wife Rebecca, and Isaac's son Jacob and Jacob's wife Leah. Both Islam and Judaism hold these tombs of their patriarchs sacred, but though this building houses a mosque and a synagogue, do not mistake that for a sign of unity. It's a sign of bitter partition.

Ellie and I left the bright empty street and entered the Haram el-Khalil with Hijazi, where we took off our shoes and put on the blue woven cloaks with hoods provided for female visitors. We saw the entrance to the burial caves, over which this building had been constructed, covered by a marble flower-shaped disk, its center a glass porthole. Then we sat quietly on the plush Persian carpets in varying shades of red while Hijazi prayed, bending his body in submission to the will of God. An Israeli soldier plodded through, though he kept to the long plastic runners "so the mosque remains pure," as Hijazi explained after his prayers. "The soldiers won't take their shoes off."

As we were leaving, he pointed out the *mihrab* where, in February of 1994, during the overlapping holidays of Purim and Ramadan, Baruch Goldstein, an Israeli settler, an emigrant born in Brooklyn, wearing his IDF reserve uniform, opened fire with his

army-issued assault rifle, murdering twenty-nine unarmed Palestinians and wounding another hundred and twenty-five. After he
ran out of ammunition, he was beaten to death by the survivors.
Though the massacre was officially condemned by Israel, for a time
Goldstein's grave became a site of pilgrimage. Soon after the massacre, the division of this building took place.

In order to enter the synagogue, which we, not being Muslim,
could do, we exited the mosque, parted from Hijazi, and passed
through a turnstile and a metal detector. Israeli soldiers looked at
our passports and asked us uninterestedly, "Do you have a knife?
Something sharp?" "No, nothing like that," we said. They nodded.
"Go on through." Then we entered the synagogue on the other side
of the building.

Though Fabri and the Christian pilgrims with whom he traveled, like all infidels and Jews, could not enter this same walled
mosque above the cave of the tombs, they were allowed to pray
on the steps outside. But what impressed Fabri most was the hospital for the poor, attached to the mosque, whose annual revenue
amounted to more than twenty-four thousand ducats. "Every day
twelve hundred loaves of bread are baked in its ovens, and are
given to those who ask for them; neither is charity refused to any
pilgrim, of whatever nation, faith, or sect he may be. He who asks
for food receives a loaf of bread, some oil, and some *menestrum,*
which we call pudding," Fabri notes admiringly. And in the tradition of Abraham's hospitality to strangers and wayfarers, "In the
serving out of the loaves of bread, they sent a basketful to our inn
for our use, albeit we had never asked them for anything."

We reunited with Hijazi and walked through the souk of the
Old City of Hebron, such as it was. Many of the green metal doors
were shuttered. Cut off from other Palestinian areas because of
the separation wall, and with almost no tourist trade to speak of
anymore, the district urgently needed customers. But Ellie and I ar-

rived entirely unprepared for the onslaught. I carried just enough cash to pay Hijazi and buy lunch, little more, and though I purchased rosewater candy and some cheap earrings for Mary Martha and Sabine from the vendors, that didn't seem to be nearly adequate, and their desperation as they tried to get us to look at their wares made me feel panicked and desperate myself.

In the souk, we met two members of a Christian Peacemaker Team, probably a little older than Ellie, who told us how they walked Palestinian children to and from school to protect them from Jewish settlers who harass them. Farther on, Hijazi pointed to the green wire netting that stretched across the space between the limestone buildings of the souk. Jewish settlers lived in the apartments above—a Jewish settlement *within* Palestinian structures. The netting was for catching the trash the settlers would otherwise toss down onto their Palestinian neighbors. That settlement and the others like Har Homa in the hills have running water continuously, water subsidized by the Israeli government. The Palestinians have water tanks on the tops of their houses. Sometimes they run dry. "Abraham paid for the land where his wife was buried," Hijazi turned to us and said. "He did not confiscate it. I feel for them. They should come out of this trauma. Come out of these gates. This is not good for them or for us."

That evening, when Ellie and I were back at Ecce Homo Convent, Carol Ann called to see how our day in Hebron had gone. I told her about the souk in the Old City, how guilty I felt, being unable to help, because *if I do not stop to help this man, what will happen to* him? But she told me, "Nothing you could have spent today would change *anything*. What you mainly need to do is bear witness to what is happening."

Earlier that day, when we were at the traditional site of Mamre north of Hebron, Hijazi had said to us, in that neglected place of thorn and thistle, "The stones are talking here, but nobody listens." But *I* was listening. I couldn't *stop* listening. Everywhere we went, the stones were telling me stories—stories from scripture and from Fabri's account, stories told by guides and interpreters, by everyone we met who wanted to persuade us of the truth of his narrative. The world was layered with meaning, like the Field of Damascus. And in the landscape of my mind, I thought, there was room for all of the stories, even though they conflicted.

But even the landscape of my mind was becoming over-crowded and confusing. I felt small and naive and ignorant in this ancient place of ancient grudges, in this cauldron of resentment and guilt and literalism and searching. What could I possibly understand in the short time we would be here? In the limited geography we could cover? Everywhere we'd gone, old hatreds had been present—the Balkans, Cyprus, now here. I had heard so many stories and had been trying to piece together what was just and true. And I was looking, as Ellie had put it, for *imaginative spirituality amid all the concrete statements*. But in this material world the stories could not all fit. So they jockeyed for position and claimed territory and set up walls of separation and tried to silence one another.

I was full of other people's stories of how they'd been wronged. I felt I could no longer take anything else in. I'd have to cry for days to make room for more. Once, when she was little and obsessed with amphibians, Sabine asked me, glasses on her face, frog boots on her feet, "Did you know that sea turtles have glands instead of ears?" When I said, No, sweetie, I did not know this, she explained that sea turtles can only sense vibrations. They don't actually hear. And then she told me a theory she had about these glands. "When they sip up the salt water," she said, "the water goes into their glands and the salt sticks to other pieces of salt and comes out as tears from their eyes." That's how I felt. I was trying to swallow this vast sea rushing into me, but it was emerging as tears from my eyes.

The next morning, I sat in the lounge and tried to Skype with Terry. It was a Saturday, and he was home from work. He'd just woken up and he was still in his T-shirt and boxers, his hair sticking up and out. Years ago, when he'd been in Cuba, we'd written letters to each other every day. But it had grown harder and harder on this journey to connect. Instead of writing to him, I was writing in my notebook. Phone calls were outrageously expensive and so mainly for emergencies. Days and days would go by without speaking. But here we were, finally face to face. I wanted to be cheerful and grateful. But since I couldn't pretend, I wanted at least to tell him how overwhelmed I felt. But it was all too much to explain—the bitter man with a face lined like the Judean hills, the broadsides in Mea Shearim, the merchants in Hebron, the nets for catching trash. Instead what I kept saying was "I don't know why I'm doing this. I don't know why I am here. I don't know why I came," and though he tried to sympathize and be encouraging, he no longer said as forcefully as he had before, "You're supposed to be doing this."

Terry was overwhelmed himself. His intricately mapped Excel spreadsheets of daily activities for Mary Martha and Sabine had given him a false sense of order. The actuality of getting the girls to where they had to be and feeding them when they were home and walking the dogs and keeping the house relatively clean in addition to getting his own work done—he was managing to do it all, but barely, and the chaos that always threatened was taking a toll. "But it's more than that," he told me, sitting at my desk in my office, all my books on the shelves behind him, which I could see on the computer screen as we Skyped. "I'm always worrying now about the girls. I keep wondering, *Are they safe? Are they happy?* There is this pressure that I never felt before because you were always there."

Terry's anxiety had the effect of making me feel both crucial to this private ecosystem he and I had fashioned with our own hands and trapped within it. What did I want? To be essential to other human beings or to be free to live a *bohemian-explorer-intellectual kind of life?* These were mutually exclusive options, even if we were pretending with this trip that I could have both. I'd chosen motherhood. I'd chosen Terry. I'd chosen the old house in the city. I'd chosen to worry about the girls. *Are they safe? Are they happy?* That was *my* job. But I kind of liked this freedom, despite how overwhelmed I felt. I kind of liked talking to strangers on the streets of strange cities while Ellie sat in the lounge and read. I kind of liked being by myself.

On the bus from Hebron back to Jerusalem after we'd parted from Hijazi late that afternoon, I sat silently staring out the window, Ellie's head on my shoulder. When we'd boarded the bus full of Palestinian women in head scarves, they'd looked at us skeptically. We took our seats beside them. Who was I in their eyes? And what were they to me? We all shopped for food and cooked dinner for our children and tried to be good mothers. And yet, I was on a journey, free from all of that, at least temporarily, and they were trapped behind concrete walls they couldn't easily escape. Were we really *rooted in one another?* Were we *in relation?* Was God in the space between?

In the clarifying light of late afternoon, Arabic music played mournfully. It was filled with longing, with something ancient and inaccessible to me. We passed through villages whose names I could not read—fruit stands, flats of herbs, dusty rows of marble sinks and car seats, a shop full of frilly dresses of layered lace, piles of trash and rubble, laundry hanging out to dry on the roofs of distant houses. We passed a Bedouin on a donkey. We passed a donkey beneath a tree. We passed fig trees and terraced fields of grapevines. *House of Meat. House of Bread.* Every once in a while, a wall of concrete, and Israeli flags, and a watchtower with cameras pointed in all directions. Then, like Fabri, *we came into a wide valley full of ploughed fields and meadows,* small plots separated by low stone walls. And beneath green shoots I finally saw the red earth, the *adamah,* the living dust, the hungry dust from which we were all made and that I'd been seeking.

THE POOLS OF BETHESDA

ELLIE HAD BEEN a good sport about climbing Mount Quarantal, and about walking the Via Dolorosa with the Franciscans, and about seeking the Field of Damascus, and about visiting all of the churches and mosques we could find that Fabri had seen—sacred houses that were becoming indistinguishable from one another. And the farther away we moved from the familiar world, the more the small tensions that existed between us seemed to dissipate. In a way, it was as if we'd returned to the beginning, when it had been only her and me. There was no one else with whom she needed to compete for my attention. There was no one else to distract me from her. Perhaps, too, this peace was simply resignation: we couldn't go back across the sea and we still had the desert before us. But it seemed larger than all that to me. I think we both sensed that it was just the two of us now, working our way through strange lands alone. The foreign surroundings made us turn toward each other for reassurance. We could confirm who we were if we began to forget.

In her notebooks, Ellie was making lists continually, lists that probably calmed her during the uncertainty of traveling, the way her presence did for me. She had always made lists, it's true. Favorite Bands. Favorite Writers. Favorite Movies. Boys I've Liked. Top Ten Things About Ellie. That last list, from middle school, included these items: "She has a made-up style called Vintage Electric. She loves writing novellas. She has two families. She kicks butt at Karate." Her New Year's Resolutions, also from middle school: "1. Kiss a boy. 2. Make a friend. 3. Be alive." And on a Summer List before she started high school: "Read Mom's library. Write more poems, stories, letters. Come to terms with everything."

I found that Summer List years later, when Ellie gave me her diaries from that troubled time. She wanted to burn them. To leave no monument to that suffering. I read some of the entries but hadn't the heart to read them all. That list stayed in my mind. What was contained in the *everything* she was pleading to come to terms with? The summer day she rode her bike to the house of a boy who forced her to do things she was ashamed to do? The cutting, the cutting, the cutting? Or was there more in it? Did it go farther back? The rush of moves from place to place, away from her father? The bewildering onslaught of siblings? Or maybe it went even farther back; maybe contained in that *everything* was the restlessness she'd inherited, growing fat in the womb with my own longing so that it filled every cell of her body. Or the anger at the burden of that restlessness which she could not explain. And had she done it? Had she *come to terms with everything?*

As we traveled now, Ellie's lists signaled a growing urgency. In Croatia, she'd made a list of Things to Do in Austin once she returned ("Swimming at Barton Creek. First Thursdays on SoCo. Concerts at Stubbs, Emo's, etc. Kayak Town Lake"). At Rhodes she'd made a list of Possible Side Trips from Madrid, where she was thinking of spending a semester in the coming year studying abroad ("Paris. Dublin. Prague. Istanbul. Casablanca. Berlin."). But in Jerusalem she seemed to make lists nearly every day. Possible Classes to Add to Fall Schedule. Things to Do Before School Starts. Things I Have. Things I Need. She made a list of States Visited (thirty-one) and Countries Visited (thirteen) and Places I Want to Go To, which took up an entire page. Her mind was elsewhere, far away from me, making plans, trying to organize the chaos, longing for what would come next. For me, this trip *was* the next thing, that for which I'd always longed. For Ellie this was just a stop on the way to where she really wanted to be.

One afternoon, Ellie and I drove through the Judean Desert toward the Jordan River, as we had with Carol Ann, but this time, instead of turning north toward Jericho, we headed south along the salt-rimmed shore of the Dead Sea. To the west, the muted red cliffs of Israel tumbled down toward the flat land. To the east, the chalky tiered mountains of Jordan. We stopped at Mineral Beach to swim. There, the air lay thick and hazy over the water, which was viscous and blue. Everywhere signs warned us not to splash, not to submerge our faces, to ease slowly in, to contact a lifeguard if we swallowed any water.

We eased in, as instructed, but could not hold our legs down. They kept sweeping out from under us to the surface like popped corks. We looked ridiculous, which made us laugh. A group of Slavic men bobbed nearby with their round white bellies protruding from the water, like an archipelago of deserted sand-swept islands in the sea. Closer to the shore, women laved themselves with the salty muck and chatted in Hebrew. I put my tongue to my hand just to see what would happen, and my tongue burned for a long time afterward. Floating on the Dead Sea, I thought about how the weight of our bodies depends on the context in which they exist, which seemed like a metaphor for something, but the bromide that the salt water released into the air was making me too sleepy to think of what.

After we had showered and as we were walking across the parking lot to the rental car, Ellie, exhilarated, her cheeks bright from the sun and the salt, turned to me and said, "Well, I can cross off the Dead Sea from my list of Things to Do Before I Die. But now my list has only one word: *Everything*."

We drove back north to Jerusalem, the late sun etching shadows into the cliffs around us. The land, like us, grew pensive. "I'm just afraid I'm going to die before I can do everything I want to do," she told me. "I still feel that way," I said. "But you have your work and all of us and a husband who loves you," she said, partly to soothe me but also probably partly in rebuke. "I don't have any of that yet." And what she said was true. "But you will find all that too, sweetie," I told her as we drove the black road through the desert beside the Dead Sea. "You have your whole life ahead of you. You will make that kind of world for yourself. But this world that I've made, with Terry and you and Mary Martha and Sabine, it's not going to be together much longer, at least not in the way that I want it to be." And I guess I was soothing her and rebuking her too. Ellie was quiet. I knew there was no way she could understand this loss I was trying to explain, even though she was trying. Because of course the loss of her, so painful for me to contemplate, was precisely where the possibility for *everything* she wanted to see and do on that list began.

In some way I felt I had been trying to prepare myself to let Ellie go—to *come to terms with everything*—since the moment I laid her on the bed beneath the window in Lawrence, Kansas, and stared and stared. Maybe even before, when she was born and the umbilical cord joining us had to be cut. My love as her mother was always infused with that necessity. Maybe all mortal love is like that— haunted by the fear of its loss and of the void that will surely follow. But there is something about the love I bear for my daughters that is different from the love I bear for Terry, or my parents, or my siblings, or my friends. I am the omphalos for my daughters, the seam between this world and whatever existed before. But unlike the journey of the pilgrim toward the omphalos of Jerusalem, my daughters would have to wander away from me, as I did from my mother, as she did from hers. It's a sort of Sisyphean exercise: we are always discarding those who raised us and chasing the generation that comes after us, always longing to hold on to the young that we create, just as they will their own. Each of us engaged in a quest for this unrequited love.

On one of our last afternoons in Jerusalem, I walked the Via Dolorosa east toward Saint Stephen's Gate, which led out to the Mount of Olives, and beyond that to the separation wall, and beyond that to Bethany, and beyond that to the Judean Desert and the road to Jericho. But just inside the walls of the Old City near the gate, I passed through a doorway that opened out onto a leafy green courtyard and the Church of Saint Anne, built over the grotto in which they say the Virgin Mary was born. The ruins of the Pools of Bethesda were in this complex too. Once filled with healing waters, in the Gospel according to John, angels went down at a certain season into the pools and troubled them, and Jesus cured a man infirm thirty-eight years.

The name Bethesda—*Bet Hisda* in Aramaic; *Bet Hesed* in Hebrew—means House of Mercy or House of Grace, which is what seekers hoped to find in coming here. After the Jewish uprisings of the early centuries of the current era, when Jerusalem was razed by the Romans and then rebuilt by Hadrian into Aelia Capitolina, the sanctuary became a temple dedicated to Asclepius, god of healing, to which pilgrims could again come to be cured of their ills. Among the archaeological remnants is part of a marble foot, like the *milagros* at Chimayó, dedicated by one Pompeia Lucilla, though whether in hope or in gratitude it isn't known. By the middle of the fifth century, a Byzantine church had been built over the pools, thereby appropriating the pagan site by commemorating the miracle witnessed in John's Gospel and by marking Mary's birthplace, traditionally located nearby. The arched ruins of the white limestone church and the pools they once covered stand opened up now to the sky and the unrelenting sun, deep chasms stippled with weeds and empty, in their own way, as the rock tomb of Jesus.

As dark and brooding as was the Holy Sepulcher when I'd entered it that first morning in Jerusalem, the Church of Saint Anne seemed a vessel of resonant light. Near the doorway, I lit a candle, as I always did for those at home, then turned to find the French nun from Ecce Homo just entering. It somehow felt destined that I would see her there. We embraced and then sat together in a pew near the back. "*Ça va?*" she asked me, and I told her, "*Je suis un peu triste, mais je ne sais pas pourquoi.*" I was a little sad, but I didn't know why.

The acoustics in this church were renowned and people had lined up along the side aisle waiting their turn to take center stage on the steps to the altar. When we first sat down, a couple from Brazil were crooning a jazzy little number in Portuguese. But then, to my astonishment, an American choir took their places and sang "Amazing Grace," at which point I began, inexplicably, it must have seemed to the French nun, to weep. I tried to explain to her in French how I used to sing this hymn to my daughters as a lullaby when they were little—along with "Love Me Tender" and Doc Watson's "Midnight on the Stormy Deep" and a bunch of Lucinda Williams songs. But I could not remember how to properly conjugate my verbs and everything came out in the present tense, as if I were still singing to my girls, who were still babies, as if I were still holding them in the dark in the rocking chair beside the white iron bed, as if Mary Martha were still reaching up to grab hold of my hair and rub it against her little round cheek, which, metaphysically, I suppose, was actually the case, all of this was still happening, it was always happening, as long as I could remember it. The French nun seemed to understand even though I made no sense, and we sat together, *in relation,* as I cried and the choir sang, "Amazing Grace, how sweet the sound, / That saved a wretch like me. / I once was lost, but now am found, / Was blind, but now I see."

But I wasn't found at all. In this place of healing, just off center from the navel of the world, I longed to feel something move inside me other than my own thoughts, but there was no angel to trouble the waters. There were no waters. Only the empty Pools of Bethesda, House of Mercy, House of Grace—an abyss with weeds.

Sitting there in the church of the mother of mothers, I had this palpable sense of how the earth was always in motion, trundling toward some inevitable end. Maybe that's what I had first understood that afternoon on the carpeted floor in my bedroom in the house on Echo Street when the world turned suddenly to shadow and I became aware that I was tired. The earth is in motion, and only gravity holds my little family together, though soon not even gravity will help. The universe is expanding, after all, the distance between bodies filling out. Whether God is the dark machinery of the world or the space between us, the distinction will eventually grow irrelevant. We are even now being pulled, like taffy. Soon, we'll be pulled apart. We'll become fragmented. We'll be fragments of a shattered universe. God has been broken into pieces and He won't be made whole again.

It was all gone—the iron bed, the lullabies, walking to the old brick elementary school, sewing clothes with Mary Martha for her dolls, the tadpoles we rescued from a tire rut filled with rainwater and placed in a clear bowl until they grew legs. Gone was the intimacy of life with little children, the rituals of our days together— eating and bathing and reading and sleeping—rituals that kept the chaos of the profane world outside at bay and held us together in *communitas.*

Once, when the girls were in their teens, I dreamed that I was lying on the couch in the sunroom reading and I happened to look up to find Sabine standing in the doorway, but as a toddler, holding her blankie and sucking on her binkie. And I thought to myself in the dream, *Yes, that's exactly how she was. I remember now.* (It was like the dream I had of my grandmother after she was gone, when I knew that she was dead even as she pressed me to her.) I called to Sabine and she came and lay down on my chest, not as a toddler now but as a newborn. And then, afternoon sunlight filtering through the curtains, Mary Martha was there too, both of them cradled in my arms, where I could marvel at their perfect faces once more. The grief of being pulled out of that dream upon waking was, I imagined, what Orpheus must have felt when he turned and the darkness tore Eurydice from him again forever as they labored up toward the light of the living world.

Fabri notes the tradition, recorded by the Church Fathers, that after her son's death and resurrection, the Virgin Mary returned every day to all those places "wherein our redemption was wrought. Though she was in the spirit," Fabri elaborates, "yet as long as she lived in the flesh she was moved by fleshly feelings, and therefore was refreshed by visiting those places, and was daily inflamed with fresh feelings of love, all the more powerfully the more she was illuminated within by divine visitations." The Virgin Mary lived fourteen years after her son's ascension, "which years," says Fabri, "she passed as a pilgrim, moving actually in the body from place to place." This story of pilgrim Mary trudging from site to site every day in her blue robe and white veil, stopping here for a drink of water from a well, stopping there at a wayside church to say a prayer, remembering all the while the beloved child who was gone—this story breaks my heart.

Because when Ellie was born, no Magi came bearing gifts and no angels sang of her arrival, yet for me she was a savior nevertheless. What mother's child is not? Though I thought I longed for some *bohemian-explorer-intellectual kind of life,* one in which I might follow a man because *I liked the way he looked at the desert,* I saw once I had her and the daughters who followed how empty my life, my arms, had been before. "You are the one / Solid the spaces lean on, envious," says Sylvia Plath in "Nick and the Candlestick," a poem addressed to her son. "You are the baby in the barn." The babies are our consolation, the gifts the gods give us to help bear the inevitable pain of the mortal world.

Then they become the pain itself. I tried so hard to pay attention, to bear witness, as if by memorizing their little faces, as if by writing down their dreams and the things they said and did, I could somehow keep them with me. But they were not stones. Their cells replicated furiously even as I held them. And anyway, my attention always strayed. Now the empty space in my arms was like an amputated limb. Where, I wondered, in this ancient place of healing, where was the *milagro* for that?

V. INTO THE VOID

Sinai Desert

My soul thirsteth for thee, my flesh longeth for thee
in a dry and thirsty land, where no water is.

—Psalms 63:1

PRELUDE TO THE WILDERNESS

BEFORE HE LAUNCHES into his account of the journey from Gaza south across the Sinai Peninsula to Saint Catherine's Monastery at the base of Mount Sinai, Friar Felix Fabri ruminates upon "the State of the Desert or Wilderness"—its qualities and characteristics, its cultural history, what it has come to symbolize. For the desert wilderness of the Sinai is sacred territory, the parched earth where God spoke out of the fire to man. Though their bodies are at the mercy of this brutal place, the pilgrims cross a spiritual landscape that exists beyond time, beyond the physical world that can inflict such suffering.

"This country is called the desert because it seems to be...deserted by God, by the heavens, and by the world," Fabri begins his catalog. "It is empty and void, as though God had used it to improve or adorn the rest of the universe. The country seems also forsaken by the heavens, for it lacks the kindly influence of the stars, and seems to be viewed angrily by them, and, as it were, turned into iron, while the heaven above seems harsh, pitiless, and brazen. In consequence of this the country is also deserted by mankind, who depart from it as from a useless thing."

Fabri goes on to enumerate other associations: Barren and waterless, it's an image of death. A land of serpents and scorpions, fauns and satyrs and devils. A site of testing and temptation. But it's also a place where God bestowed the commandments upon His wandering people. One can get lost here. It is a pathless sea of sand. But one can also here be found. For the desert is where manna rained down, and water burst forth from stone. It's where divine comfort was given. It's a place to do penance.

Back home in Houston, when I'd first discovered Fabri's *Book of Wanderings,* his descriptions of the desert journey had been my favorite part. They'd been, in fact, the part that most compelled me to follow him. Everywhere else Fabri traveled, the landscape had become encrusted with sacred places commemorating what had happened there until it turned to stone. But here, the land was stripped bare and always shifting beneath him. And that barrenness and mutability seemed to free him to see. I had somehow known already that I would never find God or the spiritual rest He stood for in the churches and cathedrals built by human hands that longed to house He Who, if He existed, could not be contained. Yet back in Houston, reading Fabri and imagining my own journey, I had thought that perhaps in the vast emptiness of the desert, I might confront some desert deep within myself, where God would appear like an oasis that would not be a mirage.

But the Sinai Desert was a wilderness for Ellie and me, a place of blank blue skies and an immensity that exhausted us, of mountains from whose summits we saw only more mountains of red mounded earth raked by wind. It was a place of "no water but only rock / Rock and no water and the sandy road" of Eliot's *Waste Land,* "The road winding above among the mountains / Which are mountains of rock without water," the road that seemed to lead nowhere. We could not decipher the desert. We could not hear what it was trying to say. We could not read the landscape or the people through which we wandered, lost, as if in a reverie. The desert was an ocean in which we drifted, becalmed. Home was a dream remembered, some place I knew once, a long time ago. Our days passed slowly and in silence. Only my daughter beside me felt real.

The journey from Jerusalem to Gaza that late August of 1483 takes four days. Four days through the spare, pale hills, the olive groves and fig trees arcing toward wide plains and vineyards, which arc toward the sea. In Jerusalem, the pilgrims provision themselves for the journey across the desert to Saint Catherine's: sacks of biscuits and jars of wine and skins of water, baskets full of eggs and coops with live cocks and hens, hampers holding saucepans, kettles, dishes. They have mattresses sewn and stuffed with cotton. All these supplies, along with the pilgrims' trunks, are loaded onto camels, and then the pilgrims depart Jerusalem, the Holy City, center of the civilized world. They enter Gaza, at the edge of the wilderness of the desert, four days later at dark.

The Gaza Fabri describes in no way resembles the Gaza that exists today—or at least the Gaza that exists in my mind from images in the papers and on TV: the rubble of bulldozed buildings, young men in ski masks or kaffiyeh scarves holding Kalashnikovs, beloved bodies being carried by stunned relatives, children mangled and bleeding and burned. In the weeks and months after the revolution in Tahrir Square, as I nervously scanned *Al Jazeera English* dispatches on the Web, wondering if we'd still be able to travel to the Sinai, I would read about the smuggling tunnels at Rafah dug along the border of Egypt and the Gaza Strip in an attempt to circumvent the Israeli blockade. Now, in defiance of Israel, the Egyptians had begun to ease border restrictions put into place under Mubarak in cooperation with the Israelis. For years before, these were some of the things Israel would not let the Palestinians have: lentils, pasta, tomato paste and juice, chocolate, ginger, crayons, stationery, soccer balls, appliances, lightbulbs, matches, needles, blankets, sheets, shoes, mattresses, batteries for hearing aids, wheelchairs. Also, almost any kind of construction material, almost any item that could rebuild a house or build a bomb. Carved out of basements or beneath silvery olive groves, these tunnels were used by smugglers to carry all those banned goods from Egypt into Gaza.

Though the waves of the Mediterranean just beyond have always washed in and out like breath, the Gaza that Felix Fabri enters at dark on August 29, 1483, is unrecognizable from the one depicted in the news. A cosmopolitan port city, it houses "a wondrous mixture of nations," he says with admiration: Ethiopians, Arabs, Egyptians, Syrians, Indians, Eastern Christians, and, among all of these, many merchants who sell their wares. No city to which Fabri has been sells so much for so little. "In vulgar speech, it is a ditchful of butter," he writes, "and all things needful for human life are abundant and cheap there." The houses, it is true, are built of mud. And no wall protects the city, a city twice as great as Jerusalem. But still, the towers rise so tall they obstruct the sky, and the mosques and the public baths are elaborately vaulted and tiled with polished marble.

But for Ellie and me, there was no possibility of traveling through Gaza into the desert as Fabri had done. The government websites told us this. The guidebooks told us this. Steve Langfur told us this. Common sense in the guise of Terry insisted on this. Which is how Ellie and I found ourselves talking with Joel from Alabama as we boarded a bus to the Red Sea city of Eilat in southern Israel, the nearest town to the only border crossing into Egypt and the Sinai open to us, the one at Taba.

Joel, on his way to Petra, was tanned and compact, wearing aerodynamic Oakley sunglasses and those traveling pants that become shorts when you unzip the legs. On the bus ride south through the Negev Desert, the Dead Sea on our left, pied mountains of rust and ocher and ash to the right, the flat black road before us, Joel told me that he had originally planned to take this trip to the Holy Land with his father. Then his father died a few weeks before they were to leave. Despite the fact that Joel has six children, ages two through fourteen, his wife still encouraged him to go. During Joel's travels around Israel, he told me, he had always tried to connect what he prayed for with the place in which he prayed. In Bethlehem, at the Church of the Nativity, for instance, where God was made flesh "and did so much to change the course of the world," he appealed to the Lord to help him change the course of his own small life. He'd taken pictures and kept a journal of his prayers to share with his six children and his wife.

Ellie listened to music on her iPod and ate candy-coated almonds we'd bought in the Old City. Through the bus window, I watched the Negev scroll past. Signs for camel crossings. Hebrew words I could not read spelled out in stones against the bare hills. Interminable miles of power lines. Clumps of thistles and branching acacias that looked as if God had taken His hand and flattened them from above. From time to time we would pass a date palm grove, the trees like rows of feather dusters planted in the ground, and strange abandoned villages of greenhouses, their aluminum arched frames covered in sand-colored nylon, with nothing, as far as I could see, growing inside. Israeli soldiers with their guns slung across their shoulders would get off or on the bus at stops that seemed connected to no visible outpost. To the east lay the Dead Sea, flat and still. The mountains to the west were like waves suspended mid-arch, just as they were cresting.

"So what do you do?" I asked Joel, and he told me he was a lawyer for military contractors. "I represent those people who can disappear into these deserts and kill the bad guy," he told me. I wondered who he thought the bad guy was. His wife, at home taking care of the six children, was a major in the air force reserves. They'd met when they both worked in military intelligence. All of this information seemed somehow integral to my surreal desert reverie; I just couldn't quite make the connection. Joel asked how long we'd been traveling, and when I told him we'd been gone from home almost two months, he said, "You must miss your family." I knew the proper response to this, but the proper response was not exactly the truth anymore. "I love my daughters and my husband," I told this total stranger. But then I tried to explain how home was becoming a vaguely remembered dream.

In traveling, we collide with other bodies briefly. And in these chance encounters, we exist in a concentrated state in which the detritus of our daily lives is not cluttering the countertop or stacked upon the bedside table and therefore does not interfere. Because of this concentration, and because we know the encounter will not last, we often bare ourselves to strangers. Talking to them, without the usual reticence and social inhibitions, sometimes becomes just a more audible way of talking to oneself.

In the heat and haze of late afternoon, Ellie and I walked from the bus station in Eilat to our hotel, bent like peddlers from the weight of our backpacks. The female Israeli guard at the entrance, hair pulled back severely in a ponytail, stopped us, looked fiercely into our eyes, and demanded to know if we were guests and where our room key was—all before we had even checked in. Our backpacks could easily have concealed bombs, after all. These Red Sea resorts have been popular sites for suicide attacks over the years.

That evening, we walked along busy Arava Road, past the small airport, and down to the Bay of Eilat at the northernmost tip of the Gulf of Aqaba, that finger of the Red Sea that was itself an inlet of the Indian Ocean. From a distance, the water appeared rust-colored, perhaps from an algae that blooms near the surface, perhaps from the mountains, which wash slowly into the gulf when it rains. As the sun's light dissolved and the sunbathers departed, we

walked along the curved harbor gathering white coral like fragments of bone.

When we arrived at the Egyptian passport control at Taba early
the next morning, the cheery man examining our documents
looked at my passport through his bifocals and then at me and
asked, smiling and leaning in, conspiratorial, "Julia Roberts?" And
to Ellie, "Angelina Jolie?" One brief moment of vanity ticked by
before I realized that he probably says this to all of the Western
tourists. But by then the passport officer had turned serious. Looking me straight in the eye over his glasses, he told me, "Be careful.
Don't be naive." Perhaps we should have taken it as a sign of
what was to come, of the potential for misinterpretation, when the
young man in the white djellaba approached us, once we made
it through passport control, as if he knew us, and we naively let
him pick up our backpacks and carry them, thinking he was the
guide who was supposed to be waiting for us. He wasn't. And he
demanded five Egyptian pounds for his kindness. When our guide
finally arrived, late, I wasn't sure how to confirm it was really him.

But it was, and for days, on the circuitous way to Saint Catherine's Monastery, we navigated the wadis, dry riverbeds running
through the desert, in the jeep of Sheikh Swelam, a sinewy chain-
smoking Bedouin in djellaba and kaffiyeh and Ray-Bans who
brought with him both his sullen twelve-year-old son and Mohammad, an Egyptian interpreter, fresh from the revolution in Tahrir
Square. We did not travel directly from Taba to Saint Catherine's,
however. Back in Houston, I had sent Erez, founder of Desert Eco
Tours, a map of Fabri's journey down the Sinai Peninsula and asked
him to organize a four-day trip that would allow us to see as much
as possible of the variegated landscape Fabri described.

For weeks upon weeks, Ellie and I had entered sacred spaces
marking miracles whose literal meaning had been quite easy to
interpret. Here, on this very spot, we were told at each of the

churches and monasteries and historical monuments we visited, some wonder had occurred. Maybe a martyrdom or a sermon. Maybe a last supper. A birth or death or resurrection or ascension. A wrestling with the devil. This literalism bored us. It deadened everything. By the time we crossed from Israel into the wilderness of the Sinai Desert, our capacity for wonder was severely frayed. The blankness, the emptiness all around us, came as a relief.

As we drove across the bottom of what was once an ancient ocean, we stared out the open windows at pale sandstone formations, some crouched on the desert floor like sphinxes, others lying like fallen temples. Some of the red stone hills in the distance seemed chiseled and carved like friezes. Others were round, as if turned on a potter's wheel. But sphinxes, temples, and friezes are just similes; *like* or *as*. In reality, there were no monuments here trying to stay the passage of time. No monuments marking anything at all. And in this vast desert, we seemed to be the only breathing, moving things picking their way across its surface. *Landscape with Mother and Daughter. Landscape with Abyss.*

It's a motley crew that is traveling south toward Mount Sinai in September of 1483 with their Saracen guide, Elphahallo. All in all, Fabri counts forty persons in this caravan, along with twenty-five camels and thirty asses. The pilgrims—nobility; clergy; knights; Conrad, who is lute player, barber, and manciple in one; a printmaker from Utrecht; "two poor German Jews" hired to help with the cooking—are all divided into three companies, each assigned its own pavilion-like tent to guard against the heat of the sun.

It will take the pilgrims almost two weeks to traverse the desert to Mount Sinai and the walled monastery there. Two weeks at just over two miles an hour for twenty-five, twenty-six miles a day. Twelve hours, from well before sunrise until late afternoon spent on the march. And this in a season of drought, when the summer's heat has parched what grazing grounds exist, when the water holes have nearly all run dry.

Day by day, as the pilgrims move farther into the desert wilderness, the pitilessness of the terrain, their own relentless thirst, the breadth of the endless waste take hold. "In these plains we saw neither men nor beasts, neither villages, houses, trees, grass, nor bushes, but only the sandy earth, parched by the sun's heat," Fabri writes. One afternoon, they enter a land of swelling hills. In the valley between them, the travelers pitch their tents. The camel drivers head off with jars and water skins to fetch fresh water from a cistern while the pilgrims spread out in search of firewood. They find only dry bushes—*seneh,* after which the Sinai may be named— which they pull up by the roots.

"This place was called in Arabic *Chawatha,* and here we found many proofs that once human dwellings had stood there," Fabri writes, "for we found above us twelve great ancient walled cisterns, round about which lay many broken bricks, broken pots, and ashes from smiths' forges. . . . In the cisterns we saw the dead bodies of great and terrible serpents, and of animals unknown to us." On the morning of the twelfth, they load the camels early, before daylight, and depart from Chawatha together in the dark.

That first evening, we stayed at Ein Khudra Oasis, managed by the Muzena Bedouin, one of the seven South Sinai tribes and the one that Sheikh Swelam belongs to. The Muzena have set up Ein Khudra for tourists, though that word associated with this place does not fit, conjuring as it does hordes of fanny packs and rolling suitcases. We descended on foot through sand—*sandy road, the road winding above among the mountains which are mountains of rock without water.* From the plateau, we could look down on the green palm trees fed by an underground spring, where we were headed. The sun was sinking behind a red ridge bordering the oasis.

All the Comforts of Home and More, a hand-painted sign pro-claimed at the entrance to the camp. Which was true, I suppose, if your home included a pit latrine. But we were grateful for that latrine, and for the open-air huts, their supporting columns made of palm tree trunks, their plywood roofs overlaid with palm branches, their walls hung with immense swaths of striped fabric. Over the sand, layers and layers of woven rag rugs were strewn with pillows and cushions in dingy florals. Throughout the oasis clustered eucalyptus and acacia trees and trees of palm and pome-granate and olive. For some reason I could not fathom, a purple sequined dress hung from a peg in one of the columns. It was all quite cozy, in its way.

As Ellie and I settled into a corner, unloading our backpacks, laying out our sleeping bags, we noticed a little girl with black hair sitting forlornly in front of a rug laid with cheap jewelry. "Come see?" she asked, but we were tired and did not want to be reminded of the corrupt world of spending and buying and trinkets and clut-ter out here in the desert purified by the sun. "Come see?" she asked, but we could not. By dinner she was gone.

Why did it not occur to me at the time that this girl had perhaps been sitting there waiting for us for hours? That there were no other tourists she could hope for? That we were it? Why hadn't I just bought a little something? Why had I chosen to take a stand against consumption with this little girl, who could have been my own daughter, could have been Mary Martha or Sabine in that other world far away? When she returned home empty-handed, what did she say to whoever had sent her off to sell cheap baubles to the Americans? Was she okay?

Most Bedouin of the Sinai, as well as of the Negev we'd passed over to get here, are the descendants of nomadic tribesman who, beginning in the fourteenth century, migrated westward from the

Arabian Peninsula over the course of hundreds of years. Sheltered by tents, riding camels, wandering over the barren land in search of pasture and water for their flocks of fat-tailed sheep and black goats, the Bedouin lived much as their ancestors in the eastern deserts for four thousand years had, and their values continue to reflect that which is essential for survival in this landscape: hospitality to guests and travelers, unswerving allegiance to one another within the tribe, revenge when peace or honor is violated. Until the middle of the twentieth century, the Sinai Bedouin had little contact with the outside world, and what interaction they did have came most often from conducting pilgrims across the desert— Muslim pilgrims in caravans from Cairo east to Mecca along the Darb al-Hajj, the Pilgrimage Road; Christian pilgrims from Cairo and Jerusalem south to Mount Sinai and Saint Catherine's. Supplying camels and other provisions and services to the pilgrim caravans brought in welcome income for the Bedouin, so much so that in 1884, when the newly established British rulers of Egypt effectively closed off the Darb al-Hajj by transporting pilgrims down the Red Sea toward Mecca in British steamships instead, rebellion was whispered among the Sinai tribes.

The Arab-Israeli War of 1948—the *nakbah* for Palestinians— was the real turning point, though, says Clinton Bailey, an American-born Israeli scholar and the foremost expert on the Bedouin of the Sinai and the Negev. He lived among the Bedouin on and off for two decades and documented their culture as it was beginning to be irrevocably extinguished. The war in 1948 forced the flight of the vast majority of Negev Bedouin to the Gaza Strip, the West Bank, Transjordan, and Sinai. In the Sinai Peninsula itself, modernization accelerated after the Six-Day War, during Israel's fifteen-year occupation between 1967 and 1982. The highway that Israel built along the southeastern coast opened up the region to tourism and contact with Westerners.

When Egypt resumed control of the Sinai, the government tried to settle the Bedouin and develop the area economically. "Modern times have broken into the ancient sanctuary of the desert, with motor vehicles, highways, radios, schools, and nontraditional lifestyles and an opportunity to obtain them," Bailey laments in his book *Bedouin Poetry from Sinai and the Negev.* Some Bedouin want to preserve their nomadic lifestyle, but they find that difficult to do under the political powers that now control the land, land that for thousands of years had been theirs. "These governments want the Bedouin settled," Bailey explains, "so that they can lay claim to the desert vastness and control a population that traditionally evaded effective supervision through dispersion and mobility.... The Bedouin have ceased to be masters of their own deserts and destinies."

Did Sheikh Swelam and the little girl selling trinkets view Ellie and me as bringing sustaining income to them and the other Bedouin of South Sinai, like pilgrims over the centuries before us? Or were we, with our backpacks filled with Gap clothes and Colgate toothpaste and novels of the Western canon, signs of the end of their way of life? Probably we were something in between.

I have implied there were no tourists out here. But as Ellie and I settled into our corner of the open-air palm-tree hut in Ein Khudra Oasis, and as Sheikh Swelam and Mohammad unloaded the jeep, a large man in safari attire—olive-drab Bermuda shorts and a khaki shirt with lots of pockets—and his preteen son materialized, following a young and muscular Egyptian, their guide, as it would turn out, and a thin man with a mustache and a machine gun. "Security," Mohammad told us confidentially.

In the dry evening breeze, Ellie lay on her sleeping bag and read *Moby-Dick,* in which Ishmael wanders over the sea, which is another desert wilderness of spiritual longing. From time to time, she flicked the flea-ridden kittens roaming the camp off her legs. She seemed to be quietly distressed and trying hard to contain herself. We hardly spoke, but I could see that another deeper silence was settling in her. Just like our capacity for wonder, this nomadic existence we'd been living for almost two months now was wearing thin. Even more so for her, who was in control of nothing, than for me. Ellie was not on a spiritual quest. She missed her boyfriend and her life at school. Her iPod had died; she'd had to go to the bathroom in the sand; and the little bit of Arabic she'd learned the year before was turning out to be of no use. When, for example, would you need the word *milk* in the desert? And how rude you would sound if, knowing no niceties to soften things, you blurted, *"Ana areed akul dajage"*—"I want to eat chicken."

I did not know how to help Ellie now that we were out here in the Sinai, utterly dependent on these strangers whose language, spoken and unspoken, we could not understand. I felt a little guilty. I also felt she might distract me from whatever revelation surely was at hand. But I mostly felt a profound need to protect her, which I tried to do by being exceedingly polite to our hosts and guides, providing cover for her so that she could collapse, my excessive and unnatural cheerfulness a diversion, a shield.

That evening, I sat beside her on my sleeping bag laid down over the rag rugs covering the sand and tried to text Terry about "Security" striding through our camp with a machine gun and about Ellie collapsing and about me wandering through the dreamscape in which I couldn't really tell anymore if I missed him. Had I known that just afterward, my phone would cut out and that this would be the last he'd hear from me until we arrived at Saint Catherine's and that he would be paralyzed for days with doubt and grief, I would never have sent it. The separation we'd felt in Jerusalem had widened, but for different reasons for each of us. For me, memories of my life at home were receding into the elemental sand and stone of the immeasurable desert. I felt a helplessness before that loss, even if I knew it was only temporary. But I think for Terry, my disappearance must have felt concrete. There were the places my body used to be—the counter where I stood in the morning reading the paper, making coffee, stretching; the chair near the window in the sunroom where I liked to read. He could see with his own eyes the absence. It must have felt to him the way I had imagined it before our departure: as my own afterlife, the days in that particular place coming and going without me in them. Actually, I wonder now if we were both feeling the same thing after all, irrational as it might have been: the impossibility that I'd ever come back.

The breeze cooled and the sun set. We ate dinner—chicken, bone in, with peas in tomato sauce over rice—sitting at low tables lit by candles stuffed in plastic water bottles with their tops cut off and weighted with sand. The bottles kept melting in the heat. After dinner, Sheikh Swelam brought out a plate of watermelon and we ate the slices, spitting the seeds in the sand. My mind drifted back to the jeep ride that morning. Before turning inland to the desert, we had driven along the coast of the Red Sea, on that highway built by the Israelis, to Nuweiba. On the road, we passed a woman, veiled in black with a shift of blue beneath, walking alongside a donkey pulling a cart piled with scrap wood. In the distance, beside the sea, was a high-end tourist camp halted midconstruction—domes and inverted arches and towers, like a deserted village or a city abandoned long ago. Across the road stood a cluster of EU-built housing for the Bedouin—cement-block homes painted white and trimmed in blue.

As we drove, Mohammad told us that we could talk about anything with him—politics, religion. He said that he always talked openly. That Mubarak thought the people were afraid, but Mohammad and the people in Cairo were not afraid. Mohammad had green eyes that frightened me a little, though I couldn't say why. He had been in Tahrir Square. I had to trust him, because there was no one else, so I did.

In Nuweiba we'd picked up supplies and were served sweet tea in small plastic cups as we sat in the back of the jeep while goats milled around in the hard-packed street behind us. There are those who believe that the actual Mount Sinai is in Arabia and that the beach at Nuweiba is where God parted the waters of the Red Sea so that the Israelites could escape their enslavement and get to the Promised Land. Here, they say, the Egyptians and their pharaoh were swallowed up as God's hand smoothed back the waters over the part He had made. "For the horse of Pharaoh went in with his chariots and with his horsemen into the sea, and the Lord brought again the waters of the sea upon them" goes the song of praise for this act of mercy and triumph, "but the children of Israel went on dry land in the midst of the sea."

Security, Mohammad told us, was a member of the Egyptian police, and after dinner, as we sat at the low tables and the darkness enveloped us and the candles could do nothing to stop it with their fragile, spare light, Mohammad tried to convince him that the police force of one million could not compete against a population of eight million. Then Mohammad turned to me and Ellie and told us a story from Tahrir. A policeman shot at the people protesting until his clip ran out. Then the people put him in a box and set him on fire. When I cringed in horror, Mohammad looked at me with those clear green eyes and said, "I want to explain something. When the volcano erupts, it cannot control where it flows and who it washes over." As the men continued talking, I looked at Ellie through the darkness, willing her to be soothed by my eyes.

All night long as I lay in my sleeping bag on the rugs in the sand, the diseased and hungry kittens that prowled through the camp kept trying to nestle near my feet, and I kept shooing them away. I remembered camping with Terry and the girls in the canyon lands of the American West, of which this landscape reminded me, both being the bottom of a primeval sea. Once, in the Black Hills of South Dakota, the air so hot and still when we'd tried to sleep, I'd rubbed my daughters' small bodies with a cool wet rag, and we'd lain there all of us in the tent together, too hot to touch. Sometime in the night, a windstorm had stirred the air and dragged itself through the canyon, our tent breathing in and out like a lung, and us inside it.

All night long at Ein Khudra, I could hear the wind coming in through the canyon from a long way off, rolling toward us and washing over us like a flood, like lava, like the desert darkness, like the waters of the Red Sea.

WHAT THE DESERT SAID

MID-SEPTEMBER 1483. The pilgrims have crossed a sandy delta and entered a wilderness Fabri calls Hachseve. They are looking for water. Their guide had given them a choice: travel one wadi for three days in peace but without the possibility of wells or take another wadi and hope to find water at a well that he knows exists. But even if they were to find the well and there was water in it, Elphahallo warned, it might be guarded by Bedouin who would refuse them access. The pilgrims decided on the latter course nevertheless.

So now, as if entering a circle in Dante's *Inferno,* the pilgrims have come to a congregation of tents leaning together on a wide plain, with fires burning here and there, and beasts and men passing back and forth. The pilgrims "tremblingly went down towards them, and they, when they saw us, stood at their tent-doors awaiting us, with spears in their hands." When the pilgrims are about a stone's throw from the tents, they pitch their own and unload their camels. Children, "naked and black, scorched by the heat of the sun, ran up to us," Fabri recalls, "and to them we straightway gave biscuits, which they received with great joy, and went back to their tents." After these children come more children, and then women, some pregnant, others with babies in their arms. "By so doing we turned the hearts of these Arabs," Fabri proclaims, "who asked us to come and get water for ourselves and our beasts, and we filled our water-skins and jars without the slightest hindrance, a thing which we had never hoped to do."

For three hours, the pilgrims remain there at the well and make merry with the Bedouin. They run races together and lift great stones. The knights dance with the young men upon the plain. Finally, the pilgrims load their camels again, but as they are about to depart, they call an elder of these people to them and bestow upon him a ducat, "because he had dealt so peaceably with us." The elder receives the offering with great respect. At sunset, they enter the wilderness called Minschene, the stones white as if the land had been burned like lime. They gather dried camel dung, fuel for a fire.

In the morning, they will enter the region of Wadi el-Arish, which Fabri calls Larich. On their right will rise mountains of exceeding whiteness; on their left, an expanse of black stone and sand, "scorched as though a fire had lately burned everything that would burn therein." Fabri will imagine: "The boundary of these plains is said to be near the mountains of the earthly paradise, and therefore the flashings of the fiery sword, which the Lord has placed before the entrance to paradise, has scorched these plains and forbids all approach."

Though the days of camel caravans, like the days of miracles, are over, I had insisted on riding camels in the desert. So Sheikh Swelam arranged for us to ride one afternoon. In a Bedouin encampment, we ate lunch and drank tea with the driver sitting on rugs in a reed arbor attached to a small stone hut. From the ceiling of the arbor hung a sheepskin bag, head and hooves still attached, filled with tea and other supplies. The sheep hung upside down by its legs, near a single lightbulb.

The sheikh wrapped Ellie's scarf around her head like the Bedouin do, and she wore the striped harem pants she'd bought at Mahane Yehuda Market in Jerusalem, where we'd gone with Carol Ann. We mounted the kneeling camels, decked out in brightly woven rugs beneath their saddles, and the driver prodded them to stand. I felt myself lurching perilously forward and then wrenched back as my camel lumbered up, hind legs first, out of the sand. But once we were launched, I found the pitching and swaying almost rhythmic, and I remembered vaguely something I'd heard once about the connection between the gait of a camel and a certain kind of desert song.

Often we paused to let the camels graze on clumps of spiny grasses, their heads on their necks moving periscopically, their gaze, like their chewing, ruminative. We passed through the detritus of an abandoned Bedouin camp: nylon fencing, wood scraps, oil drums, empty and tattered rice bags. Later we saw acacia trees tied with bits of fading fabric, precarious stacks of flat stones. "Signs," said Mohammad, though of what he did not say. Of the presence of humans? The way through the desert? Portents of the divine? We tried to read the engravings on the desert walls— camels and goats scratched into the sandstone surface, strange rows of vertical lines, fragments of Arabic nearly worn away: *Bismillahir Rahmanir Rahim.* "'In the name of Allah, the Most Beneficent, the most Merciful,'" Ellie translated—the only lines she could recognize.

Another day, we came across a wizened elderly sheikh and his plump younger wife in the shadow of a rock formation, the shade like the curve of the lunule of a fingernail. They sat on a rug beside their jeep. As we pulled up, the woman covered her head. Over a small fire, she made us sweet tea in a tin vegetable can rinsed clean, then poured the tea into two small, clear glasses. Later, when the glasses were rinsed and refilled for Sheikh Swelam and Mohammad, and again for the sullen son, I realized that these were the only ones they had. While Sheikh Swelam and the couple talked,

Ellie and I looked out together on the endless floor of the former sea, lined by bisque-colored buttes and mesas, sky and sky
and sky. Mohammad said the couple were speaking together with
Sheikh Swelam in an older Arabic, one brought by their ancestors
when these desert nomads came, like Abraham, with their camels
and goats and their wool tents and woven rugs from Arabia centuries ago. In some unfathomable way, that ancient tongue they
spoke seemed connected to the faded etchings on the walls of the
canyons.

I am a teacher of literature. Ellie is an English major. Our job
is interpretation. But though I had come here hoping for insight,
hoping for meaning, I could read nothing properly in the desert.
And many situations I thought I understood, I totally misread. For
Fabri, there was a land beneath this landscape, described in scripture, that gave the surface he passed over meaning. He could read
that surface all the way to God. The crust of the earth might be
scabbed and scorched, but it would lead to a paradise guarded by
flaming swords. I could not penetrate the surface. Sand was sand
was sand. I felt like one of the children of Israel of whom pharaoh
said, "They are entangled in the land, and the wilderness hath shut
them in."

I could not read the marks on the desert walls, I could not
read the landscape, I could not read the people. One afternoon,
somewhere in Wadi Zalaka, the sun's descent smearing the shadows of tamarisk shrubs across the russet dust, we spotted a cluster
of camels, two nursing babies and their mothers. Sheikh Swelam
stopped the jeep so that Ellie and I could get out and take some
photos. In the shade of a tamarisk sat two Bedouin men, one
young, one old, wearing skullcaps and pale djellabas and looped
cloths around their necks. Sheikh Swelam squatted in the shade
with them and smoked while we stared at the gangly camel calves
staring at us and then suckling from their hobbled mothers' teats.

The tenseness and exhaustion Ellie and I had been feeling, over-whelmed by the vastness of the desert, dissipated. I smiled at her smiling and cooing at the camels. I remembered when the girls were little and I would take them to the petting zoo.

When Sheikh Swelam rose to leave, I tried to gesture from afar a thank-you: hands clasped in gratitude. The old man, whose eyes I could now see were bleary from cataracts, motioned for me to come to him, I supposed to tell me good-bye, to wish us a safe journey— desert hospitality. I asked Mohammad to come with me so that he could translate my thanks. But when we stood before him, the old man didn't look at me with his cloudy eyes. Instead he said some-thing harshly to Mohammad. He wanted money, not pleasantries. This was no petting zoo.

A more dangerous misinterpretation was this: In the villages we would stop at, on the sides of some of the flat-roofed cinder-block houses, were certain paintings: Arabic script, an airplane, a black building, its base surrounded by black carets, which seemed to stand for flames. This, of course, could be referring to only one thing: the destruction of the World Trade Center towers on September 11, 2001. Were the people whose houses these were re-joicing at that terrible destruction?

But as we stood beside one of these cinder-block structures, I finally asked Mohammad to translate the pictures for us, and he explained that they were depictions of the pilgrimage to Mecca. The black building was the Kaaba built by Abraham and Isaac, the most sacred site in Islam, and the holy place toward which all Muslims everywhere turn five times each day to pray. The plane had flown the person who lived in the home to Saudi Arabia. The carets were pilgrims performing the hajj—pilgrims like us, bent in prayer, submitting to the will of God.

*   *   *

September 18, 1483. Departing from the wilderness of Meschmar and the Catachrysia Mountains, the pilgrims see, to the right, mountains white as though covered with snow; to the left, mountains red as though dyed with blood. As the pilgrims descend down onto a wide plain, leaves on the shrubs appear wet with dew. One pilgrim tears off a bough and puts it to his mouth, but the water tastes sharp with salt. "Thus we learned by experience that this is the 'salt land' spoken of by Jeremiah (xvii. 6) where God saith unto the sinner that he shall be like the heath in the desert, which has bitter leaves covered with salt dew," remembers Fabri.

Out of a thirst now physical, not spiritual, the pilgrims open up the jars they'd filled back in Gaza for times of need such as these. But the water is putrid. Not even the asses will drink it. So they continue on. "If there were water we should stop and drink," says the traveler in *The Waste Land*. "Amongst the rock one cannot stop or think. Sweat is dry and feet are in the sand."

They come into a flat plain where, at a crossing of the Darb al-Hajj, the Pilgrim's Road that leads to Mecca, they meet a caravan of merchants with their long filament of camels behind them bringing spices and wares from the Red Sea, possibly from Tor on the coast, northeast through the desert to Palestine. "These men had been for many days without water, and importunately entreated us to give at least one draught of water to each of them, because they were just at the point of fainting," Fabri writes. "So we gave them what was left of our water, because we were to come to some marshes before evening."

At last the pilgrims reach the verge of a deep wadi lined on either side by sheer walls of rock, "so deep and narrow a gulf, that to look down into it struck us with horror." They leave the beasts at the top of the mesa and clamber down the rocks to the valley below, where they find water in the fissures and clefts left over from the rainy season, when the wadi had run full. The water is warm, thick, bituminous. It's green and muddy, full of worms. But the pilgrims are so thirsty that they fall upon their bellies and gather the water with their hands and drink greedily. After they've had their fill, they strain the water through cloths and fill empty jars and water skins and wash their bodies and their clothes. They sit in the shade of the caves carved out by the water and lined by willows. That evening, they make a fire in the valley and cook their food with great rejoicing.

In the desert, time slowed and stretched, or maybe condensed, thickening like a reduction in which all excess is boiled away. Or perhaps that is only how it was in my mind, or now, in my memory of it. In the mornings, Sheikh Swelam, a cigarette dangling from his lips, makes milky Nescafé over a fire of a few twigs, washing out the clear glasses with a swill of water, elegantly whirling and rubbing with his thumb at the same time. We sit on the rugs from the jeep in silence, eating flatbread and soft white cheese and jam. Then all day we drive the wadis, me sitting in the front seat with Sheikh Swelam so that Ellie can lie down in the back and read. To her, the desert is all the same and she just wants it to end. We stop from time to time at one Bedouin camp or another, where we drink tea and Sheikh Swelam and Mohammad smoke cigarettes with men possessed of piercing eyes and stained teeth. Later, in the shade of an acacia tree or a sandstone cliff, lunch and a rest. Then we drive on.

Every now and then, Sheikh Swelam veers off the wadi to a well he remembers, and he fills the water jugs, protected by cloth covers embroidered by the women—distant figures always around corners where we can't see them, or against the hills in black shawls and long black robes, young children on their hips, surrounded by shaggy goats. At the wells, Ellie and I bend over while Sheikh Swelam pours the cold water down our necks, wetting our hair, keeping us cool in the intense desert heat, heat like a kiln, heat without relief. Later in the afternoon, when he spots a band of shrubs in the parched riverbeds, we get out of the jeep and, like the medieval pilgrims, gather dried branches of the desert bushes to burn. Toward evening, in a gully or at an oasis, Mohammad and the sheikh and his wordless son pull out the sleeping bags and the food and the pots and plates, and while Ellie and I try to find a hidden place to wash the desert sand out of the pores of our faces, they cook for us—chicken and vegetables, flatbread, a thick fava-bean stew. We fall asleep beneath the stars as the fire dies down. No voice calls out from the midst of the burning.

Back in the late afternoon of the fourteenth of September, the pilgrims had entered a region Fabri called Magareth near some low mountains. There they pitched their tents in the sandy soil and gathered firewood with which to cook. Fabri thought he saw, at the top of one of these mountains, nearby, or so it seemed, some kind of building. Desiring to climb this mountain to investigate and see the wilderness from above, and knowing no one else would dare to join him, he gathered his courage and left the company alone, as if he were going off to pray.

It was a full hour's walk before he arrived at the base of the mountain, and it was both farther from the camp and higher than he had imagined. He pulled himself up the steep cliffs and over boulders, only to find, when he arrived at the top, a great cairn of stones and nothing more. "I stood still there and looked round about me," Fabri recalled,

> but could see nothing anywhere save a boundless wilderness, broken up by mountains, hills, and torrent-beds, wherein dwelt neither men, birds, nor beasts. I could not see our tents, because they were far away; but I saw mountains, both white

and black, and all the surface of the earth scorched by the sun's heat. I did not see any green thing, either great or small; but the curse of barrenness lay upon the land. The heap of stones on the mountain-top was a mark to point out the road, for everywhere throughout the wilderness there are piles of stones which show through which valleys men ought to go.

In a panic, and with night coming on, he descended, hoping to find his footprints, which he did, and he followed them over mounds and swellings until they disappeared, blotted out by the roving sand. Furious with himself, reproaching himself for his curiosity and presumption, fearing he was lost to all, he began to sing the penitential psalm Domine Exaudi:

Lord hear my prayer:
may my cry come to you.
Turn not your face away from me:
on whatever day I may be troubled,
incline your ear to me.
On whatever day I may call your name,
heed me swiftly.

Over and over again he sang this psalm, wandering, not knowing where he was going, until at last, on the side of a dune, he caught sight of his own footprints again. When he looked up, he saw that far off, something white rose from the ground, and from that distance he guessed it to be three Saracens or Arabs in their light desert garb. But as he drew closer he found to his profound relief that in fact these were the three pavilion-like tents for which the pilgrims had contracted back in Jerusalem.

* * *

I never knew where I was in the desert. As we passed from wadi to wadi, I wrote down their names in my notebook: Wadi Razala, Wadi Lathi, Wadi Watir. But without a map to pin them to, the names meant nothing. Lunch one day beneath a gnarled acacia tree, the only shade to be found. Tomatoes and cucumbers, canned tuna with chopped onions, white cheese, tea, unleavened bread. The only sounds: flies, the wind. Ellie and I lay on mats beneath the delicate leaves of the acacia and read. The son slept in the jeep. Sheikh Swelam and Mohammad smoked. I asked the sheikh where we were, and with a stick, he drew a map in the dirt of where we'd been, one wadi branching off into another like a bare tree in winter. Looking out across the expanse of sand and scrub, he told me he could travel this land day or night. "Everything I have in here," he said, tapping his head.

That evening we camped in a ravine, at the point where two wadis meet, one flowing to the Gulf of Suez, the other to the Gulf of Aqaba, a tipping point, a cusp of earth. As our guides unloaded the jeep and set up camp, Ellie and I wandered along this sandy rift in the late light of day, relieved to be free of the jouncing. The illuminated walls of the ravine protected us, like the walls of water on either side of the Israelites as they traversed the dry bed of the parted sea.

"I'm really feeling sad today," I confessed to Ellie as we kicked through the sand. "I feel so far away from home in a way that sort of frightens me." But I couldn't make my words convey the profundity of my emotion, born of our inaccessibility, the remoteness of this place. It seemed possible, in that moment of acute isolation, that I might never see the faces of those dear to me again, God being as impartial as this land to our reunion. It reminded me of how I'd felt in the days just before Ellie's birth. "It all seems so unreal— as if it's not really happening to me. As if it's never going to happen," I'd written in my notebook.

"It'll be okay, Mom," replied Ellie, who had been born after all, her very palpable hand now on my shoulder. "We'll be at Saint Catherine's soon and we can call them." We walked on in silence in the coppery light. I didn't want to stop. I didn't want to go back to the jeep and the men who did not speak our private language, who could not interpret the words beneath the words.

During dinner, cooked over the small fire pit fueled by splinters of *seneh* we'd collected that afternoon, Sheikh Swelam pointed to the Milky Way far south of us and said that when it was centered over the southern sky, then the fruit of the date palms was most sweet. After the dishes had been washed, and the others had closed their eyes, I lay in the dark looking up at the sky, remembering those nights after Ellie was born as she lay beside me in the white iron bed and I imagined my own annihilation in the dark abyss of death. Here in the desert beside her, I again felt microscopic, mitochondrial in the vastness.

I have said no voice called out to us from the midst of the burning fire, and that sand, in this impartial place, was only sand. But sometime in the night, I woke up in the darkness, shivering in the dry desert air. The fire had turned to cold ash, and the whole world had stilled, as if it were holding its breath, waiting for a revelation. Maybe it was only the chill that sharpened my mind, or maybe it was the divine nudging me awake so that I might see, but I opened my eyes that night to the clarity of the stars, so near my face and bright that it seemed a universe of light was trying to press itself through the curved veil of dark sky above me. I was not so much looking *at* things as looking *through* them to something beyond. The turning Earth had carried the Milky Way straight above us by this motionless hour, and, for a moment, I saw the sky as a topographical map of another world, the white, ridged cloud of the Milky Way like a chain of mountains, and the countless stars like the towns and villages and cities of a country I didn't know. I imagined that other world, gazing out at us, the desert I inhabited its firmament, any living creature there looking up in wonder at us lying in these heavens of sand. *How much is hidden,* I thought, *by the deceptive light of day. How little we actually see of what exists.*

But in the cold illumination of the morning, as Sheikh Swelam washed his face and lit a fire, it seemed again that the days of revelation might be over. That there are only, if we are lucky, small moments of clarity that open something in us amid the clamor and confusion. And then the void closes up like a wound, the ache only vaguely remembered.

The Bedouin, though largely illiterate, have a history that stretches back beyond recorded time of composing poems mentally, of reciting them, of singing them together. In his book *Bedouin Poetry,* Clinton Bailey recalls hearing a young chief of the Muzena tribe recite twenty poems, called *gasid* (singular *gasida*). "It was on this occasion [in November 1968] that I discovered the bedouin [*sic*] love of poetry and witnessed a scene, often to be repeated, of men, women, and children spontaneously gathering around the reciter in a semicircle on the ground, row upon row, listening intensely, repeating after him the monorhymes with which he unexpectedly ended the successive lines, and laughing at ironical, poetic depictions from the otherwise humdrum events of desert life."

While I scribbled notes furiously in my notebook, Sheikh Swelam had told me that he kept everything in his head. Bedouin poets do too. Bailey asked one poet, Jum'a 'Id Dakhilallah, how he composed, and the poet recalled the night he had made a *gasida* after being overturned in his felucca boat at sea. Since he was soaking wet, he changed his clothes, then made a fire and, over the fire, tea. He sat quietly, thinking about the danger he'd been in, how lucky he was not to have died. For perhaps two or three hours he sat there drinking tea and remembering. Then "I gathered up words from here and there and pressed them together, and I made a poem...I was alone."

These poems, composed and memorized and transmitted by wandering nomads as they traveled the desert, capture, as poems always do, glints and fragments of the concrete lives from which they spring—a murdered boy's father seeks vengeance; a traveler praises a hearty meal he is given in a desert tent; another is denied any welcome; a herder of camels falls in love with a girl at a well; a woman mourns a husband killed in a raid; a father mourns a daughter killed by a snake; a jailed smuggler longs for home and tea over a fire.

But beyond these glimpses of life, *gasid* also allow for the expression of certain emotions that are taboo in daily conversation. "A bedouin man, for example, rarely discusses his amorous yearnings, exploits, or frustrations, even with an intimate friend," Bailey explains, "any more than he would cry or tear his clothes at a funeral—demonstrations of grief left to the domain of women, when they visit their burial-grounds alone. If bedouin men wish to express emotions such as longing, love, grief, or despair, it is mainly in the form of a poem."

I couldn't get Sheikh Swelam to talk about anything personal. "What does he love about the desert?" I implored Mohammad to ask him one night by the light of the fire. "The silence," he replied. Perhaps ironically. So I tried, instead, to intuit what he would not say from the concrete. For example: Somewhere in Wadi Zalaka, Sheikh Swelam stopped the jeep beside a wall of stone, slightly concave, and told us how he had come here many times in winter, during the rains, and made a fire and watched the torrents fall, safely sheltered. I imagined him sitting there looking out through the bands of rain and wondered what he thought about. A woman? His children? A memory from his childhood? Only once did Sheikh Swelam reveal something to me of his internal life. That day we'd stopped for lunch beneath the acacia tree, as we sat sipping tea, he looked out on the barren land and said that here would be a good place to end your life, in this silence. Silence, which I took to mean peace.

"Everything I have in here," Sheikh Swelam had said, like one of the ancient bards who sang from memory of love and home and longing. How lightly the Bedouin travel, how little they carry, how few marks they make. Everywhere on this trip, Ellie and I had seen monuments built by human hands to commemorate and remember. Even Fabri's account was a shrine of memory, his experiences encased in words. *I never passed one single day while I was on my travels without writing some notes,* he had recorded at the outset, *not even when I was at sea, in storms, or in the Holy Land; and in the desert I have frequently written as I sat on an ass or a camel; or at night, while the others were asleep, I would sit and put into writing what I had seen.*

I had wanted to write it all down too in words that others could understand. This attempt to pluck ephemera from the flux of experience and pin them in words is also, like the building of monuments, the marking out of sacred space. It encloses the past, removes it from time, and tries to keep it alive in its own private Eden. The grief I'd felt in the Church of Saint Anne in Jerusalem was for the uselessness of this endeavor.

The Lord says to Moses on the holy mountain in the parched desert that He wants an earthen altar that will wash away, not an altar of hewn stone. In the Sinai Peninsula over which my daughter and I wandered, I saw that the only monument is the desert itself, and what's remembered is only in the mind. A few marks on the rock walls, a few stacks of stones, bright rags tied in trees. The Bedouin who inhabit this precarious land seem to recognize of necessity how flimsy are the things made, how soon they will pass away. And this recognition is, it seemed to me as we drove over the impenetrable surface of it, a humble submission to this essential fact of human existence: our fragility in this transitory world. To surrender myself to this fact, too, was the only possible cure for what I'd been seeking.

After every meal, Sheikh Swelam would scrape the plastic plates clean, wash them with water from the jugs we carried in the jeep, then throw what couldn't be saved into the fire. The scrapings he would leave on a flat stone for the desert animals.

This is what the desert said: Carry only what you need. Burn what can't be saved. Leave the remnants as an offering.

TRANSLATIONS

THE CLOSER WE got to Mount Sinai and Saint Catherine's Monastery, the end point of Fabri's pilgrimage, if not of his journey, the more impossible it seemed to Ellie and me that we'd ever get home again. Though, like the relics of saints, we were being translated, carried over, borne across the desert, we seemed to hover, lost in that unbridgeable space between where we were in body, a place whose customs and language we did not understand, and where we longed to be, which was the place we knew.

I had decided that when we got to Saint Catherine's and to some kind of Internet access, I would find a way to get us home a week early, even if it meant paying expensive fees to change our flight. I could see what I needed to see in Cairo in a couple of days and then we would leave. Though I thought at first that I'd wait to tell Ellie until I had made all the arrangements, I confessed my plan to her to make it more real. But we wouldn't tell Terry or Mary Martha or Sabine. We'd surprise them. From that point on, our secret scheme began to sustain us, the thought of being back there with them rather than here alone.

We were homesick, a word that, I see now, looking in my *Oxford English Dictionary*, was originally a rendering of the German *Heimweh*, first noted in Keysler's *Travels Through Germany, Bohemia, Hungary, Switzerland, Italy, and Lorrain*, published in 1760. In a chapter on Switzerland and the Alps, Keysler describes how Switzers, raised in the mountains, finding themselves abroad "feel a kind of anxiety and an uneasy longing after the fresh air, to which they were accustomed from their infancy, without being able to account for such disquietude." This disquietude he names *Heimweh*; literally, "home-sickness."

Heimweh reminds me of *Wehmut,* the word Sabine Mahr used to describe the pain she felt on our parting back in gray Frankfurt a lifetime before. Homesick, sick at heart; *Heimweh, Wehmut*—both a kind of melancholic nostalgia.

That's what I felt. *Homesick* as in "nostalgic," which itself comes from the Greek—*nostos*, "a return home, a homecoming," and *algos,* "pain or ache." The *Nostoi,* sequel to the *Iliad*, the story of the Trojan War, is the epic poem, now lost to antiquity, of the disastrous attempts to return home of many of the Greek heroes who fought at Troy. The *Nostoi* is followed by the *Odyssey,* the story of Odysseus's wanderings and of his longing to get back to his homeland of Ithaca and to his wife and his son, a suckling child when he left, now a boy trying desperately to become a man. "[Odysseus's] eyes were perpetually wet with tears now, / His life draining away in homesickness," Homer says of the warrior trapped on Calypso's faraway island, hidden by the vast waters. "Days he spent sitting on the rocks by the breakers, / Staring out to sea with hollow, salt-rimmed eyes."

Usually I scorned nostalgia. Nostalgia was for the gauzy sentimentalists. But my nostalgia here in the desert felt different. It centered on lost particulars: Sabine sitting on the sandy quilt in Galveston in her pink bikini, eating Goldfish crackers with her pudgy fingers. Ellie calling the moon's craters "cradles." Mary Martha explaining to Sabine that when flowers die, they go up to the trees because that's their heaven. At a campground somewhere along the Oregon coast, Terry, holding a small flashlight in his mouth, setting up the tent in the dark while the girls sleep in the station wagon, and when he's done and we carry them, one by one, inside. One morning, waking up, Sabine between us, Terry and I catching each other's eye and just staring, not wanting to look away. In the Grand Canyon, Mary Martha waking me to go to the bathroom, and us on the path through the cypress, bright moon ahead, bright star behind, and us in perfect alignment between them.

I knew that back there, in that home for which I was longing, both the home of memory and the home of the present tense, there was also doubt and frustration and resentment and fighting. Wasted days when nothing got done but the laundry, if that. But to remember the particulars of the past was to rescue them from oblivion and imbue them with a lasting beauty, because, like shards in an archaeological dig, they'd been saved. Nostalgia was a weapon against meaninglessness.

That's what I love about Odysseus as he sits weeping on the shore of Calypso's island: He aches to return to the tangible, the mortal Penelope, the rocky Ithaca with its goats and grapevines and heavy dews. The perfection of the immortal Calypso bores him. So does immortality itself, a gift the goddess offers Odysseus but that he rejects for the wife and son and high-roofed hall of home that will one day pass away.

Later, having sailed away from Calypso on a raft of alder and poplar and fir and landed on the shores of another island, battered by the sea, Odysseus says to Nausicaa, the young woman who finds him naked, stripped bare of every hard-won possession,

> *And for yourself, may the gods grant you*
> *Your heart's desire, a husband and a home,*
> *And the blessing of a harmonious life.*
> *For nothing is greater or finer than this,*
> *When a man and woman live together*

With one heart and mind, bringing joy
To their friends and grief to their foes.

That harmonious life might be a distortion born out of nostalgia. But it's what saves Odysseus. That's what I missed with Terry. Someone sharing one heart and mind—*homophrosyne,* in the Greek. Someone like-minded. Someone for whom I didn't need to translate.

On our first night in the Sinai Desert, at Ein Khudra Oasis, pestered by the diseased kittens and the innumerable flies, Ellie had made a list of her fears:

1. Getting malaria.
2. Getting hepatitis.
3. Drinking the water.
4. Eating contaminated fruit.
5. Losing my gifts for other people.
6. Running out of soap.
7. Having to dig a hole in the desert to go to the bathroom.
8. Being bit by a snake.
9. Being bit by a camel.
10. Being bit by a rabid cat.
11. Getting lice.
12. Getting worms.
13. Riots breaking out and being unable to return home for months.
14. Being killed by a terrorist.
15. Dying in general.

Having to dig a hole in the desert to go to the bathroom was unavoidable, and we got used to it, the way we got used to arriving at a Bedouin encampment and there being nowhere for us half-dressed and unaccompanied females to sit except on the rug with the men drinking tea, who seemed to resent our intrusion even though we were Sheikh Swelam's guests. But Ellie's list seemed to articulate an *algos*, an ache that became an uneasiness that we felt more and more acutely the farther away from home that we drifted. Now that we were in what the Western media consistently referred to as the "lawless Sinai Peninsula," the kidnappings and the drug smuggling in the region, as well as the recent revolution and the rape of the blond journalist in Tahrir would pass through my mind more and more, and I'd think how vulnerable we were out here, no cell phones to call for help, no GPS implants for loved ones to track our moves. How easy it would be for us to just disappear, lost in translation.

Perhaps Ellie's list was a premonition, because things began to grow strange our last night in the desert. Or at least I think they did. It's still entirely possible that I simply didn't understand what was happening, and everything was perfectly fine. Late that afternoon we had pulled into a Bedouin settlement of cinder-block houses near the base of Jebel Serabit el-Khadim, where, Sheikh Swelam said, we had been invited to tea at the home of his sister. *Here,* I thought, *maybe I'll finally get a glimpse into the real lives of Bedouin women.* I imagined Mohammad translating back and forth between me and Sheikh Swelam's sister as we sipped tea and laughed at funny little cultural differences and bonded over how similar we were inside.

But when we arrived at the low, whitewashed structure and entered the courtyard formed by walls of the same cinder-block bricks, what we encountered was an impromptu marketplace and not the intimate welcome I had expected. Women and girls emerged from doorways hauling what turned out to be pillowcases full of cheap jewelry and beaded scarves, which they spread out on the ground and then held up, unsmilingly and forcefully, for us to see. I felt ambushed. And having hardly any cash, I felt panicked as well.

I looked desperately over at Sheikh Swelam, who was drinking tea with a woman I assumed was his sister though we had not been introduced. He seemed to be avoiding my eyes. I looked at Mohammad, but he told me only, "You don't need to buy anything. It is your choice." Ellie and I looked at each other. We both felt confused and betrayed. I knew that, being a white Westerner who lived in a two-story, three-bedroom air-conditioned house, probably a member of the 1 percent if extrapolated worldwide, I was supposed to feel sorry for these women and their children. But I felt used instead. Used and naive. Was this justified? Had Sheikh Swelam brought us here not for tea but so that the women in his clan could make a little money? And if he had, was that bad? Shouldn't I want to be magnanimous? Here was my chance to make up for ignoring the little girl in the campground our first night in the desert. I started to buy what I could—some coppery bangles for Mary Martha and Sabine, a bent-up silver cuff for myself, a Bedouin headdress for my niece like the one worn by the bride in the photo in the album at Basti's. I wanted to purchase something from everyone, but I ran out of Egyptian pounds before I could and I kept waving my empty hands, meaning "That is all," but this didn't seem to translate. Finally, Sheikh Swelam stood up abruptly, or so it seemed, and we left.

That night, in a deserted campground for tourists next to the Bedouin settlement, as Ellie and Mohammad and I lay on our sleeping bags around a small fire beneath the black sky, Sheikh Swelam having returned to the home of his sister, we got into a rambling conversation with Mohammad. He claimed, among other seemingly extremist notions, that the Palestinians were Arabs, and Arabs were not to be trusted. That they sold their land after the war in 1948 and could not now ask for it back. Also, speaking of backtracking, if you converted from Islam to Christianity, this was acceptable. But if you then wanted to return to Islam, you should be killed. "But why? Is this in the Qur'an?" I asked as Ellie looked on with disgust. And Mohammad quoted a pronouncement made by a caliph ages ago. "But I still don't understand why this is so problematic, if you realize you've changed your mind. It seems like Islam would want you to come back," I insisted. "I mean, what about mercy? What about forgiveness? Maybe you make a mistake, but if you realize it, and try to change, then you can be absolved." "This changing back and forth, it shows you have no conviction," Mohammad said. "But why do you have to be *killed?*" I asked. "Because"—he repeated his critique of Arabs and Palestinians— "you cannot be trusted."

The next day, nearing Saint Catherine's, we stopped at an oasis so Sheikh Swelam could prepare a final meal for us as we sat on woven rugs in the shade of a pavilion roofed with palm leaves. Mohammad told us, when he and the sheikh were unloading the jeep for lunch, that he needed to settle a problem with some acquaintances while we were here. His responses to me had been curt that day, and I didn't know if this was due to our discussion the evening before or the problem that needed settling. He claimed to have a headache. I offered him Advil. I just wanted to get to the monastery so I could call Terry. If I could hear his voice, I would know that the home for which I was so sick still existed. That it was not all a dream.

After lunch, Sheikh Swelam went off to pray and nap. Ellie and I sat in the shade, too restless to read or sleep. Mohammad spoke among the palm trees at some distance with two Bedouin in white, settling, I assumed, whatever problem was between them. A little while later he came over to the pavilion and invited me and Ellie to drive a short way to the home of one of the men to have tea prepared by the man's wife. Though I had resolved never to say no on this trip, I didn't quite want to go. I felt uneasy, though I couldn't articulate why. But because I couldn't explain my resistance to myself, I went.

Half an hour later, Ellie and I found ourselves looking nervously at each other as we careened down a two-lane asphalt road between the red mountains in the back of a beat-up Mercedes without working seat belts along with Mohammad, the two Bedouin in the front seat. The dash was decorated with fur. An evil eye with tassels swung frantically, dizzyingly from the rearview mirror. We arrived in the disheveled town whose name I never caught and pulled up to the home of the Bedouin driving the Mercedes—a big jocular guy. He kicked a mangy dog out of the way, which seemed unduly violent, and opened a gate in a chain-link fence. "Welcome," he said in English as we entered the main room of his house, painted minty green, its floor laid with a rust-colored rug and cushions. There was one small window and, though no furniture, a huge flat-screen TV.

The wife was there, but we only smiled at her in greeting and watched her disappear into what must have been the kitchen. Her husband emerged with a two-liter bottle of Coca-Cola and clear glasses on a silver tray. Other than the word *welcome,* neither of the Bedouin spoke English, so perhaps that is why the television was turned on—the lingua franca of this brave new world. As we sat against the wall on cushions sipping our room-temperature Cokes, the Bedouin whose home we were in kept flipping between channels—a soap opera in Arabic, an American B movie I didn't recognize, hypersexual music videos, still photos of Mubarak on the news, a mullah expounding upon what I assumed was a theological point. My instincts told me I really should leave, but I kept wondering if my instincts were right. Was I judging another culture through the lens of my own, making these hospitable Bedouin the Other? Was the tension I felt in Ellie's body as she sat close to me unjustified? Or was all this, in fact, really weird?

To try to relieve my uncertainty and turn our attention away from the scantily clad women gyrating to synthesized music on-screen, I asked Mohammad to ask the men if they knew any guides at Saint Catherine's, since I had read that the only way we could hike Mount Sinai would be with a local Bedouin. An intense discussion in Arabic ensued, and when it was over, Mohammad said that the Bedouin here, not our host but the other one, young and slight, would be our guide, and that we had been invited back to the house with the mint-green room and the flat-screen TV for lunch on the following day. We would be picked up from Saint Catherine's in the beat-up Mercedes, but Mohammad would have returned to Cairo by then, so it would be just me and Ellie and the man who kicked the dog and the wife we'd barely seen. Not one part of me wanted to say yes. *"Shokran,"* I said instead. "Thank you." Meaning *Please take my daughter and me safely to Saint Catherine's, after which I will make up an excuse to get out of this invitation,* although I don't think that translation was clear.

The rush of women and girls with their trinkets at the home of Sheikh Swelam's sister; Mohammad's unsettling comments as we lay on our sleeping bags; the fur-lined Mercedes and the flat-screen TV; Mohammad's insistence, as we drove the last length of the road to the monastery guesthouse, that I write a letter to Erez at Desert Eco Tours praising Mohammad (which I did, using a piece of lined paper torn from my notebook, because how could I refuse with him looking over my shoulder, literally)—my perspective on all of this might, it's true, have been influenced by what I found out after we arrived at Saint Catherine's and parted from Mohammad and Sheikh Swelam and the wiry, mute son. What I learned, once our backpacks were dropped on the beds of our first-floor room overlooking the monks' garden just outside the walled monastery fortress, and once our guides had driven away, and once Ellie and I were finally alone, was that Mohammad had tried to sell Ellie hash the previous night while I was washing up, just before he told us that converts to Islam had to be killed because they could not be trusted.

"I didn't even know what he was trying to sell me at first," Ellie told me. "I had obviously heard of hash, but I thought it was like heroin, and that totally freaked me out." I considered Ellie's naïveté a small victory against the particular world we inhabit. When I said this to Ellie, she pointed out that her gullibility could have led to the opposite outcome. "I could have thought hash was some kind of Middle Eastern candy." "What, like Turkish delight?" I asked and we laughed, trying to dispel the disquiet.

"Anyway, Mohammad started off by asking me if I partied, like if I was interested in that sort of thing," Ellie explained when I asked her to tell me exactly what had happened. "And I went through all these excuses to try to get him to drop it. But he kept insisting, and I didn't know what to do. First I said I would be afraid to carry it back on the plane, but he told me, 'You wouldn't have to take it back to the U.S. You could just do it here.' Then I said that I wouldn't want my mom to find out, and he said, 'She wouldn't have to know anything.'" That must have been about the time I returned from washing my face, and Mohammad said that changing back and forth shows you have no conviction.

I remembered then a moment somewhere in Wadi Zalaka when I'd first noticed small patches of green plants in the midst of the desert and I'd asked Mohammad what was being grown. Mohammad had smiled broadly and then pinched his thumb and index finger together and brought them to his pursed lips in the universal code for pot. "Hashish," he said, laughing, then explained the joke to Sheikh Swelam in Arabic, and the sheikh laughed with him.

And I remembered the other green fields, too, that I then started to notice all over the southern Sinai, and black hoses hundreds of yards long snaking from plot to plot across the sand. And I remembered the white trucks near the fields, the Bedouin squatting down in front beside small fires with teapots nestled in the coals. And I remembered Mohammad and the two Bedouin talking beneath the palm trees, and the tricked-out Mercedes, and the flat-screen television in the otherwise dusty settlement. And suddenly, it all made sense. We were Americans on vacation. We had money. We'd been invited to tea in the house of a Bedouin drug lord by his dealer. And yet we hadn't been interested in the hash they were selling. This must have given the dealer a headache that my Advil could not cure. How could I have been so blind? It's exactly what the officer at passport control in Taba had warned me against. "Don't be naive!" he'd said.

I was so glad to be in the refuge of the monastery guesthouse near the protective walls of Saint Catherine's, and from this place of safety, knowing Mohammad was on a bus back to Cairo, I called him on my cell phone, which was now back in service, and confronted him with everything Ellie had told me. He denied it all. Thankful for an excuse, I canceled all of the arrangements he'd made for us with the Bedouin here, including lunch and the hike up Mount Sinai, as well as some tentative plans we had to tour Cairo with Mohammad in the coming days.

Then I called Terry and poured out to him the story of our nostalgia, our ache to return home, and about the hashish. Out went the secret plot to surprise him and the girls. I told him how we wanted to leave early. Could he, who fixed everything, arrange that for me? But I had forgotten about the last text I'd sent him, a text that had made him, quite literally, sick. He'd stayed home from work, worried, and had called Erez to make sure we were safe, given Security, with his machine gun at Ein Khudra, and Ellie's emotional collapse, and the uncertainty of whether or not I really missed him, whether or not I'd wake up from the dream I was in. But we were safe now, we were safe and I was homesick for him.

I guess it was a few hours later, after Ellie and I had showered for the first time in almost a week and then eaten dinner in the guesthouse refectory—nearly empty except for a middle-aged couple of uncertain nationality who ate in silence—because it was almost dark outside and I was talking to Terry, who had checked into the possibility of our flying home early and found that there was none, when we heard a pounding on our door. I looked out the narrow window, open to the cool night air, and what my eyes saw, empirically, was five dark-skinned men with mustaches wearing long white djellabas and red-and-white-checked kaffiyehs, one of whom was the slight Bedouin who was supposed to have been our guide up Mount Sinai until I'd canceled those plans. But what my mind said before I could reason with it, before I could remind it that those images in the Western media of angry Arabs dressed like this and holding effigies or burning American flags just perpetuated divisive stereotypes, before I could tell my mind any of this, it gasped, *Terrorists!* (See Ellie's List of Fears.)

In my right ear, Terry urged me to tell the men to go away. "Please go away!" I told them through the open window. "I cannot speak with you!" In my left ear, the men were saying something, and I don't know if it was because I so desperately did not want to confront them or be confronted by them or because they actually spoke no English, but I couldn't understand a word they uttered. *Maybe this is just some cultural misunderstanding,* my mind was telling my frantically beating heart. *Maybe you should try to explain what happened with Mohammad. Maybe they think you broke a contract with them and they require compensation. And maybe, in this place, they're absolutely right.* "Do you have any furniture you can use to bar the door?" my always-so-reasonable husband who could fix anything was asking me, which alarmed me even more. "Please go away! Please go away!" I kept shouting at the men. Ellie lay on the bed clutching *Moby-Dick* like an amulet, like a shield, to her chest.

In the night, while Ellie and I slept fitfully, Terry again sent e-mails to Erez asking him, on my behalf, if I was overreacting, if we were safe. "There is absolutely no reason to worry," Erez wrote back. Erez must have also spoken with Mohammad and dismissed him from future tours because all the next day I kept getting angry text messages from him: *I have no work now so I hope you are happy that you get what you want. Have a good day.* Which was not what I had wanted at all, and which made me worry more. *When the volcano erupts,* Mohammad had warned, *it cannot control where it flows and who it washes over.* Were we now in its path?

Ever since we'd wandered through the souk in the Old City of Hebron, unprepared to buy as much as we perhaps should have, everywhere we went, though we wanted only to express goodwill and be respectful of others, we kept screwing up. Here in the Sinai, we'd left disappointment in our wake: the little girl at Ein Khudra with her dirty rug laid with cheap jewelry; the old camel driver with cataracts; the women and girls with their pillowcases of trinkets; the young Bedouin with whom we'd broken a contract; Mohammad, whom we'd unintentionally gotten fired. I was not fully consoled by Terry when he reminded me, "That's just weird in any culture, five men coming to a woman's door at night." Or by Ellie, who said with no doubt whatsoever, "They were sketch, Mom." Because my actions, or my inaction, had had economic consequences in the lives of others to varying degrees.

Or maybe my distress was due to something more self-serving: I had wanted to have real interactions with real people, a genuine life experience, and they hadn't cooperated. I had conveniently forgotten that our traveling through their territory was a monetary transaction. The ancient laws of Bedouin hospitality did not really apply. Even if we were all pretending that I was their guest, I was their customer. I paid them money to take care of me and my daughter. We did not speak the same language, and I had not wanted to acknowledge this at all.

REVELATION

A BRIEF HISTORY of *The Monastery of Saint Catherine at the God-Trodden Mount Sinai,* according to Evangelos Papaioannou, doctor of theology and philosophy.

Yearning to be near God and far from the persecutions of Rome, Christian ascetics began filtering into the desert, arriving at Mount Sinai beginning in the third century. Attacked from time to time by marauding bands of nomads, surviving alone in caves, gathering on holy days near the site of the Burning Bush, these monks spent their precarious lives in prayer at the edge of existence.

Meanwhile, in cosmopolitan Alexandria north of Cairo on the Mediterranean coast, with its library housing all the knowledge of the world, a young woman, a virgin of high birth, educated in philosophy, rhetoric, poetry, music, mathematics, astronomy, and medicine, virtuous and incomparably beautiful to boot, was converted to Christianity by a monk, who baptized her as Catherine. She then promptly and publicly accused the pagan emperor Maximinus II of worshipping idols. Wise men from all over the empire gathered in Alexandria to try to dissuade her away from her new faith, but instead, using the Greek philosophy she knew so well against their logic, Catherine persuaded them of the error of their ways. For this presumption, she was tortured on the wheel, but she would not die, and so she was beheaded. Then holy angels retrieved her martyred body and translated it across the desert, laying it in a hollowed niche at the top of a peak just to the west of Mount Sinai.

In 313, Constantine legalized Christianity throughout the Roman Empire, ending the persecutions of hermits and the highborn alike. The desert monks crawled out of their caves, blinking, and petitioned the Empress Helena to build a church at the base of Mount Sinai at the site of the Burning Bush, just as she had built shrines and basilicas all over the Holy Land and on Cyprus. Here, legend has it, she did. And so the monks stayed and flourished, so much so that by the sixth century, the Emperor Justinian ordered the building of a walled fortress and monastery enclosing Helena's church and provided soldiers to defend them.

It was about this time that one of the monks was commanded in a dream to set out with his brethren over the hills and valleys and wadis seeking "a treasure which would be coveted by Easterns and Westerns alike," a story Fabri, too, recounts in some detail. As they wandered, Fabri recalls, the monks came to a cave in which sat an ancient holy man whose face they never saw who revealed that he'd been told to seek the same treasure. He claimed that he often glimpsed a bright, clear light emanating from the crown of a nearby mountain, a mountain they all then set out to climb with much toil. There at the top, in the niche in the rock, lay the body of Saint Catherine, preserved in oil, just where the angels had left her. Her relics needed a home, like the soul needs a body, and so the monks translated them back to the monastery and placed them in a carved stone casket. And for years, on her feast day, birds bearing green boughs from olive trees heavy with fruit would settle on the roof of the monastery church and drop the olives below where the monks could gather them and press them. "At last this miracle also ceased," Fabri laments, "either because the Age of Miracles was past, or because miracles had been abused, or because man's unworthiness and sins hindered the miracles from being wrought, or because God provided other means, since it is the rule of theologians that God does not work miracles unless there be an especial need thereof."

Some of the soldiers that Justinian sent to the desert to protect the monastery and those precious relics had come from Alexandria in Egypt, others from the territory surrounding the Black Sea— perhaps Romania or Anatolia or Macedonia or Greece; it's not entirely clear, though certainly from some distant part of the emperor's Greek-speaking Byzantine Empire. Over time the descendants of these soldiers intermarried with nomadic tribes wandering in and out of the region. When Islam arrived, in the seventh century, they converted.

But they continued to guard the monastery at the base of Mount Sinai. They were there when Fabri visited, harbored by the Eastern monks, a symbiotic relationship between people of different faiths that he simply could not comprehend. The "Arab robbers" lurk inside the monastery, he observes, camping in the courtyard day and night near the pilgrim dwellings, where they watch the visitors come and go "that they might extort their unjust dues from us." And yet, as Fabri himself admits, "They did nothing to us, either of good or evil, neither did they cry out to us, but nevertheless their waiting there was grievous to us."

These protectors of the monastery at the base of Mount Sinai harbored by the monks were there in the age of Justinian; they were there in the age of faith, and they were there when Sheikh Swelam deposited Ellie and me at the reception desk of the guesthouse. They are the Jebeliya, considered now to be one of the Sinaitic Bedouin tribes—Jebeliya from *jebel*, "mountain."

After our days in the desert, Ellie and I needed time to recuperate before we could climb Mount Sinai. In the meantime, the relics of

Saint Catherine needed to be viewed and kissed. Back in Jerusalem, Carol Ann had advised me to attend an early-morning Mass at the monastery. Afterward, the monks would present the relics and bestow upon whoever kissed them a tin ring stamped with Saint Catherine's name in Greek.

But how was I to do this? The monastery was officially open only from nine to twelve most days, and it was closed to visitors entirely on Fridays and Sundays. The Jebeliya in skullcap and Western dress at the reception desk told me to talk to the fathers, meaning the Eastern Orthodox monks, though how I might find them was left vague. Perhaps in the courtyard café of the guesthouse one evening a father might come for a coffee and then I could ask for permission, the man at reception suggested before waving me off.

I don't know why this seems miraculous to me, but that is precisely what happened. After dinner that evening, there was a father, round and bespectacled and with a long white beard, thoroughly enjoying an ice cream sandwich at a table in the courtyard café. Ellie and I greeted him and I launched into an exuberant explanation of how I had come here to Saint Catherine's from America because I was following in the footsteps of a pilgrim from the Middle Ages, a Dominican friar named Felix Fabri. Perhaps he knew of him? But the father just looked at me smilingly and said, in broken English, that he spoke no English.

So Ellie tried. Through a series of Pictionary-like drawings written in my notebook while the father looked on—stick figures of a mother and daughter, a sunrise, a church with a cross, an arrow pointing to a hand with a ring—she attempted to convey my request to attend the five a.m. Mass. The father still smiled but made no reply. Finally, some little Jebeliya boys came over and helped translate.

The next morning, early, after standing behind two bowing and weeping Russian Orthodox women, ample and wearing kerchiefs on their heads and matching polyester flower-print sweaters and skirts, I kissed the gnarled hand of Saint Catherine, draped with a string of pearls and adorned with many jeweled rings, as well as her skull—coppery-colored, just as Fabri had described it—and then a bearded monk, tall and thin, handed me the tin ring.

Our room in the monastery guesthouse overlooked the monks' garden outside the walls of the monastery proper. Beyond the garden, the red hills. In the late afternoons, while Ellie napped or read, I liked to sit on the white plastic chair outside our door and lean against the wall and look at the olive trees and date palms and desert flowers.

So did Mario Pizzuto, whose room was next door to ours. Mario was perhaps sixty, perhaps eighty, I couldn't tell, in part because I saw him only in his threadbare pajama bottoms and white V-neck undershirts the entire duration of our stay. He smoked constantly. His bushy eyebrows sprouted up from behind little round glasses, crying out for a good pruning. Though he seemed perfectly healthy, he took all his meals in his room, meals carried to him by the Jebeliya on a plastic tray. When we met, beside the garden, the sun's film of light coating the leaves of the trees, he told me he was a philosopher from Milan and that he traveled to Saint Catherine's for a month three times a year to escape the world, which he found "dee-sgusting."

One evening, after dinner in the refectory, I sat outside, not quite ready to go to bed, not quite in the mood to read, the bare overhead light in our bare room inhospitable. Mario came out for a smoke and then invited me into his room for a cup of mint tea, which he made in his bathroom with scalding-hot tap water directly from the sink. While he was preparing the tea, I sat at the chair at his desk and looked at his things—flowers from the monks' garden in a plastic bottle, a sprig of rosemary in a tin can, notes in Italian pinned to the wall, ink bottles and pens, a beer can that had been artistically fashioned into an ashtray, Fixodent, lighters, dictionaries. As he handed me the cup of tea, I asked him about an advertising postcard, tucked behind the plastic bottle filled with flowers, depicting a woman in a filmy white dress. Mario told me that in Milan, his family designed couture wedding gowns.

I also asked him about the pocket-size notebooks in various colors lined up on a narrow shelf above his desk. These notebooks—paginated, numbered, indexed, and organized by series—contained the philosophy of Mario Pizzuto. To give you some idea of the scope of this work, after ten thousand pages, he starts a new series. He's now on series three. But what, precisely, these philosophical musings contended was never totally clear to me, though this could have been a matter of translation.

"We are prisoners of *eros* and death," he said, which I assumed was a variation on Freud. He believed in God but was not religious. He sought the truth through philosophy. I countered with literature, art, religion. "Religion is a fairy tale!" said Mario, with emphasis. But so was evolution. He laughed out loud sardonically when I told him that evolution was one of the central ideas—with its insistence on chance, with its denial of any other end goal besides the passing on of genes—keeping me from believing in God. "At-ten-ti-on!" he said, grabbing my hand when I disagreed with him, and then, his cigarette hanging from his lips, he tried to convince me of his position as the ash grew longer and longer like in some cartoon. God, when He created the world, made the world beautiful, said Mario. When we see beauty, we touch God. But the world we live in now, after Eden, has been destroyed by people and is, he repeated, "dee-sgusting."

Our conversation went on for a couple of hours, until I finally extricated myself and returned to our room, carrying a Twix that Mario sent for Ellie, my beautiful daughter, through whom I touch God. But as I lay in the still room in the still land, I thought about Mario, who came to the desert to escape the denuded world, and about his philosophy, the outpourings that seemed never to get shaped into anything final, that never approached a definitive answer. His books of wandering.

Except for the Vatican Library, Saint Catherine's has the largest preserve of early manuscripts in the world—Greek, Arabic, Syriac, Armenian, Georgian, Coptic, Polish, Slavonic—as well as numberless irreplaceable icons and mosaics and reliquaries, all of these objects reaching for God in various tongues. After Ellie and I had been jostled by the impatient throngs deposited by tour buses from the Red Sea resort towns of Dahab and Sharm el-Sheikh in the monastery courtyard one morning between the hours of nine and twelve, and after we had inched forward to see the bush identified as the original Burning Bush, beneath which stood a fire extinguisher at the ready, which no one else seemed to find ironic, we escaped to the monastery museum to walk among its ancient holdings.

A young, blond Moses in tempera on wood was unlacing his sandals in front of a bush that burned with fire, its red fronds like the tentacles of a sea anemone. Across parchment pages of a Greek manuscript of the book of Job, shepherds were playing pipes for flocks of sheep and oxen and asses and camels grazing in golden fields, blind to the devastation that awaited them. Christ Pantocrator, an encaustic icon from the first half of the sixth century, was lifting his left eyebrow as if in question. Of what was he skeptical? On the illuminated image of the Heavenly Ladder, bearded men, young and old, were attempting to climb the rungs toward Christ, though some were being lassoed off by dark-winged angels in flat black silhouette. And in an icon from 1387, backed by a gold halo, Saint Catherine beguilingly stroked the wheel that could not break her, her head and hips seductively tilted.

I stood for a long time before a copy of a proclamation on tattered parchment by the Prophet Muhammad granting protection to the monastery and the monks, the original of which had been confiscated in 1517 by the Turkish sultan Selim I and is now housed in the Topkapi Museum in Istanbul. On the parchment are two hands, one in gold, one in bluish ink. The gold signifies that the Prophet touched the original. The other is the hand of the sultan. Painted around the margins of the parchment are images of the mosque with minaret that still stands within the monastery walls, the Stairs of Repentance one monk hewed into the side of Mount Sinai, and a small church that used to sit at the top of the holy mountain and has since been rebuilt on the same foundation. "This is a message from Muhammad ibn Abdullah, as a covenant to those who adopt Christianity, near and far, we are with them," it begins, and it goes on to proclaim that "no compulsion is to be on them. Neither are their judges to be removed from their jobs nor their monks from their monasteries. No one is to destroy a house of their religion, to damage it, or to carry anything from it to the Muslims' houses." And no one is to disobey this proclamation till the end of the world.

In Jerusalem, I had been exhausted by the despair of others and by their competing claims to the Holy City and the land surrounding it. My friend Fred, who traveled there soon after us, quoted Yehuda Amichai by way of describing his own experience of walking the streets of the Old City:

The air over Jerusalem is saturated with prayers and dreams
like the air over industrial cities.
It's hard to breathe.

But here at Saint Catherine's, where the Muslim Jebeliya and the Eastern Orthodox fathers lived in the concord instituted by the Prophet Muhammad, the air was clearer, at least in the long afternoons and evenings when the tourists had gone.

Once, the book of Genesis tells us, all the people of the earth spoke a single language. And they journeyed to the east, this people in exile, descendants of Adam and Eve. In the land of Shinar, somewhere between the Euphrates and the Tigris, they built a city and a tower with its top in the heavens that they might make themselves a homeland and a name "lest we be scattered abroad upon the face of the whole earth." The Lord came down to see the city, which was called Babel, and the tower that the human creatures had built, and He realized that, united as one, the people would not be restrained from doing anything they imagined. Did He feel threatened? Did He fear their attention had strayed too far from Him? Did He worry that if they had a homeland on earth, they would not need to seek His kingdom of heaven? He confounded their language so they could not understand one another and— out of irony or spite or wisdom, He did not say—scattered them abroad upon the face of the earth, the very dispersal and division they had been trying to avoid. And now for us, their descendants, riven apart, the divide can never really be bridged.

Though the rule of the Sinai monastery says its monks must be of Greek descent, I had read that there was a monk here from Texas for whom an exception had been made. As we were leaving the museum, I asked about him, mentioning our mutual home state, one of the rare times in my life that being from Texas opened doors rather than closed them. Five minutes later, we were led by a Jebeliya into the library housing all those rare manuscripts. Father Justin, originally from El Paso, where he was raised by Baptist missionary parents before entering an Orthodox monastery in Boston, now conserves and photographs and catalogs and guards these precious holdings.

A gaunt man with bright eyes, Father Justin looked kindly at us from behind round, silver-rimmed glasses. Like all the monks, his hair and beard were long, graying now. He wore the black brimless monk's cap and long cassock of the Eastern Orthodox habit. Though we had clearly interrupted him, he sat and talked with us about Fabri, whose account he knew, for half an hour in an airy room overlooking the monastery grounds below and the mountains beyond as other monks came in and out with FedEx boxes and packages from Amazon. Then he asked, "Would you like to see what we are working on here at the library now?"

Father Justin led Ellie and me into a windowless room housing the complicated apparatus of a high-resolution camera that he was using to film palimpsests and other precious manuscripts. A palimpsest is a piece of vellum or parchment paper that, once written upon, has been scraped and scrubbed clean by scribes, and then written upon again—the medieval version of reduce, reuse, recycle. With time, the ghostly remains of the earlier writing will often resurface and what was once hidden can then be revealed. Father Justin explained how the ninth-century parchment he was photographing was layered with as many as five different texts in Arabic and Syriac, how the camera can pick up the pigments of the inks that the scribes rubbed off, how scholars will now be able to tease out and translate the meanings of this ghostly babel, hoping, perhaps, to find some revelation.

Maybe it's true, as Fabri says, that the age of miracles is past. But maybe it's also true, as he says, that God does still work miracles when there be an especial need thereof. Because back on the evening of our arrival, after Ellie had told me that Mohammad had tried to sell her hash but before the men in kaffiyehs had pounded on our door, as we'd wandered the grounds of the guesthouse toward the massive stone walls of the monastery, built of the same worn red granite as the surrounding mountains, a lanky man in a pale gray djellaba and white head scarf had asked casually as he passed us, heading to the monastery as well, "You need a guide?"

I was still frazzled from the experience with Mohammad, our guide for the desert, and from all of the encounters with everyone trying to sell us something, so I brushed him off thinking, self-righteously, that since it was required here that you hire a Jebeliya to climb Mount Sinai, I would choose someone on my own terms this time. The lanky man, who had a tanned and angular face with a slant of black eyebrows and a thin black mustache, just nodded, unfazed, and kept walking.

But the next day Ellie and I walked down into the village of Saint Catherine's, a couple of kilometers away. Some say it was here that the Israelites camped out while Moses spoke to God on the mountain, as the mountain trembled and smoke went up from it as from a kiln. The town there now, with its wide, freshly paved streets and its tidy strip stores lining the flat and open space between mountains, seemed overwhelmed by the emptiness around it. After we checked e-mail for a few Egyptian pounds at an Internet café alongside Bedouin boys playing video games on the other computers, we ran into the same man in the same pale gray djellaba, and I felt inexplicably relieved.

There was something calming about him, something that suggested, after Mohammad in the desert and the men at our door the night before, that we would be in good hands. His eyes, unlike those of most everyone else we passed, did not seem to judge us. I decided to take this chance encounter as a sign, as a miracle worked when there had been a special need. We made arrangements with him to climb Mount Sinai, known to the Jebeliya as

Jebel Musa, late the next afternoon to avoid the heat of the day. His name was Mohammad Atwa Musa. Musa—like Moses.

We were nearly the only pilgrims making the ascent. After meeting Mohammad Atwa Musa in the shady stone square before the monastery, we started up the gentle rise of the camel path, past the Bedouin cameleers standing around listlessly in the sun hoping for customers, who had largely disappeared in these tense days after the revolution. As the wide trail made its switchbacks up Jebel Musa, the Mountain of Moses, the monastery, so solid and unyielding, took its proper place within the vast massif surrounding it, growing more and more vulnerable the higher we climbed.

Ellie was suffering from diarrhea and we had to stop from time to time so she could sit and rest at the little huts built into the mountainside that sold snacks and drinks along the way. The other Mohammad was texting me from Cairo as we hiked—*I have no work now so I hope you are happy that you get what you want. Have a good day.* And I was texting Terry, who was writing Erez, who was reassuring us all that we really were perfectly safe. Ellie and I told Mohammad Atwa Musa about the texts and the hash and the men at our door the night before and asked him if we should be afraid. "I tell my friends," he assured us sympathetically. His sympathy felt like an oasis. "No one bothers you again." And I somehow knew I could believe him. As we neared the summit, he pulled an empty plastic water bottle from a bag of trash left by tourists bused in from the Red Sea resort towns, people who hike in the dark of night so they can see the sunrise from the top of Mount Sinai, then tour the monastery and leave. Together, we filled the plastic bottle with red dirt from the sacred mountain, like the pilgrims with their plastic baggies at Chimayó. Then Mohammad Atwa Musa carried it for me the rest of the way.

From the top of Mount Sinai, Ellie and I looked out over the vast desert, whose ragged mountains rose up like ossified waves on a stormy sea. We'd left Mohammad Atwa Musa visiting with some Jebeliya down below at a souvenir stand. Other than a French mother with her young sons and a Bedouin who sleepily crawled out from under a woven wool blanket and opened up a wooden box filled with trinkets for our delectation, there was no other living soul anywhere we could see. From her backpack, Ellie pulled out *Moby-Dick,* narrated by Ishmael—named for that biblical exile and outcast sent off to wander the unending desert—who takes to the sea "whenever it is a damp, drizzly November in my soul." I sat beside her and scanned the ocean of stone and thought of Noah in his ark upon the devouring waters, searching the horizon for the sight of dry land for forty days and nights. And I thought of Moses and the Israelites wandering this sea of sand for forty years. And of Jesus in the Judean wilderness tempted by the devil in the cave not far from Jericho for forty days as well. Forty, meaning "a long time." How lonely are the chosen ones of God.

And we, their descendants. It suddenly struck me that, after all these years, perhaps I had been wrong about the origins of that abyss I sometimes felt inside me. Such emptiness had not taken shape when God banished Adam and Eve from the Garden, cutting them off from Him. Our yearning to connect did not start with a transgression. In the beginning, *the earth was without form, and void,* and out of that void in Himself, God made us. His breath, the breath that gave us life, was itself filled with emptiness and a deep need for connection. The umbilicus that tied us to God was His ache for us. We inherited that ache as our birthright, and it's the legacy we pass on.

Out of my own emptiness, I made my daughters. They filled a void in me. But I could not fill that same void in them. At the top of Mount Sinai, I remembered Ellie's dream as a child, of being left on the mountaintop by herself, those she loved scattered abroad by the careless wind. "I know that my dream will come true and I will be left all alone," she had told me as we sat on the floor of her room playing Sunshine Family while newborn Mary Martha napped in the white iron bed. In the mountains in the desert beside Ellie, I remembered her inarticulate fear of the abyss.

And I remembered one night just after Sabine's seventh birthday when she was lying in bed surrounded by her collection of plush stuffed frogs. She had turned toward the wall, away from Terry and me, as we bent to kiss her good night, the way she always did when she was about to cry but didn't want anyone to see. Sabine told us, "I feel like something's missing, but I don't know what it is." For just a moment, I thought, or wanted to think, that she was talking about a missing stuffed animal, because she required such a precise arrangement each night: blankie beneath her head, gray Beanie Baby kitty in her hand, baby doll perched above, on top of all the frogs. But it wasn't that sort of missing. I understood that almost immediately. This was something deeper and darker, inchoate. An inarticulate lack. An insatiable ache.

We are all alone, say the wanderers of the desert, where the emptiness without is in equilibrium with the emptiness within. It's easy to forget that in the frenetic chattering world we normally inhabit, where everyone is so desperately trying to connect via Facebook, via Twitter, via Pinterest, via Snapchat, via Instagram. Perhaps we think that if we're connected, we won't have to confront the void out of which we were created and that lives inside us still.

Even God was lonely, and fearful of the abyss. Here on Mount Sinai, He tried desperately once more to get through to us, to translate the laws that would govern a life worth living. So while Moses waited in a niche in the red hills whose color shifted with the migrating light of the sun, God wrote to us with His finger on tablets of stone the way Michelangelo's Creator reaches out to

Adam and imbues him with life. The commandments He inscribed were meant to hold us close to Him and to one another. These stone tablets—housed in an ark that traveled over the desert that was once a sea, marked by a pillar of cloud by day and of fire by night, carried by exiles who sought the elusive Promised Land— these stone tablets were the nodal point connecting human and divine. But then the tablets were lost, or destroyed; who knows? And anyway, did we ever really understand them?

My soul thirsteth for thee, my flesh longeth for thee in a dry and thirsty land, where no water is. So goes the psalm. But we are all essentially alone and somehow can't connect. The desert's blank skies, its pathless wastes, its mountains breaking like waves revealed this truth to me. In its immense silence I could finally hear it clearly, and because it was true, it brought some rest that in my restlessness I'd been seeking.

As the air grew cooler and the sun dimmer, Mohammad Atwa Musa called out to us and we followed him down the mountain, this time taking the Stairs of Repentance, some 3,750 steps carved into the stone by that monk in the age of Justinian. Somewhere near the summit, Ellie had tripped and twisted her ankle, so she limped along behind me while Mohammad walked ahead, singing verses from the Qur'an softly to himself and carrying the dirt from the holy mountain in the plastic bottle. From time to time he would pause to wait for me and I would pause to wait for Ellie and then we'd continue on. The light from the day had seeped into the red stones, so that even as the sun departed, they burned with it and then slowly went cold. We seemed to be descending into the earth as the sun descended. By the time we reached the monastery at the base of the mountain, the darkness had taken us in.

THE PEOPLE OF THE GARDEN

I COULD HARDLY remember a time when I saw myself as separate from my children or my husband, from the web, seductive and entangled, we had made. Years ago, on a fall day, I had ridden my bike to my boyfriend's house to tell him I was pregnant as the geese pulled south through the sky overhead, though even then, as I cocooned myself around the small beating heart inside me, my sense of myself as a discrete individual had come to an end. But the farther Ellie and I traveled away from the life that unspooled at the moment of her conception, the more I began to recall my former self, the one I might have been. And as Ellie withdrew into herself and her books, it struck me that we were no longer sufficient for each other. I was trying to find my own way back into the world alone without her, and like the monks translating the precious relics of Saint Catherine over the mountains of this desert, Ellie was doing the arduous and sometimes perilous work of hauling herself into adulthood, but I was in her way.

Just before Ellie was conceived, I had written in my notebook, "I wish I was brave enough to do this alone"—meaning set out into the wider world, away from everything well-ordered and safe. "Yet I know I am not, nor will I ever be." And for all the intervening years, as I feathered our comfortable nest of a house and surrounded myself with children I couldn't possibly leave, I wondered if I'd taken dictation from the gods, writing down a prophecy on leaves that had then come true. And that I'd actually wanted it to happen, more than I'd wanted that *bohemian-explorer-intellectual kind of life*.

Terry rejects my worry that I've lived a sheltered life, cozy in our house of plenty with its green teakettle and shelves full of books. He rejects the possibility that I used my family as a buffer against the world because I was afraid. "It's just so hard for me to understand this idea that you are somehow weak," he told me one time, coming into my office, where I was reading for class, holding a *New York Times* opinion piece written by a young woman struggling with the grief and remorse she felt at having had an abortion years before, when it had not been convenient to have a child. "Having Ellie took so much strength and engagement with what's real."

Still, I wanted to follow Fabri in part in order to strip something away, something naive and untested within me, something protective around me. I wanted to bare myself to the actual world, to see it and experience it for myself, not just read about it in books. In Hemingway's short story "The Snows of Kilimanjaro," a man lies on a cot in a tent dying of gangrene, realizing he'll now never write the stories he had always planned to, before he became too comfortable— women, money, drink—and stopped writing. "Africa was where he had been happiest in the good time of his life, so he had come out here to start again," he remembers. "They had made this safari with the minimum of comfort. There was no hardship; but there was no luxury and he had thought that he could get back into training that way. That in some way he could work the fat off his soul the way a fighter went into the mountains to work and train in order to burn it out of his body." It was something like that for me. On this trip, I had been trying to return to something essential within myself, maybe build some new life on that scaffolding.

The afternoon before we were to leave Saint Catherine's for Cairo, I made plans with Mohammad Atwa Musa for another hike, this time to the Monastery of the Forty Martyrs. Ellie stayed back at the guesthouse. Her stomach was still in turmoil, her twisted ankle still ached, and her legs were sore from the 3,750 Stairs of Repentance. While part of me felt I should remain with her in solidarity, I went on nevertheless. I knew Ellie didn't really want me there. And these moments of separation were reminding me that I had once been on my own and I could be again.

Mohammad Atwa Musa and I met down in the village of Saint Catherine's, and we walked through the streets of tidy, square houses, dun-colored mud brick or cinder block faced with the russet stone of the mountains or else painted red to look like stone, their wooden doors and window frames bright green and blue and orange and purple. We walked until the houses thinned out and entered Wadi el Arbain, which ran between high mountains of toothed red granite, chiseled by wind and water in some places, in other places sculpted and smoothed.

We passed a Bedouin smoking and listening to Arabic music on a transistor radio, riding a camel loaded down with canvas bags. At Hajar Musa, the rock cleft twelve times by Moses to bring forth water for the wandering Israelites, we came upon Mohammad's brother, a friend of his, and his friend's new bride. The bride sat alone, in black, around the curve of a boulder. The men offered me apricots, then spoke together while I, too, stayed alone. Later, I read that near Hajar Musa is a Bedouin proposal rock, where a man would carve an outline of his foot, and his lover, if she accepted his proposal, would carve an outline of hers next to it on the face of the stone. If they went through with the marriage, they returned and drew a circle around the two footprints.

As we continued on through the valley toward the Monastery of the Forty Martyrs, I asked Mohammad about what happens during Bedouin wedding ceremonies. He halted in the pathway of red dust and told me how the families gather together, how the man and woman join right hands and entwine their thumbs, which he demonstrated with our hands and thumbs because it was too difficult to explain in English. Then, he said, the father and the brothers of the woman speak, asking the bride and groom if they accept each other. After that, they feast. Mohammad told me, too, about a place near here where Bedouin perform a fertility ceremony. A few goats are slaughtered, the hungry earth here, like the Field of Damascus in Hebron, being fed by blood before it will give back. "A year later," Mohammad assured me, "a child comes."

In September of 1483, the Monastery of the Forty Martyrs consists of a few cells constructed of woven reeds plastered over with mud. But outside the gates of the monastery is a garden in which grows thousands of olive trees and fig trees, pomegranates and almonds, all fed by pipes that run into the garden "like living water" from wells dug by the monks. Saint Catherine's Convent gets enough oil from this garden to feed the lamps in its church and use as a relish in its kitchen. They have salad for their bread from the herbs that grow here, and hay from the grasses to feed their beasts. And every year the monks ship some of this fruit to the sultan in Cairo in recompense for his patronage and protection. "It is wondrous that there should be such a paradise in the wilderness, where everything is dried and burned up by the sun's heat, and in the barren sand no seed or root will grow; yet what cannot human industry accomplish?" Fabri remarks.

In the Qur'an, from which we'd read excerpts one fall in my class, I was struck by how often believers are called the "People of the Garden" and unbelievers "People of the Fire." From the People of the Garden, says the Prophet Muhammad, "we shall remove all malice from their hearts, and rivers shall flow beneath them."

And the People of the Fire will call out to the People of the Garden, "Pour down upon us water or else some of what God bestowed upon you." But, says the Prophet, "these shall answer: 'God forbade them to the unbelievers. They are those who took their religion lightly and in jest, and whom this present life seduced.'"

In the Sinai, this distinction between the fecundity of faith and the desert of unbelief made a concrete sense. Throughout the high mountains of this region, the Jebeliya tend a couple hundred small gardens. Here, in the garden of the Monastery of the Forty Martyrs, the caretakers and their children, six families, Mohammad Atwa Musa said, came out to greet us—the children and the men. The women stayed behind in an open-air stone structure where they made tea, which they sent out to us, along with tiny plums, slightly bitter. Mohammad sat on the low-lying wall of a stone enclosure and spoke to the People of the Garden. His hand on a wee girl's head, he asked her questions looking into her face and smiling, and joked with the little boys in their soccer jerseys. I wandered the grounds and marveled, as Fabri had done. The dusky olive trees and fig trees with their massive leaves still grew here, as did pomegranates and tomatoes. Grapevines were supported by arbors of sawed two-by-fours and limbs of trees stripped of their bark. The green living things stood out against the red earth, otherwise dusty and barren. Water channels sliced through the desert floor—*rivers shall flow beneath them*—and deep circular trenches had been dug around each tree, as if marking within that circle something miraculous, which it was.

When we arrived back in the village of Saint Catherine's, the sun's harsh light had softened and the air had cooled off. Mohammad called a friend on his cell phone to pick us up and drive me back to the monastery guesthouse so I wouldn't have to walk in the failing light. We drove through the village and passed the house of Mohammad's mother, and he waved to a gaggle of women on the balcony looking down at us in the gravel street, then asked if I wanted to go in for a short visit. After introducing me to his grandmother and his mother and his wife and small daughter, and to all the other women and little children, including the bride we'd met at Hajar Musa, he smiled broadly and said, "I love this—these women," making a circle in the air with his hands, as if I was included within it. Then he went to the men's quarters, and I entered into the women's—in this season, a balcony of concrete blocks and rebar, breezy and open, with woven mats and colorful rugs layered on the floor, which we sat upon cross-legged, beneath a palm-leaf roof overhead.

In an adjacent space, Mohammad's wife made tea on a bright blue cookstove using water from a crude tap in the wall. A sewing machine sat on a table in a corner. Hanging from pegs in the walls were embroidered bags that would be sold at a cooperative store in town founded by a Jebeliya woman named Selima. Ellie and I had bought gifts there for Mary Martha and Sabine a couple of days before. The women all wore the ubiquitous long-sleeved black shifts, but up close I could see that they hid brilliantly colored garments beneath—royal blue, teal, orange, fuchsia. Once the door to the outside world had closed, they let fall their veils from over their mouths and noses and stared at me and smiled and said things to one another I couldn't understand. I smiled back. I wondered what I looked like through their eyes. A little one toddled over and put her dimpled hands on my face. I wanted to squeeze her, bury my nose in the crook of her neck, as I used to do with Sabine and Mary Martha and Ellie, but I was afraid of frightening her. So I let her translate my strange face with her fingers until she began to cry and her mother swept her up in her arms to console her. I was nobody's mother here.

We had only two words in common. The bride, as I sweetened my tea, pointed and said, "Sugar!" I held up my small clear glass and said to all of them, *"Shokran."* "Thank you." Meaning, *You are all so beautiful, and I'm so glad you exist in the world, even though I'll probably never see you again in this life.* When Mohammad Atwa Musa knocked on the door to retrieve me, all the women, as one, deftly lifted their veils to cover themselves, the movement like the taking flight of a flock of birds. As he drove me back to the monastery guesthouse at Saint Catherine's, he told me, "Family is good," a statement that needed no translation.

In the story of Pentecost, Jesus's disciples gather together in the Upper Room of the Last Supper to celebrate the Jewish festival of Shavuot, a festival which commemorates God's giving of the commandments to Moses on Mount Sinai during the Israelites' exile in the wilderness, after the angel of death has passed over their sons and He has led them from their bondage in Egypt. Jesus is dead and risen, having been crucified during Passover, but his followers have continued to meet in the place made sacred by his presence, and on that particular feast day, the room fills with a mighty wind and the disciples fill with the Holy Spirit, which enters into them like tongues of flame. When they speak, all those Jews who have made the pilgrimage to Jerusalem for the festival — "Parthians and Medes and Elamites, those dwelling in Mesopotamia, Judea and Cappadocia, Pontus and Asia, Phrygia and Pamphylia, Egypt and the parts of Libya adjoining Cyrene, visitors from Rome, both Jews and proselytes, Cretans and Arabs" — all these strangers and wanderers hear and understand as if the words are being spoken in their own private language.

In that Upper Room of the Last Supper, the Holy Spirit knits up the gashes God hacked between people when He came down to see for Himself the blasphemy of the Tower of Babel. And for me, this story speaks to the possibility of a reprieve from the division that followed when He scattered the people like seed. For a few fleeting moments, perhaps, in a small upper room with the breeze blowing through, we can connect with one another though we speak different tongues. Out in the desert, I had seen clearly that the essential fact of our human existence is our fragility in a transitory world. Here, with the women of Mohammad's family, I felt how our transience binds us all together, despite the divisions between us, divisions that had confronted us everywhere we went.

I feel the need to travel and experience the beauty and mystery of other worlds, other cultures, I'd also written down just before Ellie was conceived. This, too, now seemed prophetic.

From the Monastery of the Forty Martyrs, Fabri labors on into the desert with some of the heartier pilgrims, where they thread Saint Catherine's Mountain before dawn, "crawling round the mass of rock, suspended from the face of the cliffs like ants climbing a tree." When they reach the top and the hollow where the angels had laid Saint Catherine's broken body, a harsh wind is blowing and their Jebeliya guides collect fagots and build a great fire until the sun grows warmer and the chill of the air grows less keen. From there, it seems they can see all the world in a moment of time. To the east, the Red Sea, and beyond that the Arabian Sea, which comes from the Indian Ocean even farther beyond. To the south, the coastal city of Tor, where ships from India anchor with their aromatic spices. In the desert on the opposite shore lies the desolate wilderness of the Thebaid, where Saint Anthony and other desert fathers formerly dwelled. To the southwest, Ethiopia, where satyrs roam and men curse the sun because of the heat. To the northeast is Arabia and Mecca. To the north, Chaldea and Babylon, land of the Tower of Babel. Looking toward the wilderness between Mount Sinai and the Red Sea, Fabri recalls the story from *Lives of the Fathers* about Postumius, who escapes into the wastelands whenever religious men travel there to meet him because "if men were to converse with me, the angels with whom I now converse would flee." Before descending, the pilgrims lay their bodies in the niche in the stone.

"We felt an especial joy on this notable spot; for hitherto our journeys had ever taken us further away from our home and native land, but from this desirable place we began to turn ourselves back, and set our faces steadfastly in the direction of our native land, our own country, and our home," Fabri recalls. "How joyous and delightful a thing this is no man understands save he who has long sojourned in distant climes, and lived an exile in a strange land among a people whom he knows not, whose manners and language he does not understand, and has dwelt awhile with a nation of a strange sect, a strange religion, that worships as it were a strange God." And then he quotes Ovid, in exile in the hinterlands of the Roman Empire: *Qua natale solum dulcedine cunctos ducit et immemores non sinit esse sui;* "Our native soil draws all of us, by I know not what sweetness, and never allows us to forget."

"Every day feels so long that when you finally lay down to sleep, it seems ages ago that you woke up," Ellie told me as we packed our bags the evening before our departure for Cairo. "Why can't I seem to let go of this extreme need to be home and just enjoy this?" I told her I was feeling the same way. "I'm beginning to wonder if I'm just a terrible homebody," I said, thinking of the home I'd made in Houston, the one etched with memory. But Ellie thought about all this a little more and said, "I don't so much miss my 'home' because I don't really even know where my home is anyway. Since I went away to school, my home has shifted. Our house doesn't feel like home anymore because it's really not. But my dorm room wasn't home either. I just hope that my apartment this fall feels more like *my* home." I realized then that *home* had different meanings for each of us, where formerly it had meant the same thing. My home was in some ways her past. Her home was still unmade and existed only in the future tense. Which reminds me now that the German Romantics, in contrast to the Swiss soldiers sick for home, coined an opposite to *Heimweh,* "homesickness." *Fernweh,* they called it, this "far-sickness," this ache to be away.

As the pilgrims prepare to depart, the fathers ask them to allow four camels loaded with fruit to journey into Egypt with their company. Every year, the monks send a gift to the Mameluke sultan of Egypt. "This fruit is packed in wooden boxes," Fabri explains, "and is gathered in the wilderness of Sinai and Horeb. The King sets great store by this present, because the fruit has grown in that holy spot, and divides it among the greatest men in Egypt, who receive that fruit as though it were a holy thing sent down from heaven."

In those last days of September 1483, the caravan of camels and asses and pilgrims and guides crosses into the desert again, this time heading north and following, roughly, the western finger of the Red Sea that points to the Mediterranean and, beyond that, home. Just past the northern tip of the gulf, they come upon the pilgrim road to Mecca and begin to follow it west toward Cairo. This is the season for the hajj, and the Christian pilgrims heading away from their Holy Land encounter large companies of Muslim pilgrims heading east to theirs. Fabri has learned from one of the drivers that Christians are permitted, even encouraged, to travel with Muslims on their pilgrimage, and though he is nearing the end of his journey, Fabri feels that *Fernweh,* that far-sickness, calling out to him like a Siren. "Often I have been tempted to visit . . . that accursed sepulchre," he remarks, not registering his own contradictions, "and if I had had but one to go with me, hardly could I have refrained."

We left the Sinai Desert for Cairo on the 6:00 a.m. bus, its blue curtains creased black with filth. From the windshield, Mickey Mouse decals stared back at us where we sat in the front seat, and the rest of the bus—all men—stared too. Arabic music played over the speaker, perhaps religious, given that the driver had a *zebiba*—a mark on his brow from touching his head to the ground in prayer so many times. The singer strung out the long syllables of his song like the sinewy black road before us, like the roads Terry and I had driven so many times west across Texas.

We left the red mountains near Saint Catherine's and passed into lower mountains and hills of dry turf. Then the hills became soft dunes, which became flat sands lining the waters of this inlet of the Red Sea. Finally we were delivered into the machinery of the modern world, into the People of the Fire: gas pipelines, and sand-colored oil rigs, and refineries like those along the Gulf Coast pumping black smoke into the air. Mostly, the Egyptian army in green fatigues waved us through the checkpoints. But in Suez, we had to get off the bus with our luggage, which the soldiers rummaged through with their guns. We stared at the goats milling about in the parking lot of a mosque beside the highway while the soldiers searched the others. In the median, a donkey pulled a green cart filled with palm leaves. Another pulled a cart of watermelons. Back on the bus and moving again, we passed rows of dull gray apartment buildings, satellite dishes of various sizes cluttering the roofs, their little alcove porches painted yellow and lime green and aqua and hung with laundry. Piles of trash, trash everywhere, clotting the spaces between.

VI. PARADISE, WHEREVER THAT MAY BE

Cairo, Alexandria

Whence then cometh wisdom?
and where is the place of understanding?
—Job 28:20

LEVIATHAN

THEY ENTER THE city at night, in the shadows, to avoid trouble. For miles they ride through throngs of men whose faces are lit by lanterns and torches. It is the season of Ramadan, with its days of fasting and contemplation, and these hours between sunset and sunrise, when a black thread cannot be distinguished from a white one, are the hours of their rejoicing. There was, recalls Fabri, "such a clamor and crowding of men that I cannot describe it. There were so many lights and torches, there was so much dancing about, it was as if it were the joy of all the world, and not just in this one place but in every quarter of the city." But the pilgrims find they cannot so easily dissolve into the darkness and the crowds. A group of young men recognize them as Christians and run after them, shouting and throwing dirt. When the pilgrims at last arrive at the home of their dragoman in Cairo, they unload their beasts and are led into a room whose walls and floor are paved in polished marble. But because of the Ramadan celebrations, they spend a sleepless night until finally, when "it began to grow light, they stopped their carousing and a great silence came over the house."

This is the home of Tanquardinus, a shape-shifting figure for the coming world. Born a Jew in Sicily, where he became a rabbi—according to a German-speaking jeweler and goldsmith living in

Cairo, who warns the pilgrims about their host—Tanquardinus abandoned Judaism for Christianity, learned Latin, and joined the clergy. But after performing in that office for some time, he "foreswore the faith of Christ, swore an oath to Mahomet and after being received into the court of the Sultan he became a rich and powerful Mameluke." From the sultan, Tanquardinus has been granted the right to serve as dragoman for Jews and Christians who arrive in Cairo. The pilgrims must wait on Tanquardinus to obtain the sultan's permission for them to travel to Alexandria, where the merchant ships will carry them across the sea and home. But, warns the jeweler, "he takes money rightly and falsely and knows how to gain the affection of pilgrims with amazing sweetness so that he can consequently empty their purses."

The season of piety that grips Cairo during Fabri's stay escapes the friar. Instead, for him, it is a city of earthly delights. And Tanquardinus's house an epicenter of the wealth and power that sustain the Mamelukes, that warrior caste made up of slaves of mainly Turkic origin who had claimed the sultanate for themselves and now ruled Egypt. The bedrooms' walls and floors are overlaid with marble and tapestries. A saddle room is hung with silver stirrups and breast straps and cruppers and embossed reins and halters. The stables hold innumerable horses—jennets, destriers, palfreys, and pacers. Lining the courtyards are cages housing a menagerie of parrots and ostriches, a civet, a leopard on a chain. Handlers arrive displaying other exotic animals: a giraffe, a lion, a dancing bear with a monkey who plays a pipe and dances too.

When the pilgrims leave the comfort of their accommodations to go out into the city, their Mameluke guide must part the crowd with his staff, often striking and knocking down those in their way, "for there is such a great number of men on all sides in the street, such a density of population, and so many merchants and peddlers that it is astounding to see and incredible to hear, and no one can just walk there without continually pushing his way forcefully through the oncoming crowd." The tumult of men and beasts stirs up so much dust that camels must be hired "from the common purse" to sprinkle Nile water over the streets, otherwise the population would suffocate. Eight thousand camels do nothing else but carry water to private homes.

About the pyramids and the Sphinx, Fabri says almost nothing. And the Eastern Orthodox churches, many dedicated to some stop or other on the Holy Family's pilgrimage during their flight into Egypt, are mostly closed to them. In the few that they enter, the pilgrims cannot always tell to which saints they've been dedicated, in part because their guides don't know Latin and in part because the knowledge of which saints' relics were buried in which tombs was lost after the Latins were expelled.

Fabri ends up, therefore, documenting small miracles of human ingenuity rather than the miracles of saints. The chick hatchery where women bring eggs to have them hatched, "just as they bring dough to the bakery to have their bread baked." The water sellers who carry ladles in their hands and water skins around their necks and walk the streets, accepting whatever pittance they are given. The sellers of street food who carry improvised stoves on their heads that they use to prepare meat and fish. "The cook takes small bowls with him and everything he needs," notes Fabri. "Foreigners and paupers content with little gather with them at some corner in the street, make their purchases and sit there and eat."

The massive public works of Mameluke Cairo also impress him—an arched aqueduct with lead pipes that passes from the Nile up a mountain to the sultan's castle; the countless lamps hung in the minarets of mosques that burn through the darkness. "Sometimes at night I climbed into the upper story of the house and looked out across the city, and often my hair stood on end because of the excessive fire of the lamps," Fabri admits. "Christian men who know it to be true say that no king in Christendom, not this one nor that one, could buy with a year's revenue all the oil that is burned in one night in that city's lamps." From a stone bridge spanning the Nile one day, the pilgrims witness slaves and condemned captives shaping mud bricks from the clay of the banks of the river and leaving them to dry in the sun. Nearly all the houses in Cairo are built of these unfired bricks and if it were ever to rain in Cairo as it does in Ulm, "the entire city would melt like wax."

The immensity of this metropolis and the multiplicity of its people confound Fabri: Saracens without number, Mamelukes, Moors, Arabs, Turks, Tartars, Ethiopians, Egyptians, Samaritans, Eastern Greek Christians, Jews. And somehow, it works. "It is certainly amazing how such a community can be governed in which there are such diverse men from all over the world, from every religion both contrary and monstrous," says Fabri. "It is amazing that they do not tear each other to pieces."

But Fabri also recognizes the suffering that is the cost of these teeming multitudes. Or maybe it's suffering that has brought them here. More people live in Cairo without house or hut or bed, he claims, than live in all of Venice. "There are large plazas in the city where the poor sleep at night in the open and during the day they sit and perform labor," he says with pity. "Poor women give birth in public in the plaza, unless by chance some passing women cover her with a cloth." Lives are cheap and disposable. In 1476, Fabri recalls, a plague fell upon the city and sixteen thousand people died every day for nearly three months. "When such a slaughter of men had been reported to the Sultan, he was struck dumb, fearing the desolation of the city, but one of those sitting with him said that he should not be afraid since, if one person died from each mosque, that would be sixty thousand men, and under each mosque there were many thousands of men."

The suffering of others runs like a musical variation throughout

Fabri's account of his stay in Egypt. And weeks later, when the pilgrims arrive in Alexandria, the wretchedness they witnessed from a distance back in Cairo will draw unnervingly near. Wandering the city one day, they'll pass by a house of prostitution. The beautiful, adorned women, Christians from France, Spain, Calabria, Italy, Catalonia, Genoa, Padua, Trevi, Venice—"daughters no doubt of good men, seduced by intemperate passions and led into the jaws of damnation"—will tell the pilgrims their stories of misery and beg them to pray for them or snatch them away from this life. Another day, they'll go down to the seashore, which is littered with sacks full of spices that the Saracen officials will pour out onto the ground to inspect before loading. In their wake will follow the forlorn of the empire: paupers, women and boys, Bedouin and African, who will dig in the sand for ginger, cloves, cinnamon, and nutmegs and then sell whatever they can recover at the city gates. But the Mamelukes will beat them with sticks and drive them away, "pitilessly injuring old men, pregnant women and children, striking them like animals, ignoring the shouts, lamentations, and cries, with which the heavens were filled. I often saw this cruelty."

But it is in the Alexandrian *fondaco* of the Tartars that Fabri witnesses the most disturbing of transactions: the sale of "the most precious merchandise, which they nevertheless sold cheaply," he says with barely disguised rage. "Those items were God's creatures"—more than sixty people, men, women, and children—"possessing reason, made in the image of God." The particulars of this "sad market" Fabri will lay bare in horrifying detail. The buyers who inspect the slaves, stripping them naked, inspecting their genitalia, forcing them to run, walk, leap in order to determine whether they are "sick or healthy, man or woman, virgin or corrupted. And if they should see any of them blush, they abuse them even more with beating, whipping, boxing their ears, so that he might do by force what he is ashamed to do willingly before everyone." There's the haggling over prices as if these creatures of God are horses. And then the clamor and the wailing when a sale is made, "for a boy is sold there as his mother looks on and cries, a mother is sold to the confusion and dismay of her son. Here, as her husband stands ashamed, his wife is played with like a whore and handed over to another man, there a little child is snatched from its mother's arms and as they feel it in the pits of their stomachs its mother is separated from it."

In the pilgrims' own hospice at the Catalonian *fondaco* in Alexandria, Fabri will record what is for me the saddest moment in his entire *Book of Wanderings*. An Ethiopian woman, a slave, chastised by her mistress and unable to bear the reprimand, will be ordered beaten by another slave. Picking up a stick, the slave will strike the Ethiopian woman "with all his strength like one would beat an ass, and [kick] her as she lay on the ground." Though she will resist—clawing back, spitting—finally she'll be bound with ropes. But then she'll turn her fury inward, "lowing like a cow, tearing herself with her teeth, banging her head on the ground and against the walls, and again and again [throwing] herself headfirst from the bench on which she was tied and in every way [trying] to end her life." In her rage, she will blaspheme God and bless Muhammad. At last, she will lie still for many hours, as if dead.

After the stillness of the desert, Cairo felt like bedlam, though maybe Cairo always feels that way to strangers. On the roads, the demarcated traffic lanes had become mere suggestions to the drivers, who ignored them while they honked at one another and jockeyed for openings and stopped and started and sped ahead. Trash in various stages of decomposition furrowed the streets. On the urban fringes, green carts pulled by burros were filled with piles of fruit—grapes, prickly pear, mangoes, limes, melons, bananas. Chickens and goats and sheep and oxen roamed the dirt streets. Slabs of meat plagued by flies hung in the open windows. Zooming in and out like gnats were the three-wheeled auto-rick-shaws called tuk-tuks decorated with Bob Marley and Che Guevara decals and verses from the Qur'an. At night, the faces of the innumerable people in the crowds of downtown Cairo were illuminated by the harsh blue cast of fluorescent strobe lights. The only still, quiet places were the mosques with their forests of pillars and their walls of cool stone and their plush red carpets, which we would walk across in bare feet.

Cairo made no sense to me. As disoriented as I had been in the immensity of the desert, here in the city, I was more bewildered by the cacophony. But like Fabri, we were staying in an oasis of sorts: a white stucco British colonial villa in the tree-lined Ma'adi neighborhood south of the city, a neighborhood of affluent Egyptians and expats. Julia and Kilian, German friends of Sabine and Martin back in Frankfurt, she a foreign correspondent for a German newspaper, he a lawyer specializing in Sharia law, had offered us a room overlooking their green lawn and banana trees and bougainvillea and oleander. In the mornings, in the garden, Ellie and I would drink Nescafé and plan what we would do that day. In the evenings, back from whatever touring we had done, we would eat dinner there and listen to the muezzin calling out over the crackling loud-speaker of the neighborhood minaret through the humid air. At night, we would lie in the bedroom and read, the window air con-ditioner drowning out the noise of the city still rattling in our heads.

Sitting on the back porch that first evening, sharing falafel and watermelon and a fresh chopped salad, Ellie and I peppered Julia with questions about experiences we had not understood in the Si-nai Desert and about her life as a Western woman navigating the Middle East. We told her about the Bedouin men we'd encoun-tered at Beer Ikna, for example, a tenuous patch of green, where we thought we had been invited to sit down on rugs along with Sheikh Swelam. But as we began to squat, one of the men motioned with his hands, flicking us out of the way. So Ellie and I sat on the edge of the circle of men, none of whom would look at us or acknowledge our presence, though we were passed bread and grilled goat meat and tea by a little girl whose mother sat behind a stone wall refilling the platter and cups.

Actually, no men would look at us or acknowledge us anywhere in the desert. Mohammad with the green eyes had told us that the men feared we would think they were leering. Looking at us was an impropriety. But Julia had a slightly different take. "They simply didn't know what to do with you. You were completely alien to them," she said. They didn't look at us or acknowledge us because they didn't recognize us—literally and figuratively. We didn't fit into any identifiable category. We were not men, though we were out in the world on our own wearing pants, our heads uncovered. And though we had breasts and were shaped like women, we didn't resemble any women they had ever known. We were like some third gender—freakish and aberrant.

Ellie and I wondered out loud what we could have done to blunt this reaction. We hadn't wanted to be offensive. "Maybe I should have learned more Arabic. Maybe I shouldn't have worn shorts. Maybe I should have drunk more tea," Ellie mused. "But even on the days when I didn't wear shorts and when I said *'Marhaba'* and *'Shokran,'* I still felt like they didn't want me there. They didn't see me as an equal." Julia replied, "As a woman who goes out at night alone, who stays in hotels alone, who goes places and interviews people she shouldn't, I am still an outsider, even though I speak their language." Then she told us how once, traveling on the train to Alexandria, she overheard the Muslim women in their hijabs mocking her short hair and joking that she must be a man. "Here you are seen not as an individual," Julia explained, "but as part of a larger whole." If you don't represent that whole properly, you are spurned. You cannot be looked in the eye and acknowledged as existing. It's a protective measure. As it was for the ultra-Orthodox Haredi in the Mea Shearim neighborhood of Jerusalem who begged women and girls passing through with all their hearts not to dress in immodest clothes, the cohesion of the community is at stake.

It was difficult to chart Fabri's path through Cairo. Descriptions didn't quite add up. Names have changed. Ellie and I hired drivers to take us to some of the spots Fabri appears to have visited. The walled Coptic Christian Quarter, with its Eastern churches and their confusion of relics, that Fabri calls Babylon. Matariyya, where he'd entered the Garden of Balsam and smelled the fragrant oil rubbed onto his skin by their guide. But the walled garden we entered was set in the midst of the urban chaos, and the precious balsam plants were now gone.

Rubiyo, who did work of some sort on old manuscripts but who was moonlighting as a driver to make ends meet, brought us to the archaeological site of al-Fustat, the first city founded in Egypt by Arabs, who'd traveled from the east across the deserts in 641. The name means "tent." For five hundred years, this was the center of Muslim rule, with its colonnaded houses and its domed mosques. Now it was an empty field with only the shadowy outlines of the foundations of buildings, their stone floors laid out in delicate herringbone. Stands of reeds marked out where an inlet of the Nile used to run. Water pooled here and there, threatening the relics buried underneath, but the ministry of culture had no money to save them. The money had disappeared.

"This is why the revolution happened," Rubiyo explained as we stood in the empty field that was once the city of the tents. "The revolution was purely economic. There was no work, there was no housing, there was no food. We know it will take months, years maybe, but we have hope that we will choose our government, and our life. We will make the income go for the people, not for Mubarak and his monsters, stealing from everyone, taxing everyone. We are not against the rich," he concluded, "but live and let live."

But five hundred years after Fabri, the poor continued to collect in the plazas of the medieval quarter. The disregarded were still the disregarded. Through the crowded squares wandered *erk sous* sellers with their silver urns topped by silk flowers strapped across their chests, pouring the licorice drink they plied into glass cups secured to belts around their waists. Young boys balanced bamboo baskets the size of mattresses and filled with flatbread on their heads. Men with lined faces shined shoes in their olive djellabas and white turbans. Large women covered all in black lingered on the steps of mosques or, trailed by little girls in pink and yellow and purple, walked desultorily through the train stations selling packets of tissues, which Ellie and I used to clean the soot that collected in our noses, the same soot that coated the buildings and the horizon.

In the English edition of *Al-Masry Al-Youm* as our trip neared its end, a vendor in Tahrir Square, epicenter of the revolution, was quoted as saying, "We can't find enough money to live on inside or outside the square. We just want the world to have mercy on those that have never experienced it, to notice us, the living dead in the streets." Everywhere we went in Cairo just months after the Egyptian revolution had deposed Mubarak, we felt a tension and uncertainty and desperation in the air like dust stirred up by the cloven hooves of beasts. Mubarak was ill and in prison somewhere near the Red Sea, and the army was in charge. Protesters were again in Tahrir Square, or perhaps they'd never really left. They camped out under tarps and blogged on laptops and demanded that former government officials be put on trial. On the sidewalks, hawkers sold pins and flags and *I ♥ Egypt* T-shirts, though the flow of Western tourists had evaporated like water in the desert sand. On the sweltering afternoon that we walked through Tahrir, a woman in a battered green army jacket was speaking forcefully in Arabic to a small crowd of young men in tight V-neck sports jerseys who cheered halfheartedly.

The revolution was ongoing.

We needed to visit the Church of Saint Sama'an in the Moqattam Hills and also the Mosque of Qa'it Bay in the Northern Cemetery, the City of the Dead. It seems pretty clear that Fabri spent an afternoon climbing up the hills to look out over the city and the Nile and the sultan's castle and then descended and passed through the cemetery. Because Julia has written extensively on the City of the Dead and the *zabbaleen* district at the base of the Moqattam Hills—both so-called informal areas—she loaned me a book in which many of her articles and those of other journalists had been collected. Informal areas—*ashwa'iyyat,* meaning "disordered," "haphazard" in Arabic—are the unauthorized settlements on the urban periphery where a majority of Cairo's population live.

In one piece, Julia tells how the *zabbaleen* (garbagemen) began arriving from the rural regions of Upper Egypt in the 1920s, settling outside the city, and collecting rubbish to feed to their pigs. As Cairo expanded, the *zabbaleen* were pushed farther and farther out. They were poor. They were Christian. They raised unclean animals. Those animals smelled. But eventually they reached an old stone quarry, an area between, quite literally, a rock and a hard place, between the cliffs of Moqattam and the City of the Dead, that no one else wanted and where no one could take offense at their presence, and there they settled for good.

Over the years, the *zabbaleen* have organized their trade. One article examines how families within the community run their businesses, with each member assigned a particular role—driver, collector, sorter, trader. They have developed relationships with residents of the endless city to pick up its endless trash. Once they collect the trash in the ubiquitous pale green plastic mesh bags we saw everywhere, and after they carry the bags piled high by wagon or by truck back to the neighborhood, the women and children sort through it for aluminum foil, animal bones, tin cans, glass, computer parts, plastic bags and plastic bottles, plastic toys and plastic chairs. These are then traded in to recyclers for cash. Of course, the wages for the *zabbaleen* also include infection—hepatitis, parasites, skin and eye diseases—wages reaped most often by the women and children who do the sorting.

The *zabbaleen* are Coptic Christians in this predominantly Muslim country, but they trace their roots to those Egyptians who embraced Christianity when it arrived here in the early days. It was important to Ibrahim, our guide to the Church of Saint Sama'an and himself a Coptic Christian, that we understand this, that we understand that the Copts were pureblood Egyptians, unlike the Muslim usurpers who had come from the east. He explained it all to us sonorously, in sentences that seemed scripted even when spontaneous, as we drove in his shiny black sedan up the mountain to the church through the district of the *zabbaleen*.

The dirt streets were narrow, and everything too close and too frantic, the sun too bright. But we were shielded, hermetically sealed away in the black sedan from the clouds of dust stirred up by passing trucks and wagons drawn by donkeys—all of them filled with bags of trash lashed down with rope. We were shielded, too, from the hungry dogs with their swinging teats nudging the garbage spilling from those bags. But as we passed brick and concrete apartment buildings in various states of dilapidation or construction, I could hardly tell which, Ellie suddenly remembered a dream she'd had almost a year before. In the dream she was in an alley, enclosed by buildings made of brick. She was propped up against one of these buildings, sitting in the dust, her legs splayed awkwardly to the sides, bleeding. She was staring at a mangy dog, knowing she'd been bit and knowing she would die of rabies. She'd been in Cairo.

From the front seat, Ibrahim was telling us, "The Bible is not just a book of fairy tales." Nor was the story of Saint Sama'an, which he recounted as we drove:

Sama'an, poor and pious, plies his trade, tanning hides and making shoes. One day, a beautiful woman comes in to have her shoes mended. As she removes them from her feet, Sama'an looks lustfully upon her delicate leg and hears in his mind the words of Matthew: "But I say unto you, that whosoever looketh on a woman to lust after her hath committed adultery with her already in his heart. And if thy right eye offend thee, pluck it out, and cast it from thee: for it is profitable for thee that one of thy members should perish, and not that thy whole body should be cast into hell." At once he seizes the awl hanging by a rope at his waist and drives it into his right eye.

Meanwhile, the caliph of Cairo, a lover of poetry and religious debate, hears that the Holy Book of the Christians decrees, "If ye have faith as a grain of mustard seed, ye shall say unto this mountain, Remove hence to yonder place; and it shall remove; and nothing shall be impossible unto you." The caliph calls the Coptic pope to him and gives him four options: move the mountain in the Moqattam Hills, renounce Christianity and embrace Islam, go into exile, or be smitten by the sword. The pope has three days. He calls upon the Virgin Mary in his hour of need, and she tells him in a dream that in the market he will find a one-eyed man carrying a jar of water. When he awakens, the pope goes to the market and takes hold of the one-eyed man, who is Sama'an the tanner. Near the mountain, a crowd has gathered, and the caliph and his men ride up on steeds. The Copts there repeat *Kyrie, eleison* four hundred times. But it is because of the faith of Sama'an, *faith as a grain of mustard seed,* that a great quaking shakes the mountain, and the mountain moves.

I hated this story. I hated the Jesus who condemns a vision of the imagination, never acted out. I hated the poor, pious tanner who follows scripture so literally. I hated the caliph who seizes upon the literalism of his subjects for his own political ends. I hated the inventor of this story who cannot see Jesus is speaking in parables. I hated the congregants of the Church of Saint Sama'an even before I met them for being so deluded. I hated Ibrahim for telling us this was not a fairy tale.

By now we had reached the parking lot of the church, and Ibrahim backed his black sedan into the shade. "I ask you please do not slam the doors, but close them gently," he told us, though this was out of a concern not for the noise but for the potential damage to his car.

When we arrived at the Church of Saint Sama'an, a massive open-air auditorium seating fifteen thousand and built into a cavern in the cliff, we noticed banners hanging from the stone walls. On the banners were the faces of nine men and boys, each in their own blue-sky-and-cloud bubble. Some were clean-shaven, some had mustaches or goatees. One wore a fur-lined blue-jean jacket and sported a mournful look and a soul patch. Another had his chin propped on the knuckles of his hand—*The Thinker.* These, Ibrahim told us, were the most recent Coptic martyrs.

We descended into the cavernous church. A Friday-morning service had just ended, and a small knot of the faithful were crowded around Abuna Sama'an, "minister to the rubbish collectors," who was performing an exorcism on a young woman. He cupped his hands around her face and told her, Ibrahim translated for us, "Seek the kingdom of God and then all will be given to you." Then he flicked holy water on her, and as the girl walked shakily past us, dazed and supported by her family, another sinner took his place before Abuna Sama'an, hoping to be cleansed. *It's a protective measure,* Julia had said of the way we, as Western women, had been treated. The cohesion of the community is at stake. I wondered if something similar was at stake here too.

Ibrahim introduced us to Aadim, an eyewitness to the massacre that had taken the martyrs whose pictures adorned the banners. Aadim closed his eyes like some ancient blind poet and began to tell us their story in Arabic as Ibrahim translated. That March, a Coptic church had been burned and destroyed in Giza, and Christians had gathered to protest, including two thousand men in the Moqattam Hills. This much was clear and verifiable. But after that, the story gets slippery. According to Aadim, Muslim onlookers began to spread a rumor that the Copts were coming to burn a mosque in retribution, and "this rumor spread like fire in the hay." Muslims came to Moqattam armed with knives and guns and Molotov cocktails and began attacking the Christians. When the military arrived, they only pushed Christians into their homes. Muslims poured into the neighborhood. The nine boys and men whose garishly sentimental photos adorned the banners had been murdered. Homes and recycling equipment were burned to ash. "But even with all these troubles, we believe in Jesus," Aadim told us, opening his eyes. "He is the same Lord who told Peter, 'On this rock of faith you will build this church.' He is the same Lord who helped Moses cross the Red Sea. Nothing will separate us from the Lord—not death or persecution. We have seen the miraculous hand of God. The mute speak, the deaf hear, the blind see. Me too—I was a gambler and a drug addict. But for the last sixteen years, I've been saved by Jesus. Amen." Then he handed me a business card with the Church of Saint Sama'an as a backdrop. I started to reach for my wallet, but Ibrahim stayed my hand and shook his head. "It makes them dependent," he said, in English so that Aadim could not understand.

Back outside the church, we climbed the stairs of an unfinished building and from up there we looked out over all of Cairo—pyramids in the polluted haze beyond the Nile, the Citadel with its dreamlike domed Mosque of Muhammad Ali, minarets puncturing the horizon like swords. But in tight focus was the district of the *zabbaleen* just below. We could see their goats and sheep, matted coats furred with dust, animals that have replaced the swine that formerly roamed the streets and consumed the refuse until they were slaughtered by the government in 2009, ostensibly because of the swine flu epidemic. We could see satellite dishes like sunflowers sprouting from the roofs, all pointing their round white faces west. We could see lines hung with clothes from the roofs of thin-walled brick apartment buildings, none of which seemed level or true.

Ibrahim asked, "Would you like to visit the *zabbaleen?*" But Ellie's stomach was still on the fritz, and now we had to contend with her dream of being bitten by a rabid dog in a street that looked eerily familiar. And besides, she whispered to me, "I'll feel like a tourist to their pain." I knew exactly what she meant. Why should we enter the streets of the trash pickers and stare like voyeurs at their poverty? What would this accomplish? Would staring make us brave? Would regarding their suffering and being able to say *We saw this* ennoble us somehow? Or did we think that seeing how the *zabbaleen* lived would help us to appreciate our privileged life? Were the poor and persecuted placed here in the Moqattam Hills merely to remind us how lucky we were?

But Ibrahim was telling me in a tone verging on scolding that the *zabbaleen* want people to see how they live. They want witnesses—that word again that Carol Ann had used regarding the Palestinians. "But, you know, it is up to you," said Ibrahim, resignedly. My pride couldn't take the suggestion, half hidden in his resignation, that I was a typical Westerner, oblivious to the tenuous lives lived by most of the rest of the world. Or, worse, that I was purposely looking away. So despite the protests of Ellie's pained expression, and the dream, down from the mountain we went.

The stench from the trash was almost visible. The atmosphere had grown heavy with it, like humid air before rain. Bags of trash piled up precariously on open beds of trucks and on carts pulled by burros driven by young, laughing boys standing on the axles. Bags piled up in the cavernous ground floors of the brick buildings. They piled up in the alleys between them. In a thousand years, the bags could not be sorted. Here was the mountain that could not be moved. Here was the underside of our voracious consumption, our unending need. And the bags kept coming.

The flies were everywhere too. And the feral cats and dogs. I walked protectively in front of Ellie. The *zabbaleen* eyed us warily. But eventually we introduced ourselves to a group who seemed to be taking a break from their work of sorting. Ibrahim explained our travels to them while Ellie bent down to talk to some little girls with the few words of Arabic that she knew. They offered us white plastic chairs. At some point, a baby named Paul was placed in my arms by a woman in an orange tunic. Paul is the name of my father and my brother. It's the name of Sabine and Martin's son to whom I am godmother. I told this to Ibrahim, who told it to those who had gathered around us. We all nodded at the significance.

"How has the revolution affected you?" I asked as the baby held on tight to my hands and stood bobbing on my legs. One man told me it had made life worse. Another, a cousin to one of the martyrs, said it had "taken away our children." As we sat in the white chairs under the bright sun and the dust, the crowd around us grew. "What are the practical things you need to make your lives better?" I asked. One woman pointed to a manhole cover. When it rains, she explained, the sewage overflows. Her eyes were pleading; her voice held a note of desperation. I suddenly wondered if she thought, if any of them thought, that I was asking these questions in order to help. Was I leading them on? Didn't they know that I could do nothing tangible to address their problems? "Do you have any hope that life will get better after the elections?" I asked. "The government doesn't care about us," said a woman, brushing away flies. "We live like animals," said a man with an open sore on his nose. "Our only hope is in God."

When you've been abandoned by the world, I was realizing, spiritual doubt such as mine becomes a luxury. And I remembered suddenly our trip one summer to the cliff dwellings in Mesa Verde in southern Colorado. For seven hundred years, the Ancestral Pueblo peoples built storerooms and living quarters and sacred kivas within the caverns of the cliffs. They grew corn and beans and squash on the flat mesas above and hunted turkey and rabbit and deer among the piñon pine and juniper. But in the late 1200s, the area suffered a severe drought and years of subsequent crop failures. Resources were utterly depleted. Turkey bones in the lower layers of the trash middens from when times were good gave way in the upper layers to the bones of rats and other rodents. These, along with more and more ceremonial objects, are signs, researchers speculate, of growing distress. A decrease in food, an increase in prayer.

I had hated the story of Sama'an the Tanner, whose faith—*faith as a grain of mustard seed*—moved a mountain. I had hated the literalism that was both its subject and its moral. *Faith that can move mountains is a metaphor!* I'd wanted to shout. But I thought about the martyred young men on the posters, and about Aadim, gambler and drug addict, and about the mother of Paul, the mothers of all the children Ellie had bent down to talk to. For them, the mountains were not metaphors. They were made of hard stone and trash at the edge of a haphazard city bordering a City of the Dead. What did the *zabbaleen* have to move those mountains, to change the crushing condition of their lives besides faith? And if he in whom they had faith told them to pluck out an eye, why wouldn't they? For in the same sermon, he had also told them, "Blessed are the poor in spirit: for theirs is the kingdom of heaven. Blessed are they that mourn: for they shall be comforted. Blessed are the meek: for they shall inherit the earth."

By this point Paul had been reclaimed by his mother and I had pulled out my notebook and was writing down everything, as if inscribing the particulars of their suffering could somehow make a difference. "To witness isn't enough," I wrote down too. But I knew, even as I recorded the name of their street—Sedky Iskander—as if I planned to come back, as if I planned to fix its sewer and bring shoes for Paul's bare feet and books to read him and food to feed him, that I, unlike their Savior, would betray them all.

After becoming tourists to the *zabbaleen's* pain, in a daze, we visited the City of the Dead, which shambles for miles beneath the Moqattam Hills. This necropolis, its dusty streets lined with domed mosques and the walled courtyards of tombs, is home to thousands of people. Egyptians bury their dead in chambers under the earth, and over these chambers sit small houses within open courtyards where relatives can take shelter and mourn in peace. Julia had explained to us how the poor had always lived among the tombs, tending to the graves. But more and more of these caretakers have begun to bring their families with them, their children and grandchildren. Many of the mausoleums now have electricity. Some have running water. There's a medical center, a post office, schools, as well as haphazardly constructed apartment buildings. The requirements of the living supersede those of the dead.

In some ways, the Northern Cemetery seemed like any other informal area. There was trash here, too, banked in drifts against the courtyard walls, and little food stands. Women in head scarves sold vegetables. Children dug with plastic food containers in the dirt. Men in skullcaps and djellabas sat in chairs pressed against the walls of shops. But it was quiet here. And there were trees and therefore shade. We passed a laundry where a wiry young man in crisp jeans and a bleached bright undershirt was pressing clothes. We passed a barbershop. We passed a glassblower's studio.

On the steps outside of the Mosque of Qa'it Bay, while Ibrahim was giving us some background, a woman in black came up to us, begging. Ibrahim didn't blink. He kept looking into my eyes, never glancing at the woman, and said in English, "Don't look at her or acknowledge her at all. And now let us go inside." Ellie and I, bewildered and embarrassed, took off our shoes and covered our heads with the scarves round our necks and entered the mosque behind Ibrahim.

Because they were Christian infidels, Fabri and the other pilgrims had not been allowed to enter this airy space of carved wood and wool carpets, but they'd stood in the courtyard outside. Through the door they glimpsed hanging lamps and "a very beautiful room in their style." Next to the mosque was "an oblong house with distinct cells as if it were a religious monastery where their priests live who day and night sing in the mosques and call from the towers. They were ululating with especially great clamor while we stood there, praising Mahomet and perhaps cursing us," Fabri describes, a little paranoid. Through the open windows we could hear aluminum plates clacking from a stand across the road, and the public radio station playing religious music and sermons.

As we returned to Ibrahim's black sedan, I saw a man racked

by some deformity, walking on his hands toward us, pulling his shrunken, useless legs behind him up the hill. It was a lurching, grotesque crawl invented in the absence of pity, invented in a world where humans must live like animals, and where the animals, too, are discarded. A dead kitten lay in a pile of trash, flies in its nostrils. Thin dogs roamed, heads down. And I remembered how, when we left the neighborhood of the *zabbaleen* and walked back up Moqattam Hill to the Church of Saint Sama'an, a girl named Rania, maybe ten, had followed us to Ibrahim's car. She had her onyx hair pulled back into a band. Over her shoulder, she carried a dainty white purse. As we passed beneath one of the banners of the Coptic martyrs, she began to recite the names of the dead for us in a singsong chant, smiling, like a madwoman crooning a lullaby over the dead child she holds in her arms. Ellie had dreamed it all already. I imagined we were wandering through a Bosch painting or a painting by Brueghel. "About suffering they were never wrong, / The Old Masters," Auden had written:

> *how well they understood*
> *Its human position; how it takes place*
> *While someone else is eating or opening a window or just walk-*
>   *ing dully along.*

So when the dark eyes of the mutilated man caught mine, I just tried hard not to look away.

THE PLACE OF THE CURE
OF THE SOUL

THE JOURNEY FROM Cairo to Alexandria that October 1483 is a slog. The pilgrims travel by boat north down the Nile to Rosetta, from which city they plan to pass west overland with beasts of burden to the seaport. But all of the camels and asses have been hired out already by merchants transporting their aromatic spices and silks up to Cairo. So the pilgrims cram aboard a small boat that will carry them along a narrow tributary to Alexandria. Again and again, however, wind and mud confound them, and the sailors must strain to drag the boat against the current or dislodge it from the sandbars that pock the shallow waters. Bedouin attack the pilgrims with lances, leaping into the boat from the shore and trying to drag the pilgrims' sacks and baggage away, until they are bought off with ducats and biscuits.

In Canopus, still eighteen miles from Alexandria, they exchange their boat for asses and five camels and a driver to carry them across the sand of the Mediterranean coast. But on the overland journey, Saracens follow and assault them, forcefully reclaiming many of the asses, though as Fabri says, "We could not understand the causes of these arguments for the most part because of the confusion of tongues, nor they us and we offended each other with passionate shouting." The sun is hot, the sand deep and soft, and the pilgrims have had no food for two days, nor more than a drop of wine or water. As they continue west, they meet several bands of Alexandrian camel drivers and their camels heading east to collect loads of spices. The Alexandrians must be bought off just like the Bedouin. Approaching a small range of mountains that extends to the sea, they turn inland away from the water to skirt the hills and pass near a broad field covered with what looks like frost—a vast saltworks owned by the sultan.

When, in the evening, they finally arrive in Alexandria, ringed on one side by the Great Sea and on the other by gardens and orchards and palms, officials unceremoniously corral them behind iron gates for the night, the customs inspectors having all gone home. Desperate, though, the pilgrims bang on the gate that leads into the city and beg the people living nearby for bread and water, passing *madini* to them underneath the threshold. "Those pagans then took the money and jugs and brought us bread, warm and fresh from the oven, and jugs of water and little bags of dates, the fruit of the palm tree," Fabri remembers with gratitude.

In Alexandria, that cosmopolitan center, that node linking East and West, Fabri and his band are housed in the Catalan *fondaco* like all Christian pilgrims. Here the merchants store their goods for transport across the sea to the warehouses Fabri had seen in Venice. "It is a *fondaco* from which merchandise flows to other countries, just as water from a fountain," as he describes it. "There are many of these *fondachi* in Alexandria, just as sometimes in some parts of the land many springs erupt at once." In the morning, saying his office, Fabri stands in the doorway watching passersby and wonders to himself at the diversity of human beings.

In Alexandria, Ellie and I walked the Corniche lining the harbor west toward the Fort of Qa'it Bay, a fortress constructed, just a few years before Fabri arrived, out of the stones of the toppled Pharos lighthouse built by the Greek Ptolemies. The blue waters of the Mediterranean lay to one side, the elegant nineteenth-century apartment buildings and coffeehouses and the onion-domed mosques of the city to the other. Like Tahrir in Cairo, Midan Saad Zaghloul was filled with protesters camped out under blue tarps. As we walked the promenade, black-robed, black-veiled matrons, some even wearing gloves on this stifling summer day, stared disapprovingly at us. Boys and young men in tight shirts and jeans followed too close beside us: "What is your name?" "Can I take your picture?" "Welcome to Egypt," the g soft, like in *Georges*. "I feel like a circus animal," Ellie told me, miserable. At the fort, we took refuge in the nooks of the stone crenellations overlooking the sea and thought of home.

Fabri, too, must have gazed out across these same waters toward the priory and the brethren he longed to see again, not knowing that the world that seemed so solid was about to dissolve. In 1492, less than a decade after Fabri's journey, Columbus would hit upon the islands of the Bahamas and think they were India. By his third voyage, in 1498, exploring the coast of present-day South America, he would acknowledge that this was, in fact, an *otro mundo,* an other world. I like to think that, had he lived into the age of exploration, Fabri might have made his way across to the New World along with all those Dominican friars from Spain. That maybe, given his wrenching descriptions of the horrors of the slave market in Alexandria and the Ethiopian woman beaten and bound, like the later Dominicans, he, too, might have become a fierce advocate for the native people caught up in the appalling machinery of an empire intent on subjugation.

But all that was in a future Fabri would not live to see. Ten years after Columbus's first voyage, he'd be dead. Then came the Reformation. In the summer of 1531, the town council of Ulm abolished the Catholic Mass. The friars were held as virtual prisoners in their own cells, while overseers from the city controlled the keys to the cellars and grain bins, the kitchen and the library, the choir from which Fabri had departed, surrounded by his brethren. That autumn, their property was formally seized and the Dominicans were expelled from the city into which they had been so thoroughly integrated for centuries. The friars had asked on September 9 to be allowed to meet with the town council to plead their case, *"oder aber wollen sie nur mit der nöthigsten Bekleidung und Büchern abziehen,"* or to depart with only the most necessary clothing and, as in Ellie's dream of our own apocalpyse, their books. Denied their request for a hearing, on September 12 the friars were exiled. They went first to Steinheim an der Murr, later to Rottweil and Gmünd and Schlettstadt. In 1616, the walls of the Dominican convent in Ulm fell down. Now a parking lot covers the friars' graves.

We had only about twenty-four hours in Alexandria. We had seen Pompey's Pillar from the taxi we took from the train station, and I decided that that would have to suffice. We walked to the Fort of Qa'it Bay. We had coffee and cake in the Trianon. Then, even though it was only late afternoon and still broad daylight, we went back to our hotel on a side street off the Corniche and laid down in the double bed we were sharing and watched Martha Stewart piping frosting and offering cake-decorating tips in an episode from the days before her imprisonment, and then a rerun of an Oprah Winfrey show on the miraculous faith healer of Brazil, John of God. "I don't know how to understand this," said the doctor brought in to provide a skeptical stance but who himself bled inexplicably after watching a "psychic surgery." "I do not feel in control." We ordered round after round of fresh guava juice from room service, and when the English-language programs ended, we turned to cooking shows in Arabic. It was the first time we'd watched TV since we'd left home almost two months before. It felt like the end of the school year. It felt like the end of a lifetime. Ellie wanted a hamburger and to sleep until our plane departed.

In the morning, I rallied myself just enough to head back out into the streets to try to find some of the churches Fabri had visited. I snapped some photos of a mural of Saint Catherine arguing with the wise men of Alexandria. I saw some relics. I was done.

Returning to the hotel, though, I was stopped at the door by a young bearded man in Levi's and a loose cotton tunic who I thought was going to ask *What is your name?* or *Can I take your picture?* or say *Welcome to Egypt,* soft *g.* But instead he turned out to be the Muslim equivalent of a Mormon missionary, complete with glossy booklets: "Women in Islam" and "Have You Discovered Its Real Beauty?," *Its* referring to the Qur'an. Why I didn't simply take his booklets—or reject them—and turn my back and enter the hotel I'm not quite sure. Maybe after all of the judgmental stares we'd gotten despite our best intentions not to judge, I was spoiling for a fight.

"May I ask you a question?" he asked me when I did not turn my back on him. "What are you? Christian? Jew? Muslim?" "I'm nothing," I replied, daring him to go on. "Do you believe God is one or divided into many gods?" he asked, undeterred. He seemed perfectly nice, really. But I knew this was a trick question. If I answered *one,* I would be pronounced a Muslim. If I answered *many,* I'd be either a Christian, indoctrinated into belief in the Trinity, or a pagan. I said that I did not know if I believed in God, but I supposed that if God existed, He would be one spirit that pervades all things. As expected, and ignoring my doubt completely, the bearded young man told me, as if diagnosing me, "Well, then, you are already a Muslim."

I wanted to explain to him that if I believed in God, I wouldn't mind being a Muslim, that I wasn't opposed to that possibility out of hand. But what about—the title of his glossy booklet—

"Women in Islam"? "Men and women are different," he told me, to which premise I agreed. "Women here are like queens," he continued. *Oh, do go on,* I thought but did not say. "Because women are so beautiful, their beauty is something that needs to be prized and kept away from other eyes." "But," I protested, "what about the beauty of men? What about female desire for their bodies?" "Men and women are not the same," he repeated. "Really?" I replied sarcastically. Ignoring me, he argued, "Women's bodies must be covered for their protection." "What happens to men if they look at a woman's body is *their* problem, not ours!" I found myself nearly shouting in defense of all my Muslim sisters, who did not need or want my defending. "*We* shouldn't have to cover *our*selves because men can't control *their* desire!"

"But this isn't the real issue," the young Muslim missionary told me, trying to defuse my mounting frustration. The real issue was my immortal soul. For a long time, he told me, he too had been wandering and searching. For a long time, he too had not been at peace. But then he found Islam and, with it, rest in God. I had heard that line before, from all the converts I'd ever talked to. It wasn't about to work here, on this busy street, with my hand on the doorknob of the hotel, and my daughter upstairs in our room waiting for me, and both of us desperate for the plane we would catch tomorrow.

But then he said, "I want you to listen to something, and tell me what you hear." And, looking into my eyes, he began to chant verses from the Qur'an. At first it was awkward, the two of us staring at each other, a total stranger serenading me with the music that I'd found so haunting in Jerusalem, in the desert, in the garden in Ma'adi. But slowly, the blur of pedestrians and the blaring of horns and the grime of the city and the heat of the sun on the crown of my head began to dissipate. I found myself closing my eyes. His voice enclosed me. His voice made a shield around me. His voice became a sword of flame. Except in it I heard not the peace and rest he had promised, but a yearning, like the pull of the water of the Nile for the sea. It seemed to travel on the knife's edge between praise and lamentation, and this wrenched something loose deep inside me. But before I could catch whatever it was, the sura ended. I opened my eyes. The city came rushing back in.

The rebuilt Library of Alexandria anchors the eastern end of the city's half-moon harbor, opposite the Fort of Qa'it Bay. After we checked out of the hotel and before we took the train back to Cairo, Ellie and I spent an afternoon in its cool, dark rooms. *The place of the cure of the soul,* an inscription on the wall of the original library is said to have read. Here was once a repository of all the world's knowledge written on papyrus scrolls in every tongue—Greek, of course, and Hebrew, Aramaic, Nabataean, Arabic, the Indian languages, Egyptian. Tradition records that Ptolemy II required travelers entering the port city, then the capital of the kingdom, to declare any manuscripts they were carrying. Those texts not already in the library would be confiscated and copied and then returned, though often the library kept the original. But all those papyrus scrolls and the library that housed them are gone, burned, legend has it, by Julius Caesar, who describes in *De Bello Alexandrino* his troops setting fire to a warehouse full of papyri near the port. More likely the destruction took place later and perhaps over time. Still, one way or another, all those manuscripts containing all that knowledge for which the Ptolemies hungered were lost.

Except, maybe, for a scrap of papyrus tucked into the folds of the linen wrappings of the mummified body of a man who probably visited the library and copied out parts of its collection to remember. We saw the facsimile of that scrap in the new Library of Alexandria, the original being housed in Vienna. But that scrap reminds me now of those who would come to the cave of the Sibyl of Cumae, who scribbled down the prophesies of the god on leaves. And of Fabri writing as he sat upon *an ass or a camel; or at night, while the others were asleep.* Or of Ellie when she was little wanting to write it all down so she could remember and explain to her children the things I explained to her. Or of me. We are gleaners of wisdom, hungry for truth, picking our way through the stubbled fields of the earth.

Also on display in the rebuilt Library of Alexandria were examples of sacred texts—Torah scrolls, the Gospels in Arabic, the Hadith, the Qur'an. There were translations of Galen and Paracelsus, Euclid and Hippocrates, a facsimile of *Geographica* by Ptolemy. There were incunabula: *De Sphaera Mundi, De Caelo et Mundo, Somnium Scipionis ex Ciceronis Libro de Republica, Excerptum, Genealogie Deorum*—all books Fabri had read, printed in the years just before he died. There were works of literature and logic and philosophy, astronomy and astrology, mathematics and medicine. Manuscripts eaten by worms, frayed and darkened papyrus, words leaching away.

"In the beginning was the Word, and the Word was with God, and the Word was God," says John the apostle. Walking through the contemplative hush of the library, I saw that these books, these words, were what I believed in. They were what I wanted to give my daughters to believe in too, something holy for them to carry with them like talismans into the void. Because in them is a struggle for wisdom and understanding that is itself sustaining the way some claim rest in God to be.

There is a radical insufficiency at the center of human existence. We exist. We don't know why. We die. We don't know what follows. We love. What we love will leave us. We suffer though we have tried to be good. These aren't questions and they don't have answers. To paraphrase Samuel Beckett, we must go on, we can't go on, we'll go on. We'll go on because doubt, and the wandering search it provokes, keeps us spiritually alive.

"At the heart of the philosophical stance toward the world is the Socratic assertion: I do not know," said my friend Iain, the philosopher, in a lecture he gave to our students on Plato's *Apology*. Starting from that position of ignorance, we arc toward understanding in dialectic with another, because together we crave to know. And like an asymptotic curve, we approach truth, though we will never arrive there in this life. Still, the soul, for Plato, said Iain, "is a kind of dynamism. When it's at rest it is not in its natural state. It urges us in the direction of deeper understanding. Virtue is a consequence of this pursuit of knowledge and truth." And that kind of examined life, says Plato, is the only one worth living for a human being. I thought about the dynamism of the soul in the reconstructed Library of Alexandria. And I thought about the rest and peace promised to me by the Muslim missionary. And I thought about the restlessness of doubt. About how doubt implies ambiguity, which can be unnerving. *There's more than one answer to these questions, pointing me in a crooked line,* the Indigo Girls had sung to me when I was young. But the ambiguity of doubt can also imply possibility. It can imply the open road. And it is, I suspect, the stance more aligned with whatever divinity exists because it reflects a humility before the mystery of the universe of which divinity would surely approve.

On the train from Alexandria to Cairo, Ellie and I looked out the window and shared a set of earphones and listened to Ralph Stanley singing "I'll Fly Away" on her iPod. It was one of the songs Terry and the girls and I had listened to over and over again on our trip through the American heartland when they were little. We'd driven on two-lane roads through cornfields and wheat fields and camped by the sides of reed-lined streams. We bought Mary Martha a pioneer sunbonnet that she wore hanging between her fragile shoulder blades. Ellie read *Little House on the Prairie* in the backseat as we drove. I made pancakes on our camp stove. Terry made a fire. At night, Sabine curled in my lap like a kitten and fell asleep. Terry and I saw that the little towns and the open land were vulnerable the way our children were vulnerable, both changing irrevocably and moving toward their inexorable end. *When the shadows of this life have gone, I'll fly away,* sang Ralph Stanley, while we were all held together, temporarily, in that vessel. Maybe that's what I had heard in the sura sung to me on the grimy street of Alexandria. Maybe that's what I had sensed when I sat on my bedroom floor as a child watching the pattern of leaves disappearing and returning, like the lives of mortal men. Somewhere in that borderland between praise and lamentation is where I most belong. I want to ply myself to the beauty that is passing in the particulars of *this* world, and find salvation there.

In the morning, Ellie and I would board the plane that would take us home to the ones we loved and to our diverging lives, but for those few last hours together, we watched the timeless images of the Nile delta at sunset as the windows darkened and the figures outside turned gradually to silhouettes. A group of women and children sitting cross-legged upon rugs laid down over the dirt. Green fields of corn. Rice paddies. Fishermen casting their lines in the canals. Date palm trees and banana trees. White ibis in the rushes. Water buffalo. A man in a djellaba and a woman fully covered, each carrying a child, passing along a narrow lane beside an open field. Mud-brick walls and reed huts and domes of mosques. Dovecotes like beehives. A man walking beside a cart pulled by a burro. A woman balancing a basket on her head. Bedouin moving among their kneeling camels. Children running through the sugarcane.

This was the fleeting world, tied umbilically by the Nile to paradise, wherever that might be. As we traveled east, the haze of the setting sun behind us transformed everything to sepia, to a lithographic print from the nineteenth century, to a faded fresco from an ancient tomb. It was as if a veil had been pulled back to reveal the cells of the beating body of the earth, of which we were two, all turning into the past before our eyes.

EPILOGUE

Home

Neither shall they say, Lo here! or, lo there! for, behold,
the kingdom of God is within you.

—Luke 17:21

THE KINGDOM WITHIN YOU

FOR THREE DAYS after our return, I couldn't get out of bed. Ellie's jet lag was offset by her enthusiasm to see the boyfriend she'd missed so much, but I lay in my bedroom with the shutters closed beneath the fan. I called no one. Terry and Mary Martha and Sabine would tiptoe in to give me kisses on my forehead or bring me something to eat and then they'd leave. All I wanted was to be still. Back in Venice, when I'd visited the island monastery of San Francesco del Deserto and taken surreptitious photos of the friar in Birkenstocks, I'd written in my notebook, "I'm drawn to the mendicant orders, to this idea of wandering. It's a kind of detachment from the world. But that internal feeling of separation and longing, that state of wandering—is that sustainable? Even the mendicant friars eventually settled down to their convents and grew fruit trees and made a life."

Slowly I awakened from my torpor and got out of bed and reentered the life that Terry and I had made, so similar to the one we'd imagined in our letters years ago. Perhaps my travels had blurred my memories of our home and its possessions because everything now looked sharper to me, as if it had just come into focus— the green teakettle on the yellow enamel stove, my thrift-store oil paintings, the artwork of my daughters, the headboard Terry built for us and painted a dark teal blue, the ancient trunk filled with relics that came from Germany on an immigrant ship, the dining table I'd inherited from my grandparents that had sat in their house in St. Louis beneath the window that looked out over the yard where my cousins and my brother and sister and I would play when my parents made the long drive up north from the Woodlands. "Home has to be a physical space with objects in it," as Ellie had said while we walked the streets of Ulm eating gelato. "Because objects have memories attached to them. And we're human beings and our physical things remind us of who we are." I was filled with gladness to be in that place again.

A week after we returned, for our anniversary, Terry and I drove down along the Texas Gulf Coast to Surfside Beach—low dunes and switchgrass and primrose, flat metallic waves. We stayed in a cheap hotel with sandy linoleum floors and a window air conditioner that couldn't quite dispel the humid air. But I knew where I was on the map. I could read all the signs. An oil refinery loomed up behind us, and some rigs were anchored out in the Gulf. We ate fish tacos and sipped our Shiner beer. Willie Nelson was singing on the radio about blue eyes cryin' in the rain.

As I looked out at the waters of the Gulf of Mexico with Terry beside me, I thought back to myself sitting on the bulwarks of the Fort of Qa'it Bay looking out over the Mediterranean with Ellie, missing here, and for a moment I had a vision of my two selves passing each other somewhere over the ocean between. Afterward, all that had become normal while we were gone started to grow strange again—the backpacks holding only the essentials, the babel of languages I couldn't understand, camping in a desert alone with men unrelated to me, drinking Nescafé, the stares. I began to feel a nostalgia for those moments and an ache for the home we had made far away and in motion.

A few weeks after we got back, Ellie returned to school in Austin. She arranged her apartment according to the diagram she'd drawn. She took the classes that she'd listed in her note-book. She broke up with her boyfriend. But she's never really come back home again. She'll drive in now and then from Austin and stay for a night or two. But the life she is making for herself is elsewhere.

We are still trying to find our way in this new dispensation. Sometimes she will call with some heartbreak—a fair-weather friend, a frustration at school, out of loneliness, disappointed in love—and the need in her voice connects us. It was also she who proposed that we send texts consisting of only a period whenever we are thinking of each other: ., she writes as I finish teaching or when I'm in the grocery store; ., I write, sometimes at night when I'm reading or knitting, sometimes when I think I'm not think-ing of her at all. But other times I feel so separate from her, as if she's an old friend I knew once, years ago. She isn't quite real. Sometimes we go days without speaking. Then, I cannot access the intimacy we once shared, when she was little and babbled on to me as if I were herself. Nor can I remember what she looked like as we stood on the Academy Bridge in Venice one warm night, a few lights daubed across the black waters of the canal below like brushstrokes, and she laughed as I pretended to take pictures of her while filming the lute player behind us instead.

She herself claims not to recall very much from our trip to-gether. "Remember in Rhodes how we took our clothes to that laundry and the Turkish family washed and folded everything for us for almost nothing?" I'll ask. "Remember the little girl in the frilly red dress in the Muslim Quarter in Jerusalem—the one who smiled at us and was dancing on those stone steps leading up to the Damascus Gate?" "No, not really," she'll say flatly. "I don't re-member that at all." Her forgetting alone doesn't bother me. It's the lack of regret that is sometimes painful.

It's been three years since we traveled together. Ellie graduated from college a few weeks ago, on her birthday, which was the day before Mother's Day this year, and it all kept coming back to me that weekend—her birth, my graduation. In a few days she'll leave for Vietnam, where she'll travel from north to south alone for a month: Hanoi, Lao Cai, Hoi An, Hue, Nha Trang, Ho Chi Minh City. She's been making lists: Vaccinations Needed, Clothing, Books. And, of course, Possible Ideas: a motorbike tour, a tour of Ha Long Bay on a wooden junk, tombs and pagodas and citadels and markets she might visit, a hiking excursion to tribal villages, the Cu Chi Tunnels where the Vietcong hid during the war, the Temple of Literature. When she comes back she'll begin law school in the east. She wants to be a public defender. *If I do not stop to help this man, what will happen to* him? said Martin Luther King Jr. thinking of the Samaritan in the Judean Desert binding up the abandoned man's wounds.

The other girls, too, are preparing to leave. Mary Martha begins university in the fall. Last summer, she traveled to Granada, Spain, by herself and took classes and walked the streets at night. Those nights, she said, were the closest she's come to a spiritual experience. Once, she sat on a balcony that looked down on a stream and listened to a man on a stone bench playing guitar, the Alhambra all lit up above. "In that moment," she wrote later, "I was not perfectly content. But I understood finally that perfect contentment is not freedom from sadness and loneliness, from internal struggle." Instead, she realized in that foreign city, all alone, that "the melancholy I have felt for most of my life is incorporated into my contentment." This summer, Sabine will be living in a remote village in the Dominican Republic for two months doing volunteer work with children, sleeping on a cot beneath a mosquito net. I plan to write her every day. Watching my daughters, I think about how, for me, certain possibilities were cut off by the choice I made to have them, those other lives I might have lived discarded. And yet, I am fragmented in them. Those other lives are being lived by part of me anyway, I try to tell myself.

When Friar Felix Fabri crossed the river Danube over the Herd-brücke in the winter of 1484 and stood at the gate of the Dominican House, he could hear the sound of his brethren's voices chanting vespers in the choir from which he'd departed, weeping. Though he beat upon the doors, they did not hear him at first. "But I had hardly knocked for the first time when the Convent dog was there, who knew me through the gate," Fabri recalls, "and not with angry barking, but with a strange joyful howling and whining scratched and bit at the planks as though he would tear the gate down, in such a hurry he was to get out to me." Then the prior and the brethren too came running, "as if to put out a fire." Crowding round, they brought him to the choir, and before the altar Fabri received "the blessing of a brother returned from a journey." And for a week, Prior Fuchs allowed the friars to keep holiday in honor of their brother pilgrim.

Then, reluctantly, because it made him look bolder, he shaved his beard, which he'd worn for eleven months. But for some time afterward, Fabri wore, unseen beneath his Dominican robes, the cross from his pilgrim tunic, and he preserved in his cell, "as a relic of my holy pilgrimage," the cotton mattress he'd used in the desert and at sea. And early in March of 1502, as he lay dying, he was granted permission to wear the pilgrim habit in which he had wandered for so far and so long.

Besides the holy dirt from Mount Sinai, brought home in a discarded plastic bottle, and stones from all the other places, this is the relic I carry with me:

When we were traveling, everywhere we went we would have to wait in lines—ferry lines, passport lines, security lines, lines for food, lines to see the Holy Sepulcher, which we never did.

Inevitably, the bureaucracy itself or the inefficiency of those in charge or the selfishness of others trying to get ahead would become too overwhelming for Ellie. She'd roll her eyes and stamp her foot and huff, totally exasperated. On the bus to Eilat across the Negev, we'd even joked together about the ideal job for her: line monitor.

But a strange calmness started to overtake me as we traveled, and it remains inside me still. It would all happen, I would think to myself, we would always get where we needed to go. And if we didn't—but we would—we'd still find our way. And if we didn't—but we would—it would be okay because not far from here was Saint Catherine of Siena's cramped marble foot, and the palace of Knossos where Daedalus sewed Icarus his wings. Not far from here was a walled medieval city gone to seed. Not far from here was the road to Jericho surrounded by hills lined like the thumbprint of God. Not far from here was the Roman fortress built beside the ancient temple of the Jews. Not far from here, a muezzin was calling the faithful to prayer from a minaret lit by green neon lights. Not far from here was the Field of Damascus with its *adamah,* the dust that made us all. I am a fleck of that dust in a thirsty desert revolving beneath a dome of desolate stars. I carry that desert within me now. It's a kingdom that feels like home.

ACKNOWLEDGMENTS

My deepest gratitude to all those who made this book possible:

To Inprint, the Brown Foundation, Houston Arts Alliance, and the Vermont Studio Center for financial support that encouraged me in my writing. To Patricia Hampl, who chose an early form of "What the Desert Said" for publication in *Ploughshares*. To my agent, Wendy Sherman, for seeing the possibilities. To my editor, Judy Clain, for agreeing and for helping to draw them out. To Amanda Brower, Jayne Yaffe Kemp, Tracy Roe, and everyone at Little, Brown for getting this book into the world.

To many of our hosts and guides during our travels: Hannelore Schüngel, Alexander Rosenstock, and Dr. Hans Eugen Specker, in Ulm; Mehmet Erginel and Sevgi Altay Erginal in Cyprus; Carol Ann Bernheim and Steve Langfur in Jerusalem; Hijazi Eid in the Palestinian territories; Mohammad Atwa Musa in the Sinai Desert; Kilian Balz and Julia Gerlach in Cairo. Most dear of all, Sabine and Martin in Frankfurt.

To readers of the early drafts, who each revealed to me part of what I was trying to say: Joni, fellow traveler and lover of oddities; Fred, generous advocate and guide; Jessica, cheerful seeker of transcendence. Also Iain, who makes me think harder than anyone else—I'm grateful for our dialectic. And steadfast Georgina, who along with Joe gave me a room of my own and a room with a view at a crucial time. To my colleagues at the Honors College at the University of Houston, too, for sharing in the essential work of interpretation.

To all of the grandmothers and grandfathers and aunts and uncles of my daughters, who babysat so I could read and travel and write, and most especially to my parents, who joyfully and generously shared the pleasures and the struggles of my early years with Ellie.

To Terry, to my girls, without whom there would be nothing.

A NOTE ON SOURCES

The Book of Wanderings owes a debt to so many scholars who have spent their lives laboring to contribute to the world's body of knowledge. I first discovered Friar Felix Fabri through the English translation of much of his account by the Palestine Pilgrims' Text Society, a Victorian learned society that published numerous translations of the writings of pilgrims and travelers to the Holy Land from the fourth to the fifteenth centuries. I'm most grateful as well to Sean Redmond for allowing me to use his unpublished translation of *Spices, Saints, and Saracens*, which picks up where the Palestine Pilgrims' work leaves off. Likewise invaluable to understanding Fabri himself was Kathryne Beebe's doctoral dissertation, "Felix Fabri and His Audiences: The Pilgrimage Writings of a Dominican Preacher in Late-Medieval Germany," now being published as *Pilgrim & Preacher: The Audiences and Observant Spirituality of Friar Felix Fabri*. For a detailed recounting of Fabri's journey and a comprehensive portrait of the medieval world through which he traveled, I found Hilda Prescott's *Jerusalem Journey: Pilgrimage to the Holy Land in the Fifteenth Century* and *Once to Sinai: The Further Pilgrimage of Friar Felix Fabri* vital. Also instrumental to my understanding of medieval pilgrimage were Jonathan Sumption's *The Age of Pilgrimage: The Medieval Journey to God* and Nicole Chareyron's *Pilgrims to Jerusalem in the Middle Ages*. Victor and Edith Turner's *Image and Pilgrimage in Christian Culture* helped me grasp Christian pilgrimage as a phenomenon more generally and see its persistence in the modern world. Finally, Karen Armstrong's *Jerusalem: One City, Three Faiths* and Jerome Murphy-O'Connor's *The Holy Land: An Oxford Archaeological Guide* helped explain the fraught and complicated history and geography of the center of faith to which Fabri traveled, and Clinton Bailey's work, in particular *Bedouin Poetry from Sinai and the Negev,* gave me crucial insights into the people among whom both Fabri and my daughter and I traveled in the desert.

CREDITS

ABOUT THE AUTHOR

Kimberly Meyer holds a doctoral degree in literature and creative writing from the University of Houston, where she was the recipient of several fellowships and grants. Her essays have been published widely in magazines and journals and have been anthologized in *The Best American Travel Writing*. She teaches literature courses in the Great Books at the University of Houston and lives in that thriving, multicultural city of no zoning with her husband and daughters.